THE ENCYCLOPEDIA OF
ASIAN AND
ORIENTAL COOKERY

COMPILED AND EDITED BY

MARGARET FULTON

THE ENCYCLOPEDIA OF
ASIAN AND
ORIENTAL COOKERY

COMPILED AND EDITED BY

MARGARET FULTON

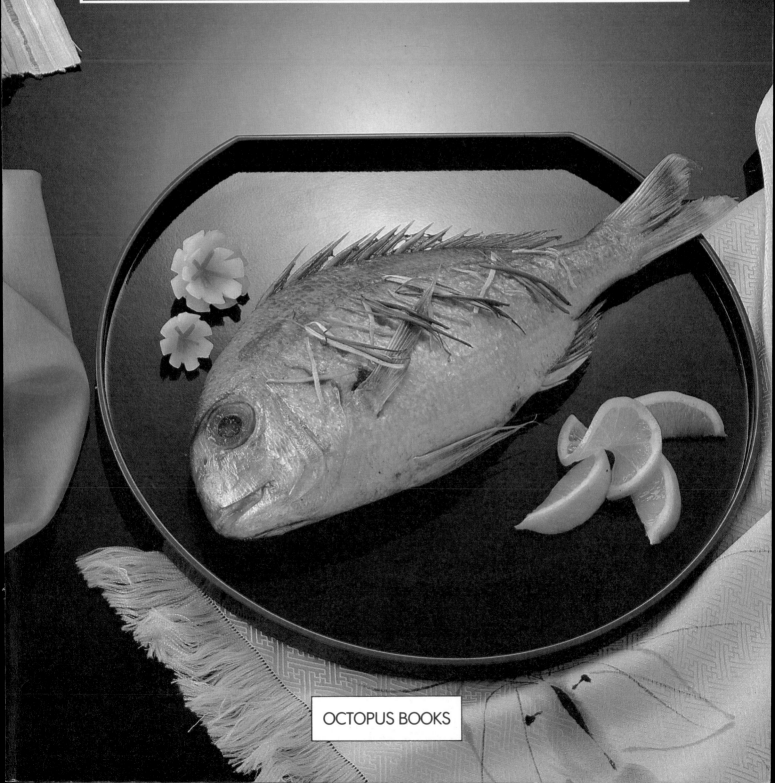

OCTOPUS BOOKS

CONTENTS

NOTES

Standard spoon and cup measurements are used in all recipes:
1 tablespoon = 20 ml spoon
1 teaspoon = 5 ml spoon
1 cup = 250 ml
All spoon measures are level.

Fresh herbs are used unless otherwise stated. If unobtainable, substitute a bouquet garni of the equivalent dried herbs, or use dried herbs instead but halve the quantities stated.

Details of specialist ingredients, marked with an asterisk, are given in the glossary (pages 184-187).

The Encyclopedia of Asian and Oriental Cookery is a revised edition of the Encyclopedia of Asian Cooking published by Octopus Books Limited

First published 1986 by
Octopus Books Limited
59 Grosvenor Street
London W1

© 1986 Octopus Books Limited
ISBN 0 7064 2780 7

Produced by Mandarin Publishers Limited
22a Westlands Road, Quarry Bay, Hong Kong

Printed in Hong Kong

14.12.88

INTRODUCTION

PAKISTAN

Karachi

Bombay

It is hard to imagine life without the lovely spiced and fragrant foods of the Orient. I have been 'hooked' on the exotic and intriguing flavours of the East for over 40 years.

My first taste of Chinese food was in the home of a Chinese school chum. It had a profound effect on my Scottish-Australian taste buds and opened up a whole new world for me. There was, I decided, an exciting and adventurous world out there, and from that moment, I knew I was going to explore every facet of it.

My first Chinese Cookery classes were in Sydney's China town in the late 40's and they were way ahead of their time. I learnt about stir-frying, sweet and sour flavour combinations, making delectable *dim-sum* and I quickly became adept at folding the little 'cloud-swallows' for the well loved short soup. Added excitement came from a police-raid. We were, it was revealed, a front for an illegal fan-tan school!

In the 50's my newspaper sent me to Hong Kong specifically to attend two renowned and serious cooking schools – for Australians were fast developing a taste for Chinese cooking. Then followed a stint in Japan where there were new and elaborate Chinese and Japanese cookery schools.

On to Taiwan for lessons from the chef at the Grand Hotel. My first visit to the People's Republic of China was two days after the death of Chairman Mao Tse Tung in September 1976. An historical time where we saw and felt the grief and mourning of one fifth of the world's population. Travelling South, East, North and West, as guests of the People's Republic, we were introduced to the simple but beautiful foods served in the communes – a carp caught and steamed with the finest angels hairs of thinly cut fresh ginger and other aromatics, as refined a dish as would be served in any top restaurant. We were also introduced to the exquisite Court dishes that were still served in the restaurants catering for heads of government and diplomats.

I returned to China in 1979, heading up the first Chinese gourmet tour. We went behind the scenes learning again first hand from the new young chefs and some of the old masters.

I have also had the honour of visiting India on many occasions as the guest of the Indian Government. Arrangements were made for me to learn 'straight from the horse's mouth' as it were. The best of Indian cooks, professional chefs, food writers and good home cooks, led me gently through their repertoire. My travels throughout the Indian sub continent have been extensive – from the lovely Vale of Kashmir at the foothills of the Himalayas to Cape Camorin on the southern tip, from Karachi at the mouth of Indus River on the West Coast, to busy, teeming Calcutta on the Ganges delta. Its food, people and customs completely captured my imagination and today I often find myself yearning for the wide and varied foods of India, easy to prepare at home when so many cooks have shared their recipes with me and taught me their skills.

Living so close to the East, I have enjoyed lovely long working holidays in Indonesia, Thailand, Malaysia. The best part of these trips has been returning home with a wonderful fund of information and recipes for the dishes of these countries.

Naturally all this love and experience should not go unrecorded. An invitation to join forces with other authorities and experts on the foods of these exotic countries was quickly grasped. It has been a pleasure to include many of my own recipes and knowledge to those so carefully prepared by such an imposing line-up of International authorities. Gloria Zimmerman, who specialises in Vietnamese and Chinese Cooking; Khalid Aziz, born in Lahore, who has written and broadcasted extensively on Indian cooking; Deh-ta Hsiung, born in Peking and has several books published on Chinese cooking; Kay Shimizu, a Japanese-American, the author of several specialist Asian Cookbooks. Jan Leeming, a journalist who has taken a special interest in Korean cooking.

Sri Owen from Indonesia; Ornsiri Selby-Lowndes from Thailand and Bach Ngo from Vietnam, all authoritative writers on the cuisines of their homelands. Together we have been able to prepare a book that is rich and varied, and authentic.

With Oriental shops in all major cities and many country towns selling both fresh and dried ingredients and with department stores, supermarkets and health food shops with Oriental sections, it is an easy matter to obtain the ingredients and special utensils required for Asian cooking.

Asia contains over half the world's population and as Australian interest in our near neighbours grows, this seems the perfect time to introduce this compendium of food lore on the Orient.

Margaret Fulton

INDIA, PAKISTAN & BANGLADESH

A visitor to India expecting to be served only burning curries is in for quite a surprise. Indian food is incredibly diverse and amazingly subtle with each region producing its own combinations of meat, rice and spices that reflect the religious beliefs of the people and availability of raw materials.

The Indian sub continent is a world apart, a land unto itself. From the lovely Vale of Kashmir at the foothills of the Himalayas to Cape Camorin on the southern tip, from Karachi at the mouth of the Indus River on the west coast to busy, teeming Calcutta on the Ganges delta and Assam, nudging into Burma, Tibet and China, India is indeed a vast country. Its food, people and customs have captured the imagination of the whole world.

The sacred earth of mother India nurtures over 600 million human beings – not to mention the cows, buffaloes, monkeys, insects and, in its jungles, those marvellous elephants and beautiful tigers. So many people living in such a vast land that includes lush and arid, tropical and temperate, mountainous and flat, naturally enough enjoy an amazingly wide variety of foods and styles of cooking.

The enormously rich and varied culture of India has evolved over the ages. Vegetarianism, linked with the doctrine of non-violence, has always been advocated and popular in India. Meat eating was never totally forbidden except in the Buddhist period. Wheat, rice, millets and pulses are the principal food grains, their popularity depending on local production. Milk, ghee and other milk products are considered necessary items for a balanced diet.

Indian cookery is famous the world over, it is so varied and subtle that it enjoys a reputation matched only by the Chinese and French. This may come as a great surprise to many Westerners who tend to think of Indian cooking as beginning and ending with curry.

One sometimes hears that curry is not really Indian or that Indians never use ready-mixed curry powders. The first claim is not true. The word curry appears in the language of both north and south India and to Indians it means a dish of meat or vegetables with a spicy sauce, not a dry dish. The claim that Indians never use a ready-mixed curry powder has more truth, for an Indian cook grinds and mixes fresh spices every day, ending up with powders and pastes like the commercial ones you buy.

To speak of Indian food as one indivisible style would be wrong. There is, most would agree, a common thread which links all styles of Indian cooking, but it is a drawstring which encompasses widely spaced points. Looking at an Indian map one will see that the first culinary differences correspond to the political boundaries between the countries which make up the area. Pakistan, when it became a state in its own right in 1948, was divided into East and West Pakistan and populated by Muslims. These two areas were separated by 1,500 kilometres of India, populated by Hindus.

It is said that there are as many differences between Hindu and Muslim cooking as there are between the religions themselves. Muslims do not eat pork, but other meat is acceptable and widely incorporated into the Muslim cuisine, as long as it is butchered in the prescribed manner (to allow as much blood as possible to drain from the carcass). However, many Hindus, particularly those from Gujrat in the south, make vegetarianism an inexorable part of their faith. For them cooking is an art indeed, designed to turn out not only tasty dishes, but a balanced diet based on vegetables, suited to the needs of an arduous life.

What was East Pakistan is now Bangladesh. Predominantly Muslim, the Bangladeshi style of cooking revolves largely around the fish that inhabit the thousands of miles of waterway that make up the Ganges delta. Fish is acceptable to Muslims, as it is believed to have already been sacrificially slaughtered by virtue of the gill slits which appear to cut the neck of the creature!

Meat, sacrificed in the proper manner for Muslims, assumes an even greater role in cuisine for Sikhs. Traditionally, Sikhs are a warlike people who make the possession of a dagger an article of faith. Their beasts have to be killed by *jhutka* – the complete decapitation of the animal, which ideally should be achieved in one blow.

Availability of raw materials is as important as religious beliefs in determining the Indian diet. In the north, temperate climes prevail. In Pakistan and Nepal, the Himalayan foothills provide lush grassy slopes for grazing. Here, broad-leaved vegetables, including spinach and cauliflower, are grown. Further south on the plains of India, a combination of baking sun and irrigation permits peas, lentils and other pulses (legumes), and tropical vegetables, such as green peppers, eggplant and okra, to be cultivated. It is here too that the spices and strong flavourings are grown – especially turmeric and chillis. Around the Indian coastline, as yet unspoilt by pollution, seafood, including all manner of shellfish, is abundant. In Bangladesh, the rivers teem with every kind of fish, including the huge Ma Sher, which is large enough to provide a feast for a village.

There are almost as many different styles of eating in the Indian sub-continent as there are styles of cooking. Throughout, the hand is used to eat with. Traditionally the right hand is used, never the left. Muslims in particular seem to make great play of this – the left hand being considered ungodly in the extreme. In polite society it is considered incorrect to allow the fingers to be soiled beyond the second knuckle joint. Traditionally, Hindus serve a meal on a *thali* – a tray-like plate

In southern India, Dosas are traditionally served as breakfast, but in the rest of India they are offered as a snack at any time of the day. Here they are prepared with the traditional Aloo Gobi filling.

INDIA, PAKISTAN & BANGLADESH

Sweets are a traditional part of Indian life and are exchanged between family and friends. Here is a selection of sweet dumplings and spirals in syrup.

usually made of metal. Each item of the meal is placed in a discreet pile around the edge of the thali — the centre being reserved as the area from which the food is eaten. In this way the diner can use the thali as a kind of artist's palette, mixing and blending flavours like colours. Today in modern India, convenience has obviated the use of the thali, but even when confronted with a plateful of curry and rice, many Indians will maintain a traditional thali-based style of eating.

The eating of both bread and rice in the same meal is frowned upon in some quarters. Usually such a choice does not arise — those in paddy-growing areas use rice to provide their carbohydrate; where wheat grows in abundance, bread is the order of the day. While day in, day out, the average peasant has to content himself with a simple meal of rice and vegetables, on holidays no expense is spared to eat the best available. During festivals, the emphasis is on abundance and flavour, and it is this festival cooking that plays the major part in

the development of Indian cuisine. Rice is still the staple food, but it will be combined with meat and stock to make sumptuous pilaus, with cardamoms and cloves adding aromatic piquancy. In the north, lamb dishes such as Korma (see page 21) and Roghan Gosht (see page 29) are made.

Throughout India, the giving and receiving of sweets has always marked celebration. Chief among these is perhaps Halwa (see page 44), a fudge-like concoction which, being easily carried, is today sent over great distances to expatriates so that they may indulge with their families on great occasions. Much use is made of milk in the preparation of sweets. In the days leading up to a festival, kitchens in sweetmeat shops and homes alike are dominated by huge bubbling cauldrons of milk being reduced to make *khoa* – a kind of evaporated milk. Khoa is then used to make all manner of sweetmeats – Kulfi (see page 44) and Gulab Jamun (see page 43), for example.

Milk is also used to make puddings for high days and holidays. On the Muslim festival days or Ids – particularly Id-ul-Fitr which follows the thirty days of fasting in the month of Ramadan – Muslims dress in their best clothes and visit one another. They offer and receive milk puddings decorated with finely beaten silver leaf, known as varak*. The most popular dishes are Sewaiian (see page 45), made with vermicelli, and Kheer (see page 45), made with rice flour.

Regional cooking styles

In the north, particularly northern Pakistan, tandoori cooking has dominated for centuries. A *tandoor* is a clay oven, conically shaped like a beehive. Three hours before cooking, a charcoal fire is lit in the tandoor and, when searing temperatures are reached inside, cooking can begin. Tandoori recipes depend on quick cooking. Meat is cut into chunks and marinated, then cooked on skewers in a matter of minutes. Poultry is dealt with in the same way, either whole or cut into serving pieces.

As the tandoor is an oven and not merely a charcoal barbecue, it offers one of the few opportunities for making leavened bread. Normally, Indian bread is a simple griddle-cooked dough of flour and water. Naan, however, makes full use of yeast to provide a product that, cooked on the inside walls of the tandoor, is lighter than most unleavened bread.

Advanced though tandoori cooking is, it is not a complete cuisine. It has developed hand in glove with the Mughal style of cooking, after the fashion of the Mughal emperors who laid great emphasis on presentation. It is within this style, which extends down towards central India, that food appears to be at its most appetizing. From Mughal cooking, a new and differing style developed around Delhi. This Delhi style is today much revered and many of the best recipes are ubiquitous throughout the land. Bombay, being a major port, developed a more cosmopolitan style, with such delicacies as cutlets and sweet and sour dishes – learnt from the Chinese. Also on the west coast, Indian Christians developed their own styles, particularly in Goa. Further south on the Keralanese coast, the use of fenugreek has been developed to a fine art, mainly to absorb odour in fish dishes.

The Tamils, further inland and on the east coast, make use of the plentiful supplies of coconut available – hardly a main dish is prepared without coconut in one form or another! A type of coconut paste is made by holding half a coconut against the rotating blade of a crude scraper, often co-owned by many families, and the resulting paste-like milk is used to give substance to Tamili curries.

It seems to be a rule that the hotter the temperature, the hotter the food. Certainly the Madrasis, who live in constantly high temperatures, prove the point. Vinda-loo, cooked with the addition of vinegar, has been treated with reverence by generations of restaurant-goers in the West, though it is the Bengalis who have

been mainly responsible for bringing Indian food to Western countries.

Inevitably, with time and the levelling effect of the British Raj, many recipes have crossed traditional regional boundaries and their antecedents have been transformed during five thousand years of cooking.

Cooking utensils

It is a fallacy that lack of utensils is a major hurdle to the Westerner setting out to cook Indian food. The sub-continent is poor, and food often has to be prepared and cooked in primitive conditions. The average Western kitchen is more than equipped to cope with the demands of Indian food. For example, using an electric blender or coffee grinder to grind spices is far easier than using the traditional stone and slab! Currying is basically a stewing process, so a large, heavy saucepan is all that is needed. Bhoona is similar to the Chinese method of stir-frying, performed in a wok. A deep-sided frying pan can normally be used for this or, where larger quantities are called for, a heavy saucepan.

Obviously a tandoor can present problems, but a charcoal barbecue will cook marinated meat on skewers. Chicken is best started in a conventional oven and maybe finished on the barbecue.

Naan is more difficult, but reasonable results can be obtained in a hot oven. Unleavened breads, such as chapattis, are traditionally cooked on a dome-shaped disc known as a *tawa*, which is heated over a fire. This utensil is perhaps worth investing in, although good results can be obtained by using any flat metal plate. When deep-frying – pakoras, samosas, puri, hoppers, for example – use normal deep-frying equipment.

Serving

When serving Indian food, balance must be borne in mind. Starters or hors d'oeuvre are not generally served as such, but crisp fried samosas with a dipping mint yogurt sauce, or pakoras can be served as an appetizer. Similarly, puddings are not normally taken with everyday meals, but again, serve them if you wish. Bread or rice are served as part of the main course, being generally preferred. Main meat dishes are best accompanied by a vegetable curry and perhaps a dal. Guests will also appreciate the coolness of a salad; green salad is more authentic because good tomatoes are generally few and far between in the sub-continent. A refreshing yogurt dish will also be appreciated.

Use hot spices cautiously; there is little point in bombarding a digestion accustomed to a Western diet with fiery hot food. To quench the thirst most Indians take water, usually well iced and sometimes flavoured with sandalwood or rose. Muslims, of course, shun alcohol although some Hindus and Sikhs take beer. Lager or wine can be served with Indian food, but it is doubtful that subtle vintages will be appreciated.

The golden rule with Indian food is that it is not static; it changes every time a cook adds a little extra something, be that cook in Bombay or Calcutta, Lahore or Madras, or even London, New York or Sydney.

GARAM MASALA

Garam Masala forms the base for much of the cuisine of India, and many people regard it as the special touch that turns ordinary cooking into golden cuisine. Consequently, there are almost as many recipes for Garam Masala as there are cooks in India. For this recipe, use either bleached or green cardamoms. Measure the spices with teaspoons or tablespoons, depending on the quantity you wish to make. If stored in an airtight jar, Garam Masala should keep for 3 to 6 months.

1½ spoons cardamom pods
5 spoons coriander seeds
1 spoon cumin seeds
1½ spoons whole cloves
6 spoons whole black peppercorns

METHOD: Remove the seeds from the cardamoms, then place on a baking tray with the remaining ingredients.

Bake in a preheated very hot oven (240°C/475°F) for 10 minutes, then leave to cool. Grind to a fine powder using a pestle and mortar, coffee mill or electric blender. Store in an airtight jar.

FRAGRANT GARAM MASALA

3 × 8 cm (3 inch) cinnamon sticks
2 teaspoons cardamom seeds
1 teaspoon whole cloves
½ nutmeg, grated

METHOD: In a small pan, roast separately the cinnamon, then the cardamom, then the cloves. Remove each spice from the pan when it begins to smell fragrant and leave to cool on a plate.

When all are roasted and cooled, grind to a fine powder in a blender or pound using a mortar and pestle. Finally, add the grated nutmeg. Makes ¼ cup.

▷ *Preparing Garam Masala from the basic spices: bleached and green cardamoms, coriander seeds, cloves, black peppercorns and cumin seeds*

DAHI
YOGURT

Dahi, or homemade yogurt, forms the base of many Indian dishes. Yogurt-making is simplicity itself, yet many good cooks seem to experience difficulty with it. No special equipment is required, but it seems to be more successful if made in quantities greater than 600 ml (2½ cups). The quantity given here is ideal.

5 cups milk
⅔ cup natural yogurt
2 teaspoons salt (optional)

METHOD: Bring the milk to the boil in a heavy pan, then boil for 3 to 4 minutes. Remove the pan from the heat and leave the milk to cool to blood heat (37°C/98°F).

Beat in the yogurt and salt (if using), then leave in a warm place, at approximately 37°C/98°F, for at least 12 hours – the longer it is left, the more separated the curds and whey become.

Use as required, keeping a little to one side in the refrigerator to start the next batch. This can be continued until the yogurt tastes 'fizzy', then a fresh yogurt should be bought and the process started again as above.
MAKES 5½ CUPS

RAETA
YOGURT WITH CUCUMBER

Westerners may have problems with Indian food because of its spiciness, this is invariably because they have never been offered Raeta as an accompaniment to their meal. There is virtually no end to the combination of vegetables that can be blended with yogurt to make Raeta, but the following recipe is a good all-rounder.

1½ cups natural yogurt
½ cucumber, cut into matchstick strips
1 small onion, peeled and chopped
1 small tomato, chopped (optional)
1 teaspoon salt
To garnish:
2 teaspoons chopped coriander leaves*
½ teaspoon chilli powder

METHOD: Put all the ingredients in a serving bowl and stir well to mix. Sprinkle with the coriander leaves and chilli powder, then chill in the refrigerator before serving.
SERVES 4

CURRY SAUCE

It is useful to know the basics of curry cookery before proceeding further with Indian food. This curry sauce is not a dish in itself, but is useful for currying leftovers.

4 tablespoons ghee*
1 large onion, peeled and sliced
2 garlic cloves, peeled and sliced
1 teaspoon ground coriander
1 teaspoon ground turmeric
1 teaspoon chilli powder
½ teaspoon salt
1 teaspoon freshly ground black pepper
1¼ cups water
1 teaspoon Garam Masala (see page 12)

METHOD: Melt the ghee in a pan, add the onion and garlic and fry gently until soft but not brown. Stir in the coriander, turmeric, chilli, salt and pepper, then add the ingredients to be curried – meat, fish, poultry or vegetables, etc. Fry for 5 minutes, then add the water and bring to the boil.

Lower the heat and simmer for 10 minutes, then add the Garam Masala and simmer for a further 5 minutes. Serve hot with vegetables, or simply spooned over a bowl of rice.
SERVES 4

BOMBAY DUCK

This is the common name applied to the Bummaloe fish, which swims in coastal waters around the sub-continent. The fish is a scavenger and is said to have derived its doubtful name from one of its better-known habitats, the docks at Bombay. The fish are usually netted and then hung up to dry in the sun; salt is added later. The taste, not to mention the smell, is an acquired experience, but they are available here and are worth trying. They should be grilled or fried for a minute or so on each side and served warm. A useful starter, but usually offered as a side dish with curries.

POPPADOMS

Poppadoms are one of the best-known Indian foods in the world. Originally they were designed as appetizers in the strictest sense of the word. With the British Raj in India the poppadom came into its own, and no colonel's table would have been complete without a pile of fresh ones. Some of the British in India developed the habit of crumbling the poppadom over a plate laden with curry and rice; but most Indians prefer to eat them from a side plate so as to savour their crispness.

Poppadoms are available both plain and spiced. The spicing is achieved mostly with crushed black pepper, but hotter poppadoms are made using chilli powder. The process of making poppadoms is so complicated that it is best to buy them ready prepared. The dough, made from besan* (chick pea) flour, is very sensitive to humidity, so it is important to store poppadoms in a cool, dry place. Deep-frying is the best method of cooking.

Heat the oil or fat in a deep pan until a small piece of poppadom, dropped into the oil or fat, immediately sizzles and rises to the surface. Before cooking, beat the

△ **From the top: Curried Pastries; Savoury Fritters; Crisp Rice Pancakes; Savoury Pancakes**

poppadom on a table to get rid of the dust.

Using a slotted spoon and a fish slice, fry the poppadoms, two at a time, for about 5 to 10 seconds, then turn them over and fry the other side. (Frying two together prevents them curling up.) Drain the poppadoms and stack them upright in a rack so any excess fat can drain away. Eat within a few hours of frying.

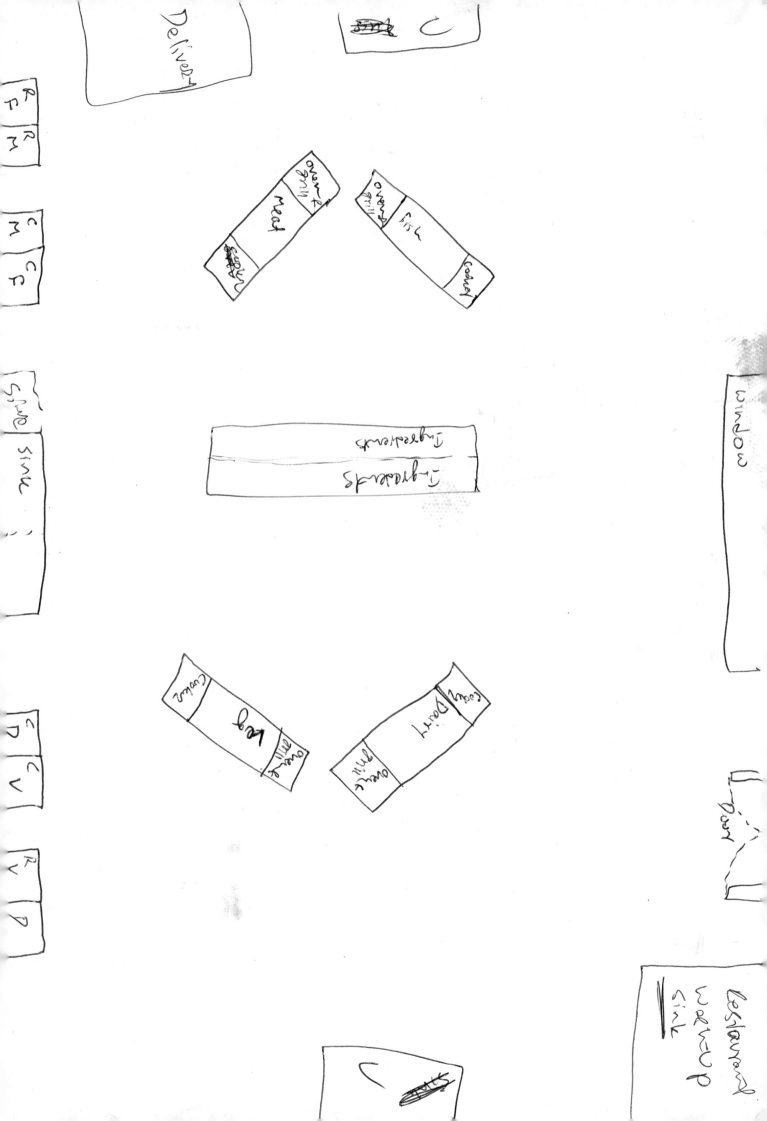

Asian — fusion food
concept

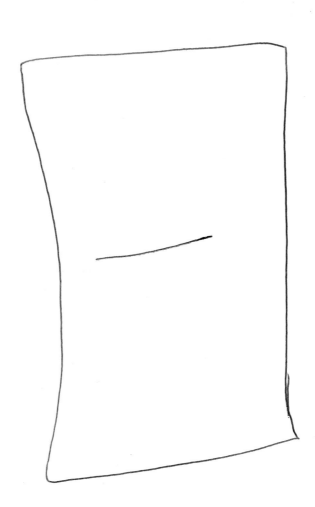

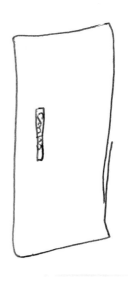

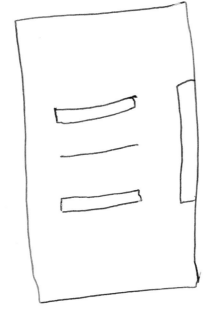

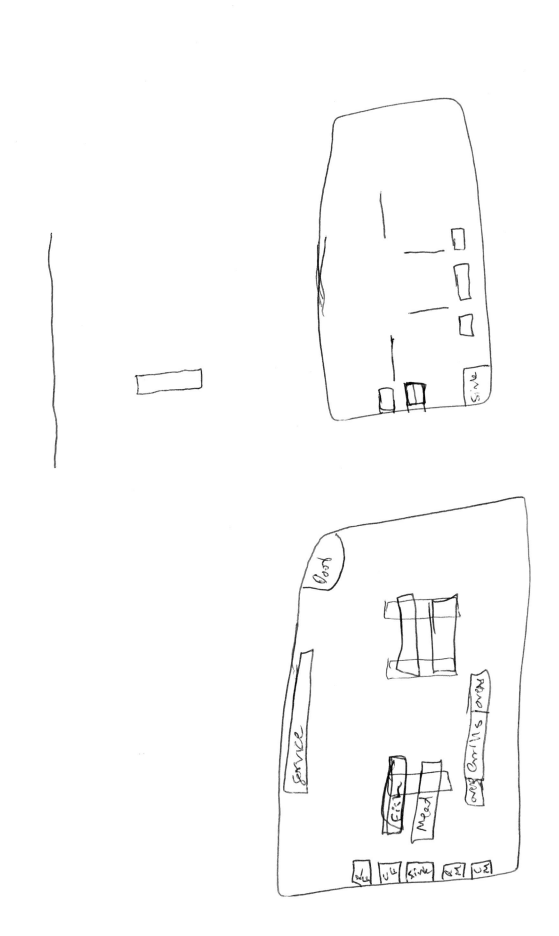

DOSAS
SAVOURY PANCAKES

A great breakfast pancake from the south of India, eaten also as a snack throughout the day. Like pancakes they can be eaten plain or with a savoury filling, such as Aloo Gobi (see page 30). Instead of wheat flour a blend of ground urhad dal* and rice are used to make dosa.

1 cup urhad dal*
¼ cup rice
2½ cups water
½ teaspoon bicarbonate of soda
1 teaspoon chilli powder
½ teaspoon salt
vegetable oil for shallow-frying

METHOD: Wash the dal and rice thoroughly, then put in a bowl with the water. Leave to soak overnight.

Place the dal, rice and water mixture in an electric blender and work until smooth. Add the soda, chilli powder and salt and stir well.

Pour in enough batter to cover the bottom of a cold, heavy pan. Put on the heat until starting to set. Pour about 1 tablespoon of oil around the edge of the dosa, then shake the pan to spread the oil. Fry the pancake for about a minute, until golden underneath. Remove from the pan and roll up each dosa, enclosing a filling if liked. Serve hot.

MAKES 12-15

SAMOSAS
CURRIED PASTRIES

These Indian savouries are semi-circular pastries filled with minced lamb, subtly flavoured with spices and herbs. They are deep-fried until golden and crisp and are wonderful with pre-dinner drinks. In India they are usually eaten as a snack – often served with tea.

Pastry:
2 cups plain flour
3 tablespoons ghee*
½ teaspoon salt
1 cup milk (approximately), soured with a little lemon juice
vegetable oil for deep-frying
Filling:
Keema (see page 24), or Aloo Gobi (see page 30)

METHOD: Sift the flour into a bowl, rub in the ghee, then add the salt. Stir in the soured milk gradually, to form a stiff dough which is velvety to the touch. Chill in the refrigerator until required.

Break the dough into pieces, about 2.5 cm (1 inch) in diameter. Roll out into very thin circles, then cut each circle in half. Spoon a little of the chosen filling in the centre of each semi-circle, then fold in half to make a triangular cone shape, enclosing the filling. Moisten the edges of the dough with soured milk, then press together to seal.

Heat the oil in a deep pan then deep-fry the samosas, a few at a time, for about 1 minute until the pastry is golden brown. Drain well and serve warm.

MAKES ABOUT 25

Note: Samosas keep quite well in an airtight container; reheat under a pre-heated grill before serving.

PAKORAS
SAVOURY FRITTERS

Vegetables are chopped or cut into bite-sized pieces, spiced and mixed with, or dipped in, a thick batter of besan* (chick pea) flour. The fritters are fried to a deep golden brown. They may be served as a snack at any time of the day and are particularly good with pre-dinner drinks. Sometimes the batter without vegetables is deep-fried and served on its own.

1 cup besan*
½ teaspoon chilli powder
½ teaspoon salt
⅔ cup natural yogurt
1 teaspoon lemon juice
vegetable oil for deep frying

METHOD: Sift the flour into a bowl, rubbing any lumps through the sieve with the back of a spoon. Add the chilli powder and salt and mix well. Stir in the yogurt and lemon juice gradually. Cover and leave in a cool place for 2 hours until the batter is thick; it should be much thicker than a pancake batter.

Heat the oil in a deep pan until a little of the batter, dropped into the oil, sizzles and rises to the surface. Deep-fry the batter in spoonfuls or use to coat fresh spinach leaves or very thin slices of eggplant, cauliflower, zucchini or green capsicums and deep-fry. Drain on kitchen paper towels, then serve fresh and warm.

SERVES 4

Note: Mix with batter, 3 cups of chopped mixed vegetables – choose from cauliflower, green peppers, peas, carrots and deep-fry until golden.

Pakoras will keep in an airtight container for a few days; reheat under a preheated grill before serving.

HOPPERS
CRISP RICE PANCAKES

Often served for breakfast, Hoppers are bowl-shaped fine rice pancakes, swirled in a hemispherical pan, a chatty – rather like a small, deep wok. Rice flour batter is poured into the chatty and immediately spun so that the batter flies to the curved sides of the pan and sizzles into a delicate filigree. You can make them in a small omelette pan, with curved sides, not quite the authentic shape but the taste is right.

2 tablespoons desiccated coconut
1 cup water
1 cup rice
½ teaspoon bicarbonate of soda
½ teaspoon salt
30 g (1 oz) butter

METHOD: Soak the coconut in the water for 4 hours. Meanwhile, grind the rice using a mortar and pestle, coffee mill or electric blender.

Strain the coconut water into the ground rice, then add the soda and salt. Beat to make a smooth batter, then leave to stand for 12 hours to allow the ground rice to absorb the liquid.

Beat the batter until well aerated. Lightly grease a hot frying pan with a little butter. Pour in a little batter, tilting the pan so that the batter spreads to the edge. Cook for about 30 seconds or until the centre of the hopper is solid. Do not turn over. Repeat with the remaining batter. Serve hot and fresh.

MAKES 25-30

JHINGA SAMBAL
PRAWN AND EGG SAMBAL

This fresh-tasting chilled dish is good for a light buffet or lunch.

500 g (1 lb) peeled cooked prawns
4 hard-boiled eggs, quartered
1 cup coconut milk*
1 small onion, peeled and minced
1 garlic clove, peeled and crushed
1 green chilli, chopped
juice of ½ lemon
pinch of chilli powder
½ teaspoon salt
To garnish:
½ cup cooked green peas
chopped coriander leaves*

METHOD: Arrange the prawns and eggs in a serving dish.

Work the coconut milk, onion, garlic, green chilli, lemon juice, chilli powder and salt in an electric blender until evenly blended. Pour over the prawns and eggs. Garnish with the peas and coriander. Serve well chilled, with poppadoms if liked.
SERVES 4

EKOORI
SPICED SCRAMBLED EGGS

The Parsees, a religious order that trace their origins back several millennia, have produced a version of scrambled eggs that make other scrambled eggs quite pallid by comparison.

8 eggs
4 tomatoes, chopped
1 teaspoon salt
3 tablespoons ghee*
1 medium onion, peeled and sliced
2 green chillis, chopped
1 teaspoon ground turmeric
1 teaspoon ground coriander
5-6 sprigs fresh coriander* (optional)

METHOD: Put the eggs, tomatoes and salt in a bowl and beat well. Melt the ghee in a pan, add the onion and fry gently until soft. Add the chillis and spices and fry for 2 minutes, stirring constantly. Add the beaten egg mixture and stir with a wooden spoon until the eggs are scrambled. Serve sprinkled with fresh coriander if using.
SERVES 4

JHINGA KARI
PRAWN CURRY

Kerala in the south-west corner of India is famous for its treatment of one of its most plentiful seafoods, prawns. They realize the importance of not masking the delicate flavour of prawns. If cooked prawns are used in this recipe take care to simmer very gently once added.

3 tablespoons ghee*
1 small onion, peeled and sliced
2 garlic cloves, peeled and sliced
½ teaspoon grated fresh ginger*
2 teaspoons ground coriander
1 teaspoon ground turmeric
½ teaspoon ground cumin
½ teaspoon chilli powder
2 tablespoons vinegar
500 g (1 lb) peeled prawns, raw or cooked
1 cup water

METHOD: Melt the ghee in a heavy pan, add the onion, garlic and ginger and fry gently until soft. Mix the spices to a paste with the vinegar, then add to the pan and fry for a further 3 minutes, stirring the mixture constantly.

Add the prawns and turn gently with a wooden spoon until coated with the spice mixture, being careful not to crush them. Stir in the water, then simmer gently for a few minutes. Serve the prawn curry immediately, with boiled rice.
SERVES 4

MULLIGATAWNY

Mulligatawny soup has no history in India before the British Raj – it was simply an invention to satisfy the needs of army officers who demanded a soup course at dinner. The literal translation of mulligatawny is 'pepper water'!

60 g (2 oz) dried tamarind*
5 cups beef stock (made with cubes)
3 tablespoons ghee*
1 large onion, peeled and sliced
2 garlic cloves, peeled and sliced
1 teaspoon grated fresh ginger*
2 teaspoons freshly ground black pepper
2 teaspoons ground coriander
½ teaspoon ground fenugreek
½ teaspoon chilli powder
½ teaspoon ground turmeric
½ teaspoon salt

METHOD: Put the tamarind in a pan, add just enough stock to cover, then bring to the boil. Remove the pan from the heat and leave the tamarind to soak for 4 hours.

Melt the ghee in a heavy pan, add the onion, garlic and ginger and fry gently until soft. Add the spices and salt. Fry for 3 minutes, stirring constantly, then stir in the remaining stock. Strain the tamarind liquid, discarding the seeds, then add to the pan and simmer for 15 minutes. Taste and adjust the seasoning. Serve hot.
SERVES 4

▽ *Prawn and Egg Sambal served with Poppadoms*

JHINGA PATHIA
SPICED PRAWNS IN COCONUT MILK

A popular dish in southern India where coconuts and large orange-coloured prawns are plentiful. A masala of spices, fresh ginger and vinegar are mixed together to a paste to give a marvellous aroma and flavour to the prawns in this dish.

3 tablespoons ghee*
1 medium onion, peeled and sliced
3 garlic cloves, peeled and sliced
2 teaspoons ground coriander
1 teaspoon ground turmeric
1 teaspoon chilli powder
½ teaspoon salt
½ teaspoon freshly ground black pepper
1 teaspoon grated fresh ginger*
2 tablespoons vinegar
1 cup coconut milk*
500 g (1 lb) peeled cooked prawns
2 tablespoons tomato paste

METHOD: Melt the ghee in a heavy pan, add the onion and garlic and fry gently until soft. Mix the spices and seasonings to a paste with the vinegar, add to the pan and fry for a further 3 minutes, stirring continuously.

Stir in the coconut milk and simmer, stirring, for 5 minutes. Add the prawns and tomato paste and simmer for 2 minutes until the prawns are fully coated with a thick sauce. Serve immediately.
SERVES 4

MASALA DUM MACHCHI
BAKED SPICED FISH

Any variety of fish, either whole or fillets, can be used for this tandoori-style dish, although white fish – such as bream, snapper or flounder – is preferable. If oily fish is used, double the quantity of vinegar.

1 cup natural yogurt
1 medium onion, peeled and chopped
1 garlic clove, peeled and chopped
1 teaspoon grated fresh ginger*
1 tablespoon vinegar
1½ teaspoons ground cumin
pinch of chilli powder
1 fish, weighing 1 kg (2 lb) cleaned, or 750 g (1½ lb) fish fillets
juice of 1 lemon
1 teaspoon salt
To garnish:
1 lemon slice
coriander leaves*

METHOD: Put ¼ cup of the yogurt, chopped onion and garlic, grated ginger, vinegar, cumin and chilli powder in an electric blender. Work to a smooth sauce. Add the remaining yogurt.

Score the fish and place in an ovenproof dish. Rub with lemon juice and sprinkle with the salt. Pour over the yogurt marinade, cover and leave to marinate in the refrigerator overnight.

Cover the fish with foil and bake in a preheated moderate oven (180°C/350°F) for 30 minutes. Garnish with the lemon slice and coriander. Serve hot.
SERVES 4

JHINGA KARI MADRASI
MADRAS DRY PRAWN CURRY

Some of the best curries of India are the dry ones, that is, the food is not swimming with sauce. From Madras come many superb seafood dishes like this prawn curry.

3 tablespoons ghee*
1 small onion, peeled and sliced
2 garlic cloves, peeled and sliced
½ teaspoon grated fresh ginger*
1 teaspoon ground coriander
½ teaspoon ground turmeric
½ teaspoon ground cumin
½ teaspoon salt
500 g (1 lb) peeled cooked prawns
1 tablespoon vinegar
pinch of chilli powder to garnish

METHOD: Melt the ghee in a heavy pan, add the onion, garlic and ginger and fry gently until soft. Add the spices and salt and fry for a further 3 minutes, stirring the mixture constantly.

Reduce the heat to very low, then add the prawns and toss lightly for 1 minute until coated with the spices. Stir in the vinegar, then increase the heat and cook for 30 seconds.

Sprinkle with the chilli powder and serve immediately.
SERVES 4

SAAG JHINGA
PRAWNS AND SPINACH

The combination of spinach and prawns is unusual, yet the two flavours complement each other very well.

3 tablespoons ghee*
1 large onion, peeled and sliced
2 garlic cloves, peeled and sliced
1 tablespoon tomato paste
½ teaspoon Garam Masala (see page 12)
1½ teaspoons ground coriander
½ teaspoon ground turmeric
½ teaspoon chilli powder
½ teaspoon ground ginger
1 teaspoon salt
500 g (1 lb) English spinach or silverbeet, washed and thick white stems removed, then leaves roughly chopped
500 g (1 lb) peeled cooked prawns

METHOD: Melt the ghee in a heavy pan, add the onion and garlic and fry gently until soft. Stir in the tomato paste and fry, stirring, for 1 minute. Add the spices and salt and fry for a further 5 minutes, stirring constantly.

Add the spinach and toss with a wooden spoon. Cook until the spinach has softened, stirring frequently, then add the prawns. Cook for a further 5 minutes, turning the prawns gently to coat with the spinach. Serve immediately.
SERVES 4

△ *Prawns and Spinach (above);*
Spiced Prawns in Coconut Milk; Madras Dry Prawn Curry

MURGH DHANSAK
CHICKEN WITH LENTILS

The Parsees are a people who trace their origins back to antiquity and Chicken Dhansak is a dish which dates almost as far back. Literally translated, it means 'wealthy chicken'. Strictly speaking, it should be made from two types of pulses – chenna dal* and moong dal*. If these are not available, use whichever dal* is most readily obtainable.

250 g (8 oz) chenna dal*
250 g (8 oz) moong dal*
5 cups water
8 tablespoons ghee*
2 large onions, peeled and sliced
4 garlic cloves, peeled and sliced
6 whole cloves
6 cardamom pods
2 teaspoons Garam Masala (see page 12)
1½ teaspoons grated fresh ginger*
2½ teaspoons salt
1 chicken, weighing 1.5 kg (3 lb), skinned, boned and cut into 8 pieces
500 g (1 lb) frozen leaf spinach
4 large tomatoes, chopped

METHOD: Wash the dals, place in a saucepan and add the water. Bring to the boil and simmer, covered, for 15 minutes.

Meanwhile, melt the ghee in a heavy pan, add the onions and garlic and fry gently until soft. Add the spices, ginger and salt and fry for a further 3 minutes, stirring constantly. Add the chicken and fry until browned on all sides, then remove from the pan and drain on kitchen paper towels.

Add the spinach and tomatoes to the pan and fry gently for 10 minutes, stirring occasionally.

Mash the dals in the cooking water, then stir into the spinach mixture. Return the chicken to the pan, cover with a tight-fitting lid and simmer for 45 minutes or until the chicken is tender. Serve hot.
SERVES 4-6

MURGH HYDERABAD
HYDERABAD-STYLE CHICKEN

This recipe, from Hyderabad, Deccan, uses coconut, and it is well worth obtaining a fresh one to make it, if at all possible.

8 tablespoons ghee*
1 large onion, peeled and sliced
2 garlic cloves, peeled and sliced
6 cardamom pods
4 whole cloves
2.5 cm (1 inch) piece of cinnamon stick
2 teaspoons Garam Masala (see page 12)
1 teaspoon ground turmeric
1 teaspoon chilli powder
1 teaspoon salt
1 chicken, weighing 1.5 kg (3 lb), skinned, boned and cut into 8 pieces
flesh of ½ fresh coconut, thinly sliced
1 tablespoon tomato paste
1¼ cups water

METHOD: Melt the ghee in a heavy pan, add the onion and garlic and fry gently until soft. Add the spices and salt and fry for a further 3 minutes, stirring constantly. Add the chicken and fry for 10 minutes until browned on all sides, then add the coconut, tomato paste and water. Stir well, then bring to the boil.

Lower the heat, cover with a tight-fitting lid and simmer for 45 minutes or until the chicken is tender. Serve hot.
SERVES 4

KUKUL CURRY
CHICKEN CURRY

A curry from Sri Lanka, the combination of spices with coconut milk and chillis makes for a fragrant dish.

3 tablespoons ghee*
1 large onion, peeled and sliced
3 garlic cloves, peeled and sliced
4 green chillis, chopped
2 teaspoons ground coriander
1½ teaspoons ground turmeric
1 chicken, weighing 1.5 kg (3 lb), skinned and cut into 8 pieces
1¼ cups coconut milk*
juice of ½ lemon

METHOD: Melt the ghee in a heavy pan, add the onion and garlic and fry gently until soft. Add the chillis and spices and fry for a further 3 minutes, stirring constantly.

Add the chicken pieces to the pan and fry gently until browned on all sides. Stir in the coconut milk, then simmer gently for 45 minutes or until the chicken is tender. Add the lemon juice and simmer for a further 10 minutes, stirring occasionally. Serve hot.
SERVES 4

KOOKARH KORMA
CHICKEN KORMA

The succulent Korma is a special kind of curry distinguished by its rich and spicy sauce. It is one of the most famous Indian dishes, which makes good use of the marinating process. The korma method can also be applied to meat; lamb korma is particularly popular in northern India.

¾ cup natural yogurt
2 teaspoons ground turmeric
3 garlic cloves, peeled and sliced
1 teaspoon grated fresh ginger*
1 chicken, weighing 1.5 kg (3 lb), skinned and cut into 8 pieces
3 tablespoons ghee*
1 large onion, peeled and sliced
5 cm/2 inch piece of cinnamon stick
5 whole cloves
5 cardamom pods
1 tablespoon crushed coriander seeds
1 teaspoon ground cumin
½ teaspoon chilli powder
1 teaspoon salt
1½ tablespoons desiccated coconut
2 teaspoons toasted almonds

METHOD: Work the yogurt, turmeric, 1 garlic clove and ginger in an electric blender, then pour over the chicken. Cover and leave to marinate overnight.

Melt the ghee in a heavy pan, add the onion and remaining garlic and fry gently until soft. Add the spices and salt and fry for a further 3 minutes, stirring constantly.

Add the chicken with the marinade and coconut, then cover with a tight-fitting lid and simmer for 45 minutes or until the chicken is tender. Scatter the almonds over the chicken. Serve hot.
SERVES 4

Note: The chicken may alternatively be cooked whole; allow an extra 20 to 30 minutes cooking time.

◁ *Chicken with Lentils; Chicken Korma; Hyderabad-style Chicken*

TANDOORI MURGH
TANDOORI CHICKEN

India's version of barbecued chicken. It gets its rich russet colour from saffron and a few drops of red dye – in India cochineal is used, red food colouring may be substituted. In recent years, there has been a growth in the number of Indian restaurants in the West offering tandoori-style food.

One of the secrets of Tandoori Chicken is the marinade – the longer the chicken is left in the marinade, the more authentic will be the finished dish. It is quite usual for the chicken to be marinated in a cool place or refrigerator for 3 days, sometimes for as long as 1 week.

This recipe has been adapted so that it can be made successfully in a conventional oven.

1 chicken, weighing 1.5 kg (3 lb), skinned and cut into 4 pieces
juice of 2 lemons
4 teaspoons salt
2 garlic cloves, peeled and sliced
1 large onion, peeled and sliced
1 teaspoon ground coriander
½ teaspoon red food colouring
½ teaspoon chilli powder
2 teaspoons grated fresh ginger
⅔ cup natural yogurt
To garnish:
1 lettuce
1-2 tomatoes, sliced
½ onion, sliced into rings
few lemon wedges

METHOD: Make 3 deep cuts in each piece of chicken with a sharp knife. Rub the flesh all over with half the lemon juice, then rub in the salt. Mix the remaining ingredients to a paste with the remaining lemon juice, using an electric blender if available. Put the chicken in a baking dish lined with foil, then pour over the marinade. Cover and leave to marinate for at least 12 hours.

Roast in a preheated moderate oven (180°C/350°F) for 1 hour or until the chicken is tender. Baste occasionally. Increase the heat to moderately hot (200°C/400°F), and roast for a further 15 to 20 minutes until browned on top. Serve hot on a bed of lettuce leaves, garnished with onion rings and lemon wedges. Serve Naan (see page 38) as an accompaniment.
SERVES 4

Note: The tandoor oven is usually about 1 metre (3 feet) high and is made of clay. Searing temperatures are maintained by a charcoal fire at the base of the oven, and the cooking is so efficient that whole young chickens can be cooked in minutes. Naan (see page 38) is cooked on the wall of the oven and meat and poultry in the centre.

MEEN MOLEE
SPICED DUCK IN COCONUT MILK

A molee is a South Indian preparation in which the main ingredient is cooked in coconut milk. This dish is from Goa on the west coast of India, although the molee style of cooking spreads far further south. It can be made with duck or chicken, although duck makes it particularly special.

6 tablespoons ghee*
1 oven-ready duck, weighing 1.75 kg (4 lb), skinned and cut into 8 pieces
1 large onion, peeled and sliced
2 garlic cloves, peeled and sliced
1 teaspoon grated fresh ginger*
1 teaspoon chilli powder
2 teaspoons ground cumin
1 teaspoon ground coriander
1 tablespoon Garam Masala (see page 12)
1 teaspoon salt
⅔ cup vinegar
1¼ cups coconut milk*

METHOD: Melt the ghee in a heavy pan, add the duck and fry until browned on all sides, then remove. Add the onion and garlic to the pan and fry gently until soft.

Mix the spices and salt to a paste with 3 tablespoons of the vinegar, then add to the pan and fry for a further 3 minutes, stirring constantly. Stir in the remaining vinegar and the coconut milk, then return the duck to the pan. Cover and simmer for 45 minutes or until tender. Serve hot.
SERVES 4

MURGH MUSSALAM

SPICED BAKED CHICKEN

The choicest cuts of chicken and careful selection of spices, including that prince of spices, saffron, combine to make this elegant curry dish.

6 half breasts of chicken, skinned
¾ cup natural yogurt
1 large onion, peeled and chopped
3 garlic cloves, peeled and sliced
3 green chillis
1 teaspoon ground coriander
3 tablespoons ghee*
2.5 cm/1 inch piece of cinnamon stick
5 cardamom pods
10 whole cloves
1 teaspoon ground ginger
1 teaspoon salt
1 teaspoon freshly ground black pepper
½ teaspoon saffron threads, soaked in 1 tablespoon boiling water for 30 minutes

METHOD: Make 3 deep cuts in each piece of chicken with a sharp knife. Work the yogurt, onion, garlic, chillis and coriander in an electric blender, then pour over the chicken. Cover and leave to marinate overnight.

Drain the chicken, reserving the marinade. Melt the ghee in a flameproof casserole, add the chicken and fry for about 10 minutes until browned on all sides. Add the spices and seasonings, except the saffron, and fry for a further 3 minutes, stirring constantly. Add the saffron with its liquid, then add the reserved marinade.

Cover the casserole and cook in a preheated moderately hot oven (190°C/375°F) for about 20 minutes or until the chicken is tender and the sauce is very thick. Serve hot.
SERVES 4

▽ *Spiced Baked Chicken (left); Tandoori Chicken*

SHIKAR KARI
PORK CURRY

The tamarind water in this recipe counter-acts the fattiness of pork.

60 g (2 oz) dried tamarind*
1 cup boiling water
3 tablespoons ghee*
1 large onion, peeled and sliced
3 garlic cloves, peeled and chopped
2 green chillis, chopped
3 whole cloves
5 cm (2 inch) piece of cinnamon stick
1 tablespoon ground coriander
1 teaspoon ground turmeric
½ teaspoon chilli powder
½ teaspoon cumin seeds
2 teaspoons chopped fresh ginger*
500 g (1 lb) boned pork, cut into 2.5 cm (1 inch) cubes

METHOD: Soak the tamarind in the water for 2 hours.

Melt the ghee in a heavy pan, add the onion and garlic and fry gently until soft. Add the chillis and spices and fry for a further 3 minutes, stirring constantly. Add the ginger and pork and fry for a further 5 minutes, stirring until the meat is coated.

Strain the tamarind, discarding the seeds, and stir the water into the pan. Bring to the boil, then lower the heat, cover and simmer for about 1 hour or until the meat is tender. Serve hot.

SERVES 4

SHIKAR VINDALOO
VINEGARED PORK CURRY

This recipe comes from the south where it is said to be best made with the pork from the wild boar that roam the area. The vindaloo method of cooking, which is rather acid because of the amount of vinegar used, can be applied to any meat; it makes a very hot curry which should be served with plenty of yogurt.

2 teaspoons chopped fresh ginger*
½ teaspoon cardamom seeds
½ teaspoon ground cloves
1 tablespoon ground coriander
2 teaspoons turmeric powder
4 teaspoons chilli powder
1 teaspoon ground cumin
1 teaspoon salt
½ teaspoon freshly ground black pepper
⅔ cup vinegar
500 g (1 lb) boned pork, cut into 4 cm (1½ inch) cubes
3 tablespoons ghee*
5 garlic cloves, peeled and sliced

METHOD: Mix the ginger, spices and seasonings to a thick paste with a little of the vinegar, then rub into the pork.

Melt the ghee in a heavy enamelled or silverstone-lined pan, add the garlic and fry for 1 to 2 minutes, stirring frequently. Add the pork to the pan and cover with the remaining vinegar.

Bring to the boil, then lower the heat, cover and simmer for about 1 hour or until the meat is tender. Serve hot with Chappattis (see page 39) and plenty of yogurt.

SERVES 4

KEEMA
SPICED MINCED BEEF

This dish is easy to prepare, and is often used for banquets and other functions.

3 tablespoons ghee*
2 large onions, peeled and sliced
2 garlic cloves, peeled and sliced
1 teaspoon ground turmeric
2 teaspoons chilli powder
½ teaspoon ground coriander
½ teaspoon cumin seeds
1 teaspoon salt
1 teaspoon freshly ground black pepper
500 g (1 lb) minced beef

METHOD: Melt the ghee in a pan, add the onions and garlic and fry gently until soft. Add the spices and seasonings and fry for a further 3 minutes, stirring constantly. Add the beef and fry, stirring, until cooked and the curry is dry. Serve hot.

SERVES 4

BHUNA GOSHT
DRY BEEF CURRY

Bhuna is a system of cooking by frying. It can be used with meat and vegetables, although it is usual to precook meat unless it is cut into small, thin pieces.

Usually bhuna dishes are dry with little sauce, and the skill in cooking them lies in not using water. However, if this proves too difficult and the meat shows signs of sticking, then you may add a little more water to the pan — as long as it is boiled off before serving.

3 tablespoons ghee*
500 g (1 lb) tender beef steak, sliced into strips
1 small onion, peeled and sliced
2 garlic cloves, peeled and sliced
1 teaspoon chilli powder
1 teaspoon ground cumin
1 red chilli, cored, seeded and sliced
½ teaspoon salt
½ teaspoon freshly ground black pepper
1 teaspoon Garam Masala (see page 12)

METHOD: Melt the ghee in a large frying pan until hot, add the beef and fry briskly for 30 seconds, turning the meat constantly to prevent sticking and burning. Remove the meat from the pan with a slotted spoon and set aside.

Add the onion and garlic to the pan and fry gently until soft. Stir in the chilli powder and cumin and fry for 3 minutes, stirring constantly. Return the meat to the pan, stir in the sliced chilli and salt and fry for a further 5 minutes or until the meat is tender. Sprinkle over pepper and garam masala, stir in and simmer 2 to 3 minutes. Serve hot, with rice and Raeta (see page 13).

SERVES 4

△ *Spiced Minced Beef; Vinegared Pork Curry, served with Chappattis (see page 39), and Dahi (see page 13)*

MADRASI KARI
MADRAS BEEF CURRY

One of the hottest beef curries.

3 tablespoons ghee*
750 g (1½ lb) beef, round, blade or other stewing cut, cut into 2.5 cm (1 inch) cubes
1 large onion, peeled and sliced
3 garlic cloves, peeled and sliced
3 teaspoons grated fresh ginger*
1½ teaspoons ground coriander
2 teaspoons ground turmeric
1 teaspoon ground cumin
2½ teaspoons chilli powder
1 teaspoon salt
1½ teaspoons freshly ground black pepper
1 cup water
2 teaspoons Garam Masala (see page 12)

METHOD: Melt the ghee in a heavy pan, add the beef and fry briskly until browned on all sides. Remove from the pan with a slotted spoon and set aside. Add the onion, garlic and ginger and fry gently until soft. Add the spices and seasonings except garam masala and fry for a further 3 minutes, stirring constantly.

Return the beef to the pan and fry for a further 3 minutes, stirring to coat the beef with the spices. Stir in the water and bring to the boil, then lower the heat and simmer gently for 1 to 1½ hours or until the meat is tender. Sprinkle over the garam masala and mix in lightly. Serve hot.
SERVES 4-6

PASANDA
SPICED BEEF IN YOGURT

This is a fine northern dish. Usually beef is used, although lamb may be substituted.

750 g (1½ lb) chuck, round or blade steak, thinly sliced
1 teaspoon salt
300 ml/1¼ cups natural yogurt
3 tablespoons ghee*
1 large onion, peeled and sliced
3 garlic cloves, peeled and sliced
2 teaspoons ground coriander
2 teaspoons chilli powder
½ teaspoon ground cumin
1½ teaspoons ground turmeric
1 teaspoon Garam Masala (see page 12)
2 teaspoons grated fresh ginger*

METHOD: Put the beef between 2 sheets of greaseproof paper and tenderize with a mallet. Rub the beef with the salt, then put in a bowl and cover with the yogurt. Leave to marinate overnight.

Melt the ghee in a heavy pan, add the onion and garlic and fry gently until soft. Add the spices except garam masala and fry for a further 3 minutes, stirring constantly.

Add the beef and marinade to the pan, then the ginger, stir well, then cover the pan with a tight-fitting lid and simmer for 1½ hours or until the meat is tender, add garam masala and simmer for a further 2 to 3 minutes. Serve hot.
SERVES 4-6

CALCUTTA KARI
CALCUTTA BEEF CURRY

There are any number of recipes for beef curry, but perhaps the best known are Madras Beef Curry (see left) and Calcutta Beef Curry.

1¼ cups water
750 g (1½ lb) beef, round, blade or other stewing cut, cut into 2.5 cm (1 inch) cubes
1½ teaspoons ground coriander
1 teaspoon ground turmeric
1 teaspoon ground cumin
1½ teaspoons salt
1 teaspoon freshly ground black pepper
1 tablespoon milk
3 tablespoons ghee*
1 small onion, peeled and sliced
1 garlic clove, peeled and sliced
chopped mint or coriander leaves* to garnish

METHOD: Bring the water to the boil in a pan, add the beef and simmer for about 20 minutes.

Meanwhile, mix the spices and seasonings to a paste with the milk. Melt the ghee in a pan, add the onion and garlic and fry gently until soft. Stir in the paste and fry for a further minute. Add the meat and half its cooking liquid, bring to the boil, then lower the heat and simmer for 1 to 1½ hours or until the meat is tender. Sprinkle with mint or coriander and serve hot.
SERVES 4-6

KOFTA KARI
MEATBALL CURRY

Minced beef is often used in Indian cooking, and kofta is a classic method. In this recipe the meatballs are sealed by deep-frying; although this takes a little extra time, it reduces the risk of the meatballs falling apart.

750 g (1½ lb) minced beef
2 large onions, peeled and chopped
4 garlic cloves, peeled and chopped
1 teaspoon grated fresh ginger*
2 teaspoons ground turmeric
2 teaspoons chilli powder
2 teaspoons ground coriander
1½ teaspoons ground cumin
2 teaspoons salt
1 egg, beaten
vegetable oil for deep-frying
3 tablespoons ghee*
1 cup water
mint or coriander leaves* to garnish

METHOD: Put the beef in a bowl and add half the onions, garlic, ginger, spices and salt. Stir well, then bind the mixture together with the beaten egg.

Form the mixture into 16 small balls. Heat the oil in a pan until very hot, add the meatballs a few at a time and deep-fry for 3 to 4 minutes. Remove from the pan with a slotted spoon, drain on kitchen paper towels and set aside.

Melt the ghee in a heavy pan, add the remaining onions and garlic and fry gently until soft. Add the remaining spices and salt and fry for a further 3 minutes, stirring constantly. Add the meatballs and turn gently to coat with the spices, then add the water and bring to the boil. Lower the heat and simmer gently for 30 minutes.

Serve hot, garnished with mint or coriander leaves. Baigan Tamatar (see page 30) is an ideal accompaniment.
SERVES 4-6

▷ *Calcutta Beef Curry; Meatball Curry served with Spiced Eggplant and Tomatoes (see page 30) and Saffron Rice (see page 38)*

DOPIAZAH
SPICED LAMB WITH ONIONS

Dopiazah is the term applied to a dish which contains double the normal amount of onions — if not more! Doh means two or twice, and piazah means onions. The main feature of the dopiazah is that half the onions are cooked with the meat; the other half are added at a later stage to give a contrast in texture.

4 tablespoons ghee*
1 kg (2 lb) onions, peeled and sliced
2 teaspoons ground cumin
1 teaspoon ground fenugreek
1 tablespoon ground turmeric
3 green chillis, chopped
750 g (1½ lb) boned lamb shoulder or leg, cut into 2.5 cm (1 inch) cubes
1¼ cups water
2 teaspoons Garam Masala (see page 12)

METHOD: Melt the ghee in a heavy pan, add the onions and fry gently until soft. Remove half the onions from the pan and set aside. Add the spices to the onions remaining in the pan and fry for 3 minutes, stirring constantly. Add the chillis, then the lamb, and fry until the lamb is browned on all sides.

Stir in the water and bring to the boil, then lower the heat and simmer for 45 minutes to 1 hour or until the meat is tender. Add the reserved onions and garam masala and cook for a further 5 minutes until the curry is fairly dry. Serve hot.
SERVES 4

MHAANS KARI
LAMB CURRY

In most parts of the Indian sub-continent, goat meat is eaten as much as, if not more than, lamb and mutton. Certainly with most recipes the two are interchangeable. If you happen to come across a butcher selling goat meat, have no hesitation in using this recipe.

3 tablespoons ghee*
750 g (1½ lb) boned lamb shoulder or leg cut into 2.5 cm (1 inch) cubes
1 large onion, peeled and sliced
2 garlic cloves, peeled and sliced
2 teaspoons ground coriander
1 teaspoon ground turmeric
1 teaspoon ground cumin
½ teaspoon freshly ground black pepper
1 green chilli, chopped

½ teaspoon chilli powder
1¼ cups water
1 teaspoon salt

METHOD: Melt the ghee in a heavy pan, add the lamb and fry briskly until browned on all sides. Remove from the pan with a slotted spoon, drain well and set aside.

Add the onion and garlic to the pan and fry gently until soft. Stir in the remaining ingredients except the water and salt and fry for a further 3 minutes, stirring constantly. Return the lamb to the pan, add the water and salt, then simmer for 45 minutes to 1 hour or until the meat is tender. Cover the pan if a curry with plenty of sauce is preferred; cook uncovered for a dry curry. Serve hot.
SERVES 4

TIKKA KEBAB
SPICED LAMB KEBABS

A fine northern Indian delicacy, Tikka Kebab are to be found over charcoal barbecues at virtually every street corner. Ideally they should be cooked over a charcoal griddle, but satisfactory results can be obtained by grilling.

750 g (1½ lb) boned lamb shoulder or leg, cut into 2.5 cm (1 inch) cubes
juice of 1 lemon
⅔ cup natural yogurt
4 small onions, peeled and quartered
3 garlic cloves, peeled and chopped
½ teaspoon turmeric
1 tablespoon vinegar
½ teaspoon salt
1 teaspoon freshly ground black pepper
1 green pepper, cored, seeded and cut into 2.5 cm (1 inch) squares
1 lemon, quartered, to garnish

METHOD: Put the lamb in a bowl and sprinkle with the lemon juice. Put the yogurt, half the onion, the garlic, turmeric, vinegar and seasoning in an electric blender and work until the mixture is evenly blended. Pour over the lamb and stir well. Cover and leave to marinate overnight.

Thread the cubes of meat on kebab skewers, alternating with the green pepper and remaining onion quarters. Barbecue or grill the kebabs, turning frequently, until tender.

Serve hot, garnished with lemon quarters, and accompanied by Naan (see page 38) and salad.
SERVES 4-6

ROGHAN GOSHT
SPICED LAMB WITH YOGURT

This dish from northern India brings out the best of the well-flavoured lamb that grazes on the temperate slopes there.

500 g (1 lb) boned lamb shoulder or leg, cut into 2.5 cm (1 inch) cubes
juice of 1 lemon
2 teaspoons salt
⅔ cup natural yogurt
3 tablespoons grated fresh ginger*
4 tablespoons ghee*
2 large onions, peeled and sliced
4 garlic cloves, peeled and sliced
½ teaspoon chilli powder
1 teaspoon ground cumin
1 teaspoon ground coriander
½ teaspoon freshly ground black pepper
1 × 142 g (5 oz) can tomato paste
1 cup water

METHOD: Put the lamb in a bowl and sprinkle with the lemon juice and salt. Add the yogurt and ginger and mix well, then cover and leave to marinate overnight.

Melt the ghee in a heavy pan, add the onions and garlic and fry gently until soft. Add the spices and seasoning and fry for a further 3 minutes, stirring constantly. Stir in the meat and marinade and fry for a further 10 minutes, stirring occasionally, then add the tomato paste and water.

Cover the pan with a tight-fitting lid and simmer for 45 minutes to 1 hour or until the meat is tender and the sauce is fairly thick. Boil off any excess liquid if necessary, then serve hot.
SERVES 4

PADINA CHATNI
MINT CHUTNEY

The word 'chutney' in India describes anything which brings out flavour and adds piquancy to food. Chutneys are usually freshly made and not bottled as in the West – bottled accompaniments are known as pickles in India. This chutney, made with mint, is very refreshing and goes well with most dishes.

⅔ cup natural yogurt
3 cups chopped mint
2 green chillis, finely chopped
juice of 1 lemon
½ teaspoon salt
pinch of chilli powder to garnish

METHOD: Put all the ingredients in a serving bowl and stir well. Chill in the refrigerator, then sprinkle with the chilli powder before serving.
SERVES 4

Note: A blender is excellent for chopping the mint.

△ *Spiced Lamb Kebabs cooking over a charcoal barbecue*

ALOO GOBI
SPICED POTATOES AND CAULIFLOWER

Aloo Gobi is a good example of the way in which Indian cuisine can adapt itself to utilize vegetables originally foreign to the area. Potatoes and cauliflowers are both available in India, although they tend to be found only in the more temperate climes. If liked use other seasonal vegetables in place of cauliflower.

4 tablespoons ghee*
1 kg (2 lb) potatoes, peeled and chopped into 2.5 cm (1 inch) pieces
2 large onions, peeled and sliced
4 garlic cloves, peeled and sliced
2 teaspoons chilli powder
1 teaspoon ground turmeric
1 teaspoon ground coriander
2 teaspoons salt
½ teaspoon freshly ground black pepper
5 cups water
500 g (1 lb) cauliflower florets
1 cup peas
2 teaspoons Garam Masala (see page 12)

METHOD: Melt the ghee in a heavy pan, add the potatoes and fry gently for exactly 1 minute. Remove from the pan with a slotted spoon and set aside.

Add the onions and garlic to the pan and fry gently until soft. Add the spices and seasonings, except the garam masala, and fry for a further 3 minutes, stirring constantly.

Return the potatoes to the pan, add the water and bring to the boil. Lower the heat and simmer for 10 minutes, then add the cauliflower and peas. Simmer for a further 15 minutes until the vegetables are tender and the sauce is thick.

Increase the heat to boil off any excess liquid if necessary. Stir in the garam masala and serve hot.
SERVES 4

SAMBAL
SPICED DRESSING

Sambal is typically southern Indian in origin, and is usually served as an accompaniment to a main dish. This recipe is for a basic sambal, which can be used on its own or with other ingredients added to it – finely shredded lettuce or cabbage, for example. If you add 2 tablespoons coconut milk or fresh milk, this will make a sambal sauce which can be used to coat prawns. Aloo Sambal is made by adding diced cooked potatoes to the basic dressing.*

2 tablespoons ghee*
1 large onion, peeled and chopped
2 garlic cloves, peeled and chopped
2 green chillis, chopped
1 teaspoon grated fresh ginger*
1 teaspoon ground turmeric
½ teaspoon ground cumin
½ teaspoon chilli powder

METHOD: Melt the ghee in a frying pan, add the onion and garlic and fry gently until soft. Add the chillis, ginger and spices and fry for a further 3 minutes, stirring constantly. Use as required.
SERVES 4

BAIGAN TAMATAR
SPICED EGGPLANT AND TOMATOES

The eggplant is a popular vegetable in Indian cuisine; there is nothing finer than its shining, purple firmness at the peak of ripening. When making any eggplant dish, select the vegetables with care; reject any that are soft and spongy.

Baigan Tamatar goes well with any tandoori meal.

6 tablespoons ghee*
1 large onion, peeled and sliced
2 garlic cloves, peeled and sliced
1 teaspoon ground coriander
2.5 cm (1 inch) piece of cinnamon stick
1 teaspoon chilli powder
1 teaspoon salt
1 teaspoon freshly ground black pepper
500 g (1 lb) eggplant, chopped into 2.5 cm (1 inch) pieces
500 g (1 lb) tomatoes, chopped into 2.5 cm (1 inch) pieces
3 tablespoons tomato paste
1 cup water

METHOD: Melt the ghee in a heavy pan, add the onion and garlic and fry gently until soft. Add the spices and seasonings and fry for 3 minutes, stirring constantly.

Add the eggplant, tomatoes and tomato paste and toss gently to coat with the spice mixture.

Stir in the water and bring to the boil. Lower the heat and simmer for 25 to 30 minutes until the eggplant are tender and the sauce is quite thick. Increase the heat to boil off any excess liquid, if necessary. Serve hot.
SERVES 4

△ *Spiced Eggplant and Tomatoes; Spiced Potatoes and Cauliflower; Spinach*

SAAG
SPINACH

Spinach is a much-prized vegetable in India. As it is very delicate, both in structure and taste, a particularly gentle spicing is used. Silverbeet can replace spinach.

3 tablespoons ghee*
1 small onion, peeled and sliced
1 teaspoon Garam Masala (see page 12)
1 teaspoon salt
1 kg (2 lb) leaf spinach or silverbeet, well washed and thick white stems removed

METHOD: Melt the ghee in a heavy pan, add the onion and fry gently until soft. Add the garam masala and salt and fry for a further 3 minutes, stirring constantly. Add the spinach and cook for about 5 minutes, covered, shaking and tossing pan constantly. Serve hot.
SERVES 4

PANIR
INDIAN CURD CHEESE

Cheese has never really had a following in the Indian sub-continent, and certainly no really distinctive varieties have developed as in the Western world. However, panir – a simple curd cheese – is a well-established dish in its own right; it is also used in vegetable curries.

5 cups milk
1 cup natural yogurt
2 teaspoons lemon juice
1½ teaspoons salt

METHOD: Put the milk in a pan and bring to the boil. Remove from the heat, leave to cool to blood heat (37°C/98°F), then beat in the yogurt, lemon juice and salt. Leave in a warm place, at approximately 37°C/98°F, for 12 hours.

Strain the curds and whey through a piece of muslin (cheesecloth) placed over a bowl – draw up the corners of the muslin and allow the whey to drip through. Leave for 30 minutes, then squeeze out as much liquid as possible.

Shape the cloth into a rectangle around the cheese, then place under a heavy weight. Leave for 3 hours, then remove the weight and cloth and cut the panir into cubes. Serve raw, or use in vegetable curries.
MAKES ABOUT 500 G (1 LB)

MATAR PANIR
PEAS AND INDIAN CHEESE CURRY

This is a basic recipe for a panir curry. The spices used are light so as not to mask the flavour of the cheese. Other vegetables can be used rather than peas and tomatoes, if liked.

3 tablespoons ghee*
500 g (1 lb) Panir (see left), cubed
1 onion, peeled and sliced
1½ teaspoons grated fresh ginger*
½ teaspoon cumin powder
½ teaspoon chilli powder
½ teaspoon salt
500 g (1 lb) frozen peas
2 tomatoes, chopped

METHOD: Melt the ghee in a frying pan, add the panir and fry until brown. Remove from the pan with a slotted spoon, drain on kitchen paper towels and set aside.

Add the onion to the pan and fry gently until soft. Add the ginger, spices and salt and fry for a further 3 minutes, stirring constantly.

Add the peas and tomatoes and stir gently until the peas are coated with the spice mixture. Stir in the panir and heat through, taking care not to break up the cubes of cheese. Serve hot.
SERVES 4

BHINDI FOOGATH
BRAISED OKRA WITH CHILLIS

A foogath is very similar to a sambal. It is a savoury dish made from a mixture of vegetables. The difference is that a foogath is cooked and is often made with leftover cooked vegetables.

3 tablespoons ghee*
1 large onion, peeled and sliced
3 garlic cloves, peeled and sliced
2.5 cm (1 inch) piece of fresh ginger*, peeled and finely chopped or grated
2 green chillis, finely chopped or minced
½ teaspoon chilli powder
500 g (1 lb) okra, topped and tailed
1 cup water
salt
2 teaspoons desiccated coconut

METHOD: Melt the ghee in a heavy pan, add the onion, garlic, ginger, chillis and chilli powder. Fry gently for 5 minutes until soft, stirring occasionally.

Add the okra, water and salt to taste. Bring to the boil, then lower the heat, cover and simmer for 5 to 10 minutes until the okra are just tender, but still firm to the bite. Stir in the coconut and serve hot.
SERVES 4

BHINDI BHAJI
SPICY FRIED OKRA

Okra are grown throughout the Indian sub-continent. They are considered to be a delicacy and a worthy accompaniment to any meal. Canned okra tends to be rather stringy and for most dishes, particularly this one, it is preferable to use the fresh vegetable rather than canned.

3 tablespoons ghee*
1 large onion, peeled and sliced
2 garlic cloves, peeled and sliced
1 tablespoon ground coriander
1 teaspoon ground turmeric
½ teaspoon salt
½ teaspoon freshly ground black pepper
500 g (1 lb) fresh okra topped, tailed and cut into 1 cm (½ inch) pieces
⅔ cup water
½ teaspoon Garam Masala (see page 12)

METHOD: Melt the ghee in a heavy pan, add the onion and garlic and fry gently until soft. Add the spices and seasonings, except the garam masala, and fry for a further 3 minutes, stirring constantly. Add the okra, then stir gently to coat with the spice mixture, taking care not to break them.

Stir in the water and bring to the boil. Lower the heat, cover and simmer for 5 to 10 minutes until the okra are just tender, but still firm to the bite. Stir in the garam masala and serve hot.
SERVES 4

▽ *Peas and Indian Cheese Curry; Spiced Fried Okra*

SABZI PILAU
VEGETABLE PILAU

In poorer areas, vegetables are often substituted for meat in traditional dishes, and for millions in the Indian sub-continent, Vegetable Pilau is very much the dominant 'special' rice dish. Other vegetables, such as potatoes and cauliflower, may be added if liked.

3 tablespoons ghee*
1 large onion, peeled and sliced
2 garlic cloves, peeled and sliced
1 teaspoon chilli powder
½ teaspoon cumin seeds
2 teaspoons ground coriander
1 teaspoon salt
1 teaspoon crushed black peppercorns
125 g (4 oz) carrots, peeled and diced
125 g (4 oz) green beans, trimmed and diced
125 g (4 oz) turnips, peeled and diced
2½ cups water (approximately)
¾ cup shelled or frozen peas
Pilau, made with 3 cups rice (see right)

METHOD: Melt the ghee in a heavy pan, add the onion and garlic and fry gently until soft. Add the spices and seasonings and fry for a further 3 minutes, stirring constantly. Add the vegetables, except the peas, and stir until evenly coated.

Stir in just enough water to cover the vegetables and bring to the boil. Lower the heat and simmer for 10 to 15 minutes until the vegetables are just tender and the sauce is thick but not dry, adding the peas for the last 5 minutes. Add more water during cooking if necessary.

Divide the curry in two. Fold one half gently into the hot pilau, then pile into a warmed serving dish. Pour the remaining curry over and serve immediately.
SERVES 4

KITCHERI
SAVOURY RICE WITH LENTILS

This is an Indian dish which has become truly international, and nowadays many think of kitcheri or kedgeree as a means of using up leftovers – usually fish. However, it is a highly regarded dish in India, particularly on the Keralonese coasts where the seafood kitcheris are famous. The following recipe is a basic kitcheri with lentils.

2½ cups rice
1 cup lentils
4 tablespoons ghee*
1 large onion, peeled and sliced
2 garlic cloves, peeled and sliced
1½ teaspoons ground turmeric
10 whole cloves
6 cardamom pods
7.5 cm (3 inch) piece of cinnamon stick
salt
1 teaspoon freshly ground black pepper
4 cups boiling water

METHOD: Wash the rice and lentils thoroughly, then put in a bowl and cover with water. Leave to soak for 2 hours. Drain.

Melt the ghee in a heavy pan, add the onion and garlic and fry gently until soft. Add the spices and seasonings and fry for a further 3 minutes, stirring constantly.

Add the rice and lentils to the pan and toss for 5 minutes until every grain is coated. Add the water and bring to the boil. Lower the heat, cover with a tight-fitting lid and simmer for 20 to 30 minutes until the rice and lentils are cooked.

Remove the lid and boil off any excess liquid before serving, turning constantly to prevent sticking. Serve immediately.
SERVES 4

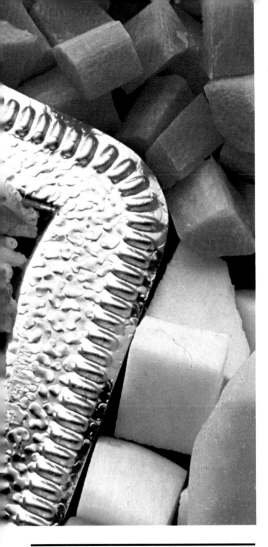

spices and salt. Fry for 3 minutes, stirring constantly until each grain of rice is coated with the mixture. Add the water and bring back to the boil, then lower the heat, cover and simmer for 20 to 25 minutes until the rice has absorbed all of the water.

Heat the remaining ghee in a small pan and fry the almonds until lightly browned. Stir in the almonds and serve hot.
SERVES 4

TARKA DAL
SPICED LENTIL PURÉE

Dal* is the collective name applied to a variety of pulses which form the staple diet for millions of people in the Indian sub-continent. Many are vegetarians, and these pulses – with a high vitamin content – are an important part of their daily food intake. The most common dal* in the Western world is masoor or lentils, although many other varieties are available in Indian food shops. Be careful when making the tarka – sesame seed oil* reaches a higher temperature than most other oils.

2 teaspoons ground coriander
1 teaspoon ground turmeric
1 teaspoon ground cumin
½ teaspoon chilli powder
1 teaspoon salt
1 teaspoon freshly ground black pepper
1 tablespoon vinegar
1 cup lentils
3 tablespoons ghee*
1 large onion, peeled and sliced
2 garlic cloves, peeled and sliced
3 cups water
Tarka:
1 tablespoon sesame seed oil*
1 garlic clove, peeled and sliced
1 green chilli, sliced
1 teaspoon coriander seeds

METHOD: Mix the spices and seasonings to a paste with the vinegar. Wash the lentils thoroughly and drain. Melt the ghee in a heavy pan, add the onion and garlic and fry gently until soft. Add the spice paste and fry for 3 minutes, stirring. Add the lentils and cook, stirring for 1 minute.

Stir in the water and bring to the boil. Lower the heat and simmer for 15 to 20 minutes until a yellow broth is obtained, adding more water if necessary.

To make the tarka, heat the oil in a small frying pan until on the point of smoking, then immediately add the remaining ingredients. Fry until the garlic has turned black, pour into the hot dal and serve immediately.
SERVES 4-6

PILAU
SAVOURY RICE

Pilau rice differs from Biryani in that the rice is sautéed in ghee* with onion and garlic before boiling. Nowadays, the term pilau is often incorrectly applied to rice that has been simply boiled in stock instead of water. This recipe is for a traditional pilau.

During the initial frying, the rice must be stirred constantly to ensure that every grain is evenly saturated with ghee*. The finished pilau should be perfectly dry, each grain of rice being separate and all liquid absorbed.

3 cups medium or long grain rice
5 tablespoons ghee*
1 onion, peeled and sliced
2 garlic cloves, peeled and sliced
10 whole cloves
5 cardamom pods
5 cm (2 inch) piece of cinnamon stick
1 teaspoon salt
5 cups boiling water
⅓ cup almonds

METHOD: Wash the rice thoroughly, then put in a bowl and cover with water. Leave to soak for 2 hours. Drain in a colander.

Melt 4 tablespoons ghee in a heavy pan. Add the onion and garlic to the pan and fry gently until soft.

Add the drained rice to the pan with the

SALAT
SALAD

Salad vegetables vary with the climate in India. Peppers feature in salads from the hotter areas in the south, whereas in the north, Kashmir and into Nepal and Bhutan, lettuces, tomatoes and cucumbers are grown. Salads are usually served with a spicy dressing.

1 lettuce, washed and dried
salt
freshly ground black pepper
½ cucumber, chopped
1 large onion, peeled and sliced
4 green chillis, chopped (optional)
2 green peppers, cored, seeded and sliced
4 tomatoes, sliced
1 tablespoon sesame seed oil*
½ teaspoon ground coriander
½ teaspoon chilli powder
1 teaspoon grated fresh ginger*

METHOD: Separate the lettuce leaves, then lay one leaf on top of another, sprinkling each one with salt and pepper. Roll up the bundle of leaves, then chop finely.

Put the lettuce in a serving bowl with the cucumber, then add the onion and chillis (if using). Arrange the green peppers and tomatoes on top. Mix together the oil, spices, ginger and salt and pepper to taste. Pour over the salad before serving.
SERVES 4-6

△ *Vegetable Pilau*

LAMB BIRYANI

Biryani is a Mughal dish and a fine example of the way Indian cooks use a wide variety of seasonings to enliven a dish and bring out its flavour without destroying its essential character. The basic formula is layers of delicately perfumed pilau rice and lamb in spiced gravy. Chicken and fish can be used but these are not what make the dish great or traditional.

First, the lamb is prepared, then cooked in the masala, or gravy, which is rich with spices and made a little acid with curd (yogurt). Finally, the pilau rice is cooked. The cooked lamb and the pilau rice are then layered together in a heavy pot, with the masala poured over, then covered and baked gently.

The biryani emerges fragrant with saffron and is unexpectedly subtle considering the spices used. It is garnished with a mixture of fried nuts and sultanas. For gala or festive occasions top with little leaves of edible gold or silver leaf (available at speciality shops supplying artists' materials).

2 tablespoons ghee*
1 lamb leg, boned, trimmed and cut into 2.5 cm (1 inch) cubes
Masala:
3 tablespoons ghee*
3 onions, peeled and thinly sliced
2 teaspoons grated fresh ginger*
3 garlic cloves, peeled and chopped
½ teaspoon ground cumin
piece of cinnamon stick
8 whole cloves
6 cardamom pods
¼ teaspoon freshly grated nutmeg
1 teaspoon salt
1 cup chicken stock
½ cup natural yogurt
½ cup cream
Pilau rice:
500 g (1 lb) basmati rice
2 tablespoons ghee*
½ teaspoon saffron threads

6 cardamom pods
1 teaspoon salt
4 cups chicken stock
To garnish:
½ cup cashew nuts
¼ cup slivered almonds
¼ cup pistachio nuts
2 tablespoons sultanas
ghee* for shallow-frying
varak* (silver leaf) (optional)

METHOD: Heat 2 tablespoons ghee in a pan and fry the lamb until lightly browned on all sides. Set aside.

For the masala: heat the ghee in a heavy pan, add the onions and fry over a gentle heat until soft and golden brown. Remove and set aside.

Add the ginger, garlic, cumin, cinnamon, cloves, cardamom, nutmeg and salt to the pan, adding more ghee if necessary, and fry lightly for a few minutes. Add the stock. Mix the yogurt and cream together and stir into the stock and spices. Cook for a

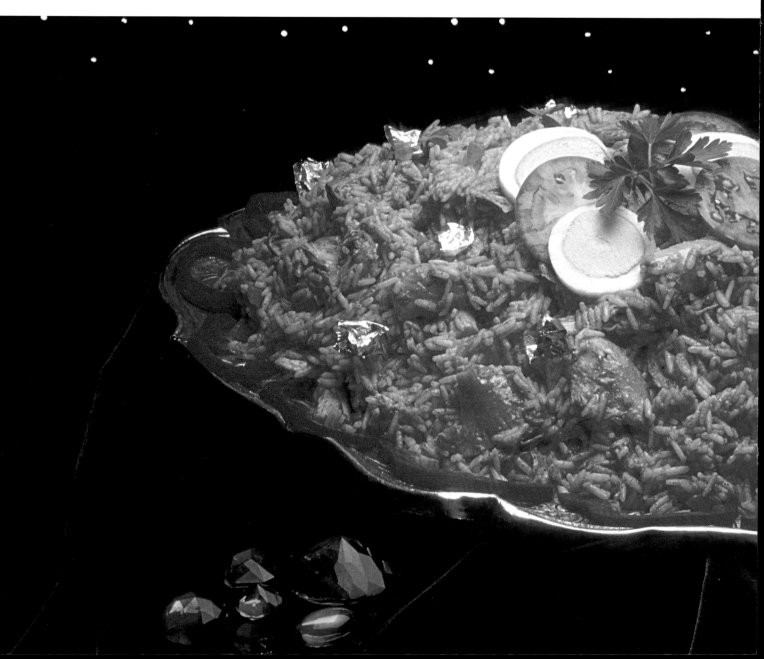

minute or two. Add the lamb and half of the fried onion to the pan, stir in, cover and cook over a low heat for about 15 minutes more. When cooked, allow to stand for about 10 to 15 minutes.

For the pilau rice: wash the rice well until the water runs clear, and drain in a colander. Heat the ghee in a heavy saucepan and add the saffron and cardamom pods. Fry for a few seconds, then add the rice and fry until the rice is coated with the ghee. Add the salt and stock and bring to the boil, stirring once or twice. Once it comes to the boil, do not stir. Reduce the heat and cook gently for about 10 to 15 minutes, in which time the stock will have evaporated and the rice be almost cooked; cover and set aside.

To put the dish together: melt a little ghee in a large, heavy flameproof casserole, swirling it up the sides. Spoon in half the rice (fork it up lightly to loosen and separate the grains first) and smooth over evenly with the back of a spoon.

Transfer the lamb cubes to the casserole using a slotted spoon, and place evenly over the rice. Top with the remaining rice. Push the masala liquid through a sieve and drizzle over the rice. Top with the remaining fried onion rings. Cover the casserole with a sheet of foil, crimping the edges to keep it in place. Cover with a lid and bake in a preheated moderately hot oven (190°C/375°F) for 20 to 30 minutes or until the rice and lamb are tender.

(If preparing the biryani for a party it can be prepared, layered in the casserole, and stored covered in the refrigerator for up to 2 days. It will then take 45 minutes to finish cooking in the oven.)

To make the garnish: fry the nuts and sultanas in a little ghee until lightly browned. Sprinkle over the biryani.

To serve, fluff up the rice with a fork and heap the entire contents of the casserole on a large heated dish. Sprinkle with the nuts and sultanas. For a festive finish, top with a few sheets of varak.
SERVES 8

Note: Gold and silver leaf (varak*) come in small squares, fitted in between leaves of a paper tissue pad. These are best kept in a refrigerator wrapped in a plastic bag. To use the foil, lift off with the tip of a paint brush and gently lay on the food. It is unbelievably thin, so take care to handle it out of a breeze — the slightest movement will make the foil fold and crimp into unwanted shapes.

BIRYANI
SAVOURY RICE WITH MEAT

In India, biryanis often steam for hours over the embers of a charcoal fire, although this is usually more for convenience than necessity, and the intrinsic flavour of the dish is the same when cooked by the following method.

1½ cups medium or long grain rice
3 cups water
2 teaspoons salt
2 cups Curry Sauce (see page 13)
500 g (1 lb) cooked meat (beef, chicken, lamb), cut into 2.5 cm (1 inch) cubes
1½ teaspoons ground turmeric
½ teaspoon ground coriander
To garnish:
1 green or red pepper, cored, seeded and cut into rings
1-2 hard-boiled eggs, sliced
2-3 firm tomatoes, sliced
coriander leaves* (optional)
varak* (silver leaf), finely beaten (optional)

METHOD: Wash the rice thoroughly. Bring the water to the boil in a large pan, add the rice and salt and bring back to the boil. Simmer for exactly 10 minutes, then drain off the excess water and set the rice aside.

Put the curry sauce in a pan with the cooked meat and heat until bubbling. Add the turmeric and coriander and cook over high heat for 2 minutes, stirring constantly. Add the rice and stir thoroughly and gently until the rice has absorbed the colour of the turmeric evenly. Cover the pan, lower the heat and cook gently until the rice is completely cooked.

Transfer the biryani to a warmed serving platter. Garnish with the pepper rings, egg and tomato slices. Top with coriander leaves and sprinkle with varak, if liked. Serve immediately.
SERVES 4

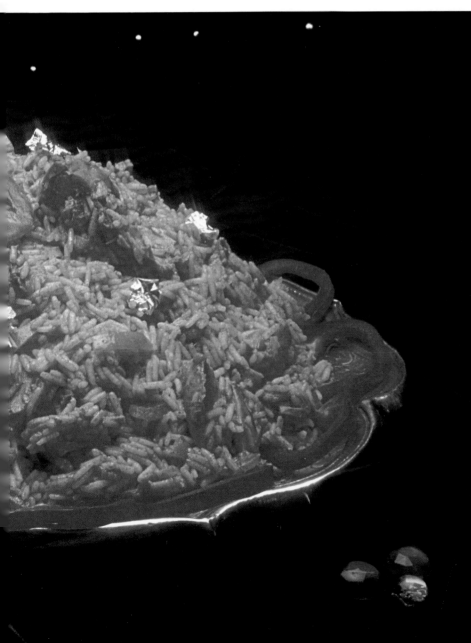

◁ *Savoury Rice with Meat*

KESARI CHAWAL
SAFFRON RICE

Saffron is the most delicate of spices, unique if only for the fact that, although used in very small quantities, its power is unrivalled. Saffron threads come from the stamens of a type of crocus which abounds on the temperate slopes of the Himalayan foothills. It is common throughout northern India, particularly in Nepal and Bhutan where it is used to colour the robes of the Buddhist priests a deep yellow.

It takes 75,000 crocus blooms to make 500 g (1 lb) saffron, but then this delicate spice can colour several thousand times its own weight. Today, synthetic food colouring is often used in place of saffron, but there is no substitute for the flavour of the real spice.

4 tablespoons ghee*
2 large onions, peeled and sliced
1½ cups rice
1 teaspoon whole cloves
4 cardamom pods
1 teaspoon salt
1 teaspoon freshly ground black pepper
½ teaspoon saffron threads, soaked in 1 tablespoon boiling water for 30 minutes
3 cups boiling water
varak* (silver leaf) to garnish (optional)

METHOD: Melt the ghee in a heavy pan, add the onions and fry gently until soft.

Wash the rice thoroughly, then drain. Add to the pan with the spices and seasonings, then fry for 3 minutes, stirring frequently.

Add the saffron with its liquid and stir well, then add the water and bring to the boil. Lower the heat and simmer for 15 to 20 minutes until cooked.

Transfer to a warmed serving dish and garnish with varak, if liked. Serve hot.
SERVES 4

CHAWAL
STEAMED RICE

The successful cooking of rice is crucial to mastering the art of Indian cuisine. The best rice in the world is considered to be basmati, although Australian medium and long grain rices are both excellent. There are many methods of cooking rice but this is an easy way.

One of the most important points to remember is that rice must be thoroughly washed under cold running water before cooking; this prevents the grains of rice from sticking together during cooking.

1 cup rice
2 cups boiling water
pinch of salt
coriander leaves* to garnish (optional)

METHOD: Wash the rice thoroughly to remove rice dust and other impurities. Bring the water to the boil in a heavy pan, then add the salt and rice. Bring back to the boil, stir once, cover with a tight-fitting lid, then lower the heat and simmer for 15 to 20 minutes until the rice is al dente – tender but firm to the bite. Do not lift lid until last few minutes of cooking. Remove from heat and fork lightly. Serve hot, plain or garnished with coriander leaves.
SERVES 4

NAAN
BAKED LEAVENED BREAD

This is very much a tandoori recipe, because the traditional tandoor clay oven is used to bake the bread. The act of slapping the rounds of dough onto the searing walls of the tandoor, and knowing exactly when to hook them out, is an art in itself. Naan can, however, be made using a conventional oven.

2 cups plain flour
½ teaspoon baking powder
1 teaspoon salt
1 teaspoon sugar
1 teaspoon active dry yeast
⅔ cup milk
⅔ cup natural yogurt
1 egg, beaten
2 teaspoons poppy seeds (optional)

METHOD: Sift the flour, baking powder, salt and sugar into a bowl. Mix the yeast to a paste with a little of the milk. Beat the yogurt into the remaining milk and heat until lukewarm. Stir in the yeast paste. Add this mixture gradually to the flour and mix to a dough. Knead well, then add the egg and knead again. Cover the dough with a damp cloth and leave in a warm place for 1½ hours or until doubled in size.

Break the dough into 6 to 8 pieces, approximately 6 cm (2½ inches) in diameter. Roll into balls and flatten with the hand. Dip the fingertips into the poppy seeds (if using) and press into the naan. Place on baking sheets and bake in a preheated hot oven (230°C/450°F) for 12 minutes or until the naan are puffed and blistered. Serve hot.

MAKES 6-8

CHAPPATTI
UNLEAVENED BREAD

Traditionally, chappattis are cooked on a convex griddle known as a tawa. If this is not available, use an upturned cast-iron frying pan.

2 cups ata*
½ teaspoon salt
1 cup water (approximately)

METHOD: Sift the flour and salt into a bowl, then add the water gradually and mix to a firm dough. Turn onto a lightly floured surface and knead well until smooth and elastic. Break the dough into 8 to 10 pieces, then form into balls. Roll out on a lightly floured surface as thinly as possible; the dough must be less than 3 mm (⅛ inch) thick.

Dust the upturned frying pan lightly with flour and place over high heat. Put a chappatti on the pan and cook for 3 to 4 minutes until blisters begin to appear. Turn the chappatti over and cook the other side for 3 to 4 minutes.

Remove the chappatti from the pan with tongs, then place directly on the heat and cook for a few seconds until black blisters form and the chappatti swells up. Keep hot in the oven or under the grill while cooking the remainder. Serve hot, as soon as possible after cooking.

MAKES 8-10

▽ *Saffron Rice; Steamed Rice; Naan*

PURI
DEEP-FRIED WHOLEWHEAT BREAD

A traditional Indian breakfast will often include puris; they are eaten simply – with plenty of chutney. Many people send to the bazaar for them, rather than cook them at home, as they are more easily prepared in bulk. As with all Indian breads, the secret is to serve them hot.

1½ cups ata*
½ teaspoon salt
⅔ cup water
3 tablespoons ghee* or butter, melted
vegetable oil for deep-frying

METHOD: Sift the flour and salt into a bowl, then add the water gradually to make a firm dough. Add the ghee or butter, kneading it in well, then leave to rest for 20 minutes.

Break the dough into 8 to 10 pieces, approximately 2.5 cm (1 inch) in diameter, then form into balls. Roll out on a lightly floured surface into rounds, just less than 3 mm (⅛ inch) thick.

Heat the oil in a pan until moderately hot. Deep-fry the puris, one at a time, for about 1½ minutes until they puff up and float to the surface, spooning the oil over them as they fry. Remove from the pan, drain and keep hot in the oven while deep-frying the remaining puris. Serve hot.

MAKES 8-10

PARATHA
FLAKY WHOLEWHEAT BREAD

A paratha is essentially a fried chappatti. A good paratha depends on the layering of fat in the dough. Some Indian cooks prefer to combine the fat in the dough-making process but, although this is easier, the final result is not so good.

Parathas are very satisfying, so allow no more than 1½ per person.

2 cups ata*
½ teaspoon salt
1 cup water
4 tablespoons ghee* or butter, melted

METHOD: Prepare the dough as for Chappattis (see page 39). Break the dough into 4 to 6 pieces and roll into balls, approximately 7.5 cm (3 inches) in diameter. Roll each out on a lightly floured surface to a 3 mm (⅛ inch) thickness. Brush with melted ghee or butter, then roll up from one side and re-form into a ball. Repeat this rolling process 5 times, then roll out to a 5 mm (¼ inch) thickness.

Warm a lightly greased frying pan over high heat, place a paratha in the pan and fry over moderate heat for about 1 to 1½ minutes on each side until lightly browned. Keep hot in the oven or under the grill while frying the remainder. Serve hot, as soon as possible after cooking.

MAKES 4-6

BESANI ROTI
FRIED BESAN BREAD

This is a kind of fried bread which has an irresistible taste. Besan* is a flour made from chick peas and its properties are therefore somewhat different from ordinary wheat flour. It is more aromatic and less starchy.

It is also quite difficult to knead into a smooth dough, but this is essential for a good result. Make sure the work surface is lightly floured when kneading.

2 cups besan*
1 teaspoon salt
1 cup water
4 tablespoons ghee*
185 g (6 oz) butter, melted

METHOD: Sift the flour into a bowl, rubbing the lumps through the sieve with the back of a spoon. Stir in the salt. Add the water gradually and mix to a stiff dough; knead in the ghee and work until smooth.

Break the dough into 4 to 6 pieces, approximately 7.5 cm (3 inches) in diameter, then form into balls. Roll out to a 5 mm (¼ inch) thickness.

Spread a little melted butter over the base of a frying pan, then cook the roti one at a time over low heat for about 3 minutes on each side. Keep hot in the oven while cooking the remainder. Serve hot, brushed with the remaining melted butter.

MAKES 4-6

▽ *Preparation of Deep-Fried Wholewheat Bread; Fried Besan Bread; Flaky Wholewheat Bread*

RASGULLAH
CREAM CHEESE BALLS IN SYRUP

Rasgullah is similar to Gulab Jamun (see opposite) but it is made with Panir (Indian curd cheese) rather than ground almonds.

Panir made with 10 cups milk (see page 32, double quantity)
¾ cup blanched almonds, chopped
¾ cup semolina
16 cubes sugar
Syrup:
4 cups water
4 cups sugar
pinch of cream of tartar
½ teaspoon rose water

METHOD: Stir the panir to a smooth paste, then add the almonds and semolina and knead well until smooth. When the palm of the hand is greasy then it is time to mould the paste. Break the dough into 12 to 15 pieces, about the size of walnuts, then shape into balls, moulding each one around a cube of sugar.

To make the syrup: put all the ingredients, except the rose water, in a heavy pan and heat gently until the sugar has dissolved, stirring occasionally. Bring to the boil, add the balls of dough, then lower the heat and simmer very gently for 2 hours. Stir in the rose water, then serve hot or cold.
MAKES 12-15

JALLEBI
DOUGHNUT SPIRALS IN SYRUP

These pretzel-like sweets are a joy if eaten fresh and warm. In Indian cities they are sold at open stalls where, by the light of a hissing Tilley lamp, the jallebi are deep-fried especially for you.

2½ cups plain flour
¼ cup rice flour*
pinch of baking powder
½ teaspoon salt
¾ cup water
vegetable oil for deep-frying
Syrup:
4 cups water
4 cups sugar
pinch of cream of tartar
½ teaspoon rose water
½ teaspoon yellow or red food colouring (optional)

METHOD: Sift the flours, baking powder and salt into a bowl. Add the water gradually and beat to a smooth batter. Cover and leave in the refrigerator overnight.

The next day, make the syrup: put the water, sugar and cream of tartar in a heavy pan and heat gently until the sugar has dissolved, stirring occasionally.

Heat the oil in a deep-fat fryer or deep heavy-based frying pan until a little of the batter, dropped into the hot oil, sizzles and turns crisp.

Put the batter into a piping bag, fitted with a 2.5 cm (1 inch) plain nozzle, and pipe spirals, about 10 cm (4 inches) in diameter, into the hot oil. Deep-fry for about 3 minutes until crisp, then remove from the pan with a slotted spoon and drain on kitchen paper towels.

Immerse the jallebi in the syrup for 30 seconds while still warm, then serve hot or cold.
MAKES 20-24

CHAAT
SPICED FRUIT SALAD

Chaat is served either as an appetizer or as an accompaniment to a main course. In the central and northern parts of India, chaat houses abound, where, for a few annas, this chilled spiced dessert can be taken with a little tea.

There is no limit to the variety of fruit that can be used in spiced fruit salad, but this recipe uses fruit which is easily obtainable in the West.

2 oranges
2 bananas
2 pears
1 apple
2 guavas (optional)
juice of 1 lemon
1 teaspoon chilli powder
1 teaspoon ground ginger
1 teaspoon Garam Masala (see page 12)
1 teaspoon salt
½ teaspoon freshly ground black pepper
varak* (silver leaf), finely beaten, to decorate (optional)

METHOD: Peel the oranges and bananas and chop roughly. Core the pears and apple and chop roughly with the guavas, if using. (Do not discard the guava seeds.)

Put the fruit in a bowl and sprinkle with the lemon juice. Mix together the spices and seasonings, sprinkle over the fruit, then toss lightly until each piece of fruit is coated. Chill in the refrigerator for 2 hours. Serve decorated with varak, if liked.
SERVES 4

△ *Cream Cheese Balls in Syrup (above); Doughnut Spirals in Syrup; Carrot Pudding*

METHOD: Put the carrots in a bowl and sprinkle with the sugar. Set aside.

Put the milk in a pan with the cardamoms. Bring to the boil and boil steadily for 45 minutes or until the milk is reduced by half. Add the carrots, then simmer until the mixture thickens.

Remove the pan from the heat, leave to cool slightly, then stir in the sultanas and almonds. Serve hot or cold.

SERVES 4

GULAB JAMUN
ALMOND BALLS IN SYRUP

This is the name given to a classic sweet in Indian cuisine. Essentially, it is dumplings infused with a rose-flavoured syrup.

2 cups plain flour
2 cups ground almonds
125 g (4 oz) butter
1 teaspoon baking powder
2/3 cup natural yogurt
vegetable oil for deep-frying
Syrup:
4 cups water
4 cups sugar
pinch of cream of tartar
5 whole cloves
5 cardamom pods
1/2 teaspoon rose water

METHOD: Sift the flour and almonds into a bowl, then rub in the butter. Stir in the baking powder, then add the yogurt gradually and mix to a firm dough. Cover and leave to stand for 2 hours.

Meanwhile, make the syrup: put all the ingredients, except the rose water, in a heavy pan and heat gently until the sugar has dissolved, stirring occasionally. Bring to just below boiling point, then remove from the heat and stir in the rose water.

Break the dough into 20 to 25 pieces, approximately 2.5 cm (1 inch) in diameter, then roll into balls. Heat the oil in a deep-fat fryer or deep heavy-based frying pan, then deep-fry the balls until they turn a rich golden brown. Remove from the pan with a slotted spoon and drain on kitchen paper towels.

Immerse the balls in the syrup while still warm. Serve hot or cold.

MAKES 20-25

GAJJAR KHEER
CARROT PUDDING

Carrots are not the usual kind of ingredient for a sweet pudding, but in this dish they are used with great effect. It is very rich and sweet, and few will have room for more!

500 g (1 lb) carrots, peeled and grated
1 cup sugar
5 cups milk
6 cardamom pods
1 tablespoon sultanas
1 tablespoon slivered almonds

SPICED SEMOLINA DESSERT

There are as many halwas in India as there are cities, and each centre of population guards the reputation of its sweetmeat. Often halwa is used as a kind of culinary envoy, being sent all over the world. It is well worth making at home, although it is said that the art of the halwai (halwa maker) is inherited and cannot be learnt!

1¼ cups semolina
4 tablespoons desiccated coconut
2 cups sugar
1 tablespoon poppy seeds
seeds of 6 cardamom pods
2½ cups water
4 tablespoons ghee*, melted

METHOD: Put the semolina in a heavy pan with the coconut, sugar, poppy and cardamom seeds. Mix well, then stir in the water. Bring to the boil, stirring, then lower the heat and simmer for at least 1 hour until every ingredient is soft, stirring frequently. Add the ghee gradually and mix well.

Transfer the mixture to a shallow tray and spread evenly. Leave to cool, then cut into triangles or diamond shapes. Store in an airtight container in a cool place.
SERVES 4

COCONUT PUDDING

2 coconuts
2 cups boiling water
1 cup sugar
1½ cups rice flour*
2 eggs, beaten
½ cup slivered almonds

METHOD: Break the coconuts in half, extract the thin milk and reserve. Grate the flesh into a bowl, then pour on the boiling water. Leave to steep for 15 minutes, then strain the liquor through muslin (cheesecloth), squeezing out the last drop of thick coconut milk. Mix with the thin milk from the coconut, then beat in the remaining ingredients.

Put the mixture in a pan and bring to the boil. Lower the heat and simmer until the mixture thickens, stirring constantly. Pour into a greased 20 cm (8 inch) round cake tin and bake in a preheated moderate oven (180°C/350°F) for about 30 minutes until the top is browned. Serve hot.
SERVES 4

ICE CREAM WITH PISTACHIOS AND ALMONDS

For centuries, ice cream has been made and sold in the streets of every major city in India. Traditionally, it is frozen in metal cones immersed in a freezing mixture of chopped ice and salt, but it can be frozen in containers used for ordinary ice cream.

4 cups milk
½ cup rice flour*
1¼ cups cream or evaporated milk
½ cup sugar
1 tablespoon chopped pistachio nuts
1 tablespoon chopped blanched almonds
green food colouring (optional)
pistachio nuts and varak* (silver leaf) to decorate (optional)

METHOD: Bring the milk to the boil in a pan, then simmer until reduced to two thirds of its original volume. Stir in the rice flour gradually, then the cream or evaporated milk. Bring to the boil again, then lower the heat and simmer for a further 15 minutes. Add the sugar; stir well to dissolve.

Leave to cool, then stir in the nuts and food colouring, if using. Transfer the mixture to suitable freezing containers and freeze until partially frozen. Beat vigorously to break down the ice crystals, then freeze until firm. Serve decorated with pistachios and varak, if liked.
SERVES 4

SWEET RICE

This dish can be made richer by adding more fruit or nuts, or both. It is traditionally served on special feast days in India.

2 cups rice
8 tablespoons ghee*
1 cup sultanas
1 cup pistachio nuts
1 cup blanched almonds
10 whole cloves
5 cardamom pods
2.5 cm (1 inch) piece of cinnamon stick
1 teaspoon ground allspice
1 teaspoon saffron threads, soaked in 1 tablespoon boiling water for 30 minutes
4 cups boiling water
½ cup sugar
varak* (silver leaf) to decorate

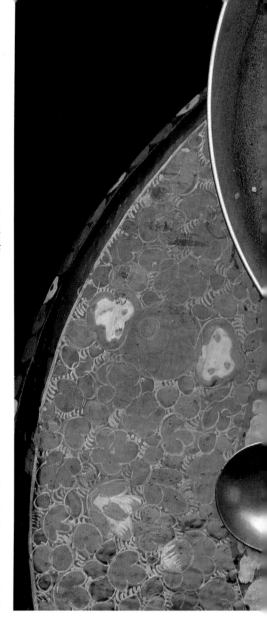

METHOD: Wash the rice thoroughly, then put in a bowl and cover with cold water. Leave to soak for 2 hours.

Melt 4 tablespoons ghee in a pan, add the sultanas and nuts and fry gently for 3 minutes. Remove from the pan with a slotted spoon and set aside.

Melt the remaining ghee in the pan. Add the cloves, cardamoms, cinnamon and allspice and fry gently for 5 minutes, stirring frequently. Drain the rice, add to the spice mixture and mix well. Stir in the saffron with its liquid, then the boiling water.

Cover the pan and simmer for 20 to 25 minutes until the rice is tender and has absorbed the liquid. Drain off any excess liquid if necessary, then add the sugar and the fried sultanas and nuts. Serve hot or cold, decorated with varak.
SERVES 4

KHEER
CREAMED RICE PUDDING

At any Muslim festival – such as Id-ul-Fitr, which is held to celebrate the end of a month of fasting – certain sweet dishes prevail. Muslims wear their best clothes and visit friends, where they will be invited to take tea and either of the traditional sweet dishes – Sewaiian or Kheer.

Kheer is based on rice flour*, which is not always easily obtainable; it can however be made at home, by simply grinding rice in a coffee mill, electric blender or by using ground rice.

2½ cups milk
½ cup sugar
½ cup rice flour*
2 teaspoons chopped pistachio nuts
2 teaspoons blanched slivered almonds
½ teaspoon rose water

METHOD: Put the milk in a pan and bring to the boil. Stir in the sugar, then sprinkle in the rice flour, stirring constantly. Add the nuts and cook until the mixture begins to thicken, stirring constantly. Remove the pan from the heat and stir in the rose water. Pour into a serving bowl or small serving bowls and serve cold.
SERVES 4

SEWAIIAN
VERMICELLI AND NUT DESSERT

There are a number of variations of this dish, some using large quantities of milk and cream. This is a very basic recipe, which can be made richer by adding cream as the dish is cooling.

250 g (8 oz) vermicelli
3 tablespoons ghee*
1 tablespoon sultanas
1 tablespoon slivered almonds
1 tablespoon shelled pistachio nuts
1 tablespoon rose water
To finish:
1¼ cups cream (optional)
2 tablespoons desiccated coconut
caster sugar for sprinkling (optional)
varak* (silver leaf), finely beaten

METHOD: Put the vermicelli in a pan and cover with water. Bring to the boil, then lower the heat and simmer for about 10 minutes until the vermicelli softens and sinks to the bottom of the pan.

Drain off enough water to leave the vermicelli just covered, then add the ghee and bring to the boil. Lower the heat, cover the pan and simmer for a further 10 minutes until thoroughly cooked; do not stir the vermicelli or it will break.

Fold in the sultanas and nuts, taking care not to break the vermicelli. Add the rose water, then transfer the mixture to a serving dish. Pour over the cream, if using. Sprinkle with the coconut and sugar, if using. Serve hot or cold, decorated with varak.
SERVES 4

△ *Coconut Pudding (above); Sweet Rice; Creamed Rice Pudding*

Even though these countries are for the most part bordered by China and India, the cuisines of Vietnam, Kampuchea, Laos, Thailand and Burma have not been influenced by their mammoth neighbours. Each country has managed to retain a unique culinary tradition that is a true reflection of their individual cultures.

Few cultures of the world have been as misunderstood in the West as those of South-East Asia. Variously dismissed as a conglomeration of Chinese, Indian and French influence, these countries essentially have cultures of their own.

Recent research indicates that such basic words as plough and seed, kiln and pottery, axe and boat, iron and gold, went from South-East Asian language into Chinese. Archaeological finds point to the probability that rice was first domesticated here 1,000 years earlier than in India or China; the same appears to be true in the making of polished stone tools, pottery and bronze implements. Scholars now ask themselves if the Chinese and Indians learned from the South-East Asians, rather than the other way round.

Today there is a great interest in South-East Asian food. Thai and Vietnamese restaurants are appearing in many cities, suburbs and country towns. Speciality food shops are making it easier to buy ingredients for those who are intrigued by the great variety of dishes that are a joy to make at home.

Vietnam

Vietnamese culture, after centuries of struggle against Chinese domination, has maintained its own distinct, sophisticated and highly complex identity.

Although there are overtones which reflect Chinese, Indian and a later French influence, authentic Vietnamese cuisine is unique. In France, home of *haute cuisine*, Vietnamese restaurants far outnumber Chinese, and Vietnamese chefs are starring in many top French restaurants.

The diversity of Vietnamese cuisine is at least partially explained by the country's geography. The extensive coastline, stretching over 2,000 kilometres along the eastern seaboard of South-East Asia, provides all kinds of fish and shellfish. Most of the population is concentrated in the north and south, which are connected by a narrow stretch of mountainous country in the centre. The Red River delta of the north and the Mekong River delta in the south provide very fertile, low-lying country.

The hallmarks of Vietnamese cuisine are lightness and subtlety, with a delicacy and clarity of flavour. Although Chinese influences are apparent, they have been so assimilated that even a stir-fried dish which looks somewhat Chinese will have a taste and aroma unmistakably Vietnamese, while their curry is quite unlike any Indian curry. The Vietnamese aversion to fats is apparent in their stir-frying technique in which even less oil is used than in Chinese cooking. Their dislike of fat is probably one reason why the Vietnamese simmer so many of their dishes. The light and delicate nature of this cuisine can be attributed to this limited use of fats and the emphasis on fresh, raw vegetables decoratively arranged on a platter and served at almost every meal.

Kampuchea and Laos

Kampuchea and Laos are relatively underdeveloped countries with very low per capita incomes. In addition, they do not have the extensive range of foods that are available to neighbouring Vietnam and Thailand and this is reflected in their relatively limited cuisines.

The Kampuchean diet is largely based on rice, fresh water and dried fish. It is heavily spiced and tends to be somewhat strong for Western tastes. Barbecuing over charcoal is a favourite way of preparing meat or fish, which is generally served with a raw Vegetable Platter (see page 56). Laotian dishes are more influenced by the Thai kitchen, although their prolific use of glutinous rice* clearly distinguishes them from others. Here, too, barbecuing is very popular, though frequently it is only the first step in the preparation of a dish. The liberal use of red chilli peppers makes for many fiery dishes.

Laos is a small, landlocked country which is relatively undeveloped and sparsely populated by a collection of tribes without a national history. Neighbouring China and Thailand have had the greatest influence on the Laotion culture.

Kampuchea, previously known as Cambodia, was a centre of power in South-East Asia about 1,000 years ago. With its capital at Angkor, the Khmer kingdom of Cambodia developed a great civilization. The remains of this can be seen today, with such enormous structures as the Temple of Angkor Wat, the world's largest religious building. From the twelfth century, the Khmer culture and power gradually declined.

Thailand

The modern name 'Thailand' or 'Moeng Tai' means 'Land of Freedom', and it is the only country in South-East Asia which has never been a colony.

Because of their independence, the Thai people, their customs and cuisine have hardly been affected by outside influences through the centuries. The majority of people are Buddhists but there are no religious restrictions in their basic diet. Different kinds of meat are eaten, as well as fresh fruit and vegetables. The favourable climate in southern Thailand allows two or three rice harvests a year, and ensures a steady supply

---

A paste of ginger, onion, chilli and garlic is the basic flavouring for many South-East Asian dishes.
A Vegetable Platter will appear at almost every meal.

VIETNAM, KAMPUCHEA, LAOS, THAILAND & BURMA

of many varieties of pak (green vegetables), tua (green beans) and fuk (squash).

Thai cooking favours the use of fresh rather than dried herbs and spices, and these are available throughout the year. Fruit is generally plentiful, raw vegetables also play an important part in the Thai diet.

Rice is the staple diet in Thailand, as it is in most of Asia. Long-grain or Patna rice may be used, but if you can obtain real Thai rice, it is well worth buying. Salt is never added to the rice. Noodles may be eaten at noon or as a snack, but all main meals are based on rice. At least four dishes are served with the rice to form a meal. For example, a soup, curry, a meat or fish dish and a raw vegetable salad with a spicy sauce.

Sweet dishes are not usually served as part of a meal, but are eaten as snacks; these are usually bought from street vendors rather than cooked at home. Fruit, plentiful in Thailand, is frequently served after meals. Pineapple and mangoes are particularly popular. Often the fruit is cut into small pieces, chilled and then served with a bowl of salt or spiced salt for dipping.

The two main types of soup eaten are Kang Chud, which is similar to consommé, and Tom Yum, which usually contains pieces of prawn, pork, beef, chicken or fish. The flavour of Tom Yum is typically Thai – a blend of lemon grass*, lime juice and fish sauce. Both soups can be served along with other dishes during a meal.

Curries are prepared with a spicy paste made from fresh ingredients, rather than a powdered dried spice base. This is because many of the ingredients, including lemon grass*, garlic, shallots, kapi*, kha*, pak chee*, lime peel and chillis have a much better flavour when used fresh. Unfortunately, the individual spices used in many of the Thai curries are not obtainable fresh outside Thailand and the dried equivalents, or the prepared curry paste sold in Oriental food stores, must be used instead.

Fish is plentiful in Thailand and normally at least one fish dish is included in every Thai meal. Boiled Pla Muek (squid) is widely used in salads; it is also fried, stewed or grilled and added to many other dishes. Choose young, small squid for preference.

In Thailand, a meal is always accompanied by iced water or iced weak tea – alcoholic drinks are not really compatible with the hot spices.

Burma

Burma is probably one of the least well-known of Asian countries. Burmese food is distinctive, although it incorporates certain elements from the cooking of neighbouring India and China and shares some common features with other South-East Asian cuisines.

A typical Burmese meal will include a wide range of tastes, each designed to balance, contrast or complement the others. A soup is nearly always included; this is not taken separately as a first course, but served at the same time as the main dish and sipped at intervals throughout the meal. Soups are usually light and refreshing to the palate. Sharp or slightly sour-tasting soup is especially popular.

The main dish will usually be a curry of meat, fish or vegetables. The basic flavouring of their curries is made up from onions, garlic, ginger and chillies pounded in a pestle and mortar. The curry is usually accompanied by a huge bowl of white boiled rice. Sometimes Coconut Rice (see page 80) is served instead of plain boiled rice. Vegetables are also served with each meal, cooked or served raw and either dipped in a sharp shrimp or vinegar sauce, or assembled into a salad, which are varied and delicious. Various condiments accompany the meal, one of the most popular being Ngapi-gyaw (see page 78).

Burmese people seldom eat desserts, but at the end of a meal they might serve a plate of sliced fruit. The Burmese have many recipes for delicious cake or pudding-type snacks called mon, which they either make at home or, more frequently, buy from a roadside stall.

Ingredients

All South-East Asian cuisines make good use of home-grown fruits and vegetables. The markets are a feast to Western eyes with their colourful display of unfamiliar fruits, vegetables and fresh herbs. A variety of mints, lemon grass* and coriander* are used in dishes.

Fish, both fresh and dried, are a major source of protein. Meat is less widely used than fish and seafood, mainly because it is relatively expensive. Lamb and mutton are hardly seen at all. Pork is cheaper than any other types of meat and is therefore more frequently eaten. Chicken and duck, much leaner than their Western counterparts, are seen on special occasions. Beef is very expensive and is served only at very special feasts. In Laos, deer and other game are hunted in the mountains and forests; these are eaten on festive occasions rather than beef.

Nuoc Cham (see page 54), also known as Nuoc Mam, is a universal condiment, used in many different ways. This clear, salty liquid is prepared by layering fresh anchovies, sardines and other small fish, with salt, in large barrels; these are then set out in the sun. As salt is to the Western cuisine and soy sauce is to the Chinese cuisine, so Nuoc Cham is to these cuisines. It is added to all kinds of dishes during preparation; it also serves as the base for sauces to be sprinkled on prepared dishes or served as a dip. In Vietnam, Nuoc Cham is combined with garlic, lime or lemon juice, sugar and fresh chillis, and used to enhance flavours of other foods. In Kampuchea and Laos, roasted peanuts are added and, in Laos, Nuoc Cham is also mixed with anchovy paste.

In Burma many dishes use a salted shrimp paste, dried shrimps or shrimp sauce, and this is a feature shared with nearly all of the South-East Asian cuisines. Many Western people find shrimp paste a difficult taste to acquire and for this reason it is not generally included in recipes, although it appears in the condiment Ngapi-gyaw (see page 78) for which it is essential. Dried shrimps and shrimp sauce impart a very pleasant flavour to soups and other dishes.

Rice is the staple food of the vast majority of South-East Asian kitchens and a bowl of perfectly cooked, steaming hot rice is brought to the table just before or after guests are seated so that it will still be hot. Prepared in infinite variety, it appears at every

meal and is, indeed, the 'bread' of life. The most unusual feature of Laotian food is the emphasis on glutinous (sweet) rice* at every meal. In this respect, the Laotian cuisine is unique. In Vietnam, Kampuchea and other Asian countries, glutinous (sweet) rice* is normally used only for sweets and snacks. For all-round use, the Vietnamese prefer rice that is very dry and flaky, in Burma a long-grain fluffy rice is first choice, in Thailand rice is preferred dry and separate.

Either peanut oil or light sesame seed oil is used for cooking, but sunflower or vegetable oil can be used instead.

A popular ingredient throughout Asia is the fruit of the tamarind tree. This adds a sharpness to food which is more subtle than the taste of lemon or vinegar. Creamed coconut and coconut milk is added to many dishes; this is made by scraping the coconut flesh, then squeezing it in hot water to extract the cream and flavour (see glossary).

Cooking utensils and equipment

All South-East Asian cuisines tend to use the same kitchen equipment, although with a different emphasis. The mortar and pestle, the wok, a sharp chopper and chopping board are common items; the electric blender and food processor can do many of their jobs.

In many Western kitchens it has been found that by careful control, switching on and off of the motor or use of the pulse buttons it is possible to control the amount of chopping, grinding and blending of spices and basic ingredients, fine, coarse, etc., that each recipe requires.

A simple charcoal stove is traditionally used for cooking. An important utensil is the wok – which may vary a little from country to country – which is used for boiling, steaming and frying. For steaming, the food is placed in a covered steamer, often bamboo, which stands over boiling water in the wok. A portable charcoal brazier is used for those delicious satays together with, today, the usual assortment of pots and pans found in many Western kitchens.

A selection of beautifully prepared tropical fruit is frequently served after a meal, particularly in Thailand and Burma.

Serving South-East Asian food

The Burmese usually sit at a round, low dining table for meals, the aim being to give a convivial atmosphere and to make sure that every dish is within reach. Each place on the table is laid with a plate and a soup bowl. A china soup spoon is provided for the soup, but the other dishes are usually eaten, very neatly and deftly, with the fingers, though the habit of eating with a fork and spoon is now becoming widespread. The Burmese use small, round serving dishes, except for one-course noodle dishes and the rice; these are put in large bowls in the centre of the table. The small dishes are constantly refilled.

In Thailand it is customary to have a soup, two or more dishes with gravy and as many side dishes as the cook can manage. Today, Thais mostly eat with a spoon and fork although many prefer the old-fashioned way, with the fingers. Everything is served at once and the diners take a little of this or that according to personal taste, combining each dish with rice, which is cooked without salt.

In neither Laos nor Kampuchea are there restaurants serving the national cuisine. The foreigner must be invited to a family meal to sample the food. Meals are served in very simple fashion and the family are seated on straw mats on the floor, as compared to Vietnam where even simple family meals are served at the table. Chopsticks are not used in Laos and Kampuchea, but food is generally eaten with the fingers. Soup is eaten with a soup spoon out of a large communal bowl placed in the centre of the serving area. In Vietnam, the Chinese influence is evident in the universal use of chopsticks, but the Vietnamese use metal spoons rather than the ceramic soup spoons favoured by the Chinese.

CRABMEAT AND TAPIOCA PEARL SOUP

VIETNAM

Fresh, frozen or canned crabmeat can be used for this soup. If using live fresh crabs, boil 1 or 2 crabs in just enough water to cover for 10 minutes, then drain and remove the meat. Reserve the cooking liquid and use in place of the chicken stock listed in the ingredients.

1 tablespoon vegetable oil
4 brown shallots, peeled and chopped
250 g (8 oz) crabmeat
5 cups chicken stock
2 tablespoons fish sauce*
²⁄₃ cup pearl tapioca, soaked in water for 10 minutes
To garnish:
freshly ground black pepper
2 tablespoons chopped coriander leaves*
2 tablespoons chopped green shallot, green part only

METHOD: Heat the oil in a pan, add the brown shallots and fry gently until lightly browned. Add the crabmeat and stir-fry until beginning to brown, then add the stock and fish sauce.

Drain the tapioca, add to the pan and boil for 5 minutes or until the tapioca is clear. Pour into warmed individual soup bowls and sprinkle with pepper, coriander and green shallots. Serve the crabmeat and tapioca pearl soup hot.
SERVES 4

·

CHRYSANTHEMUM SOUP WITH MINCED PORK

VIETNAM

Chrysanthemum choy is a cultivated edible chrysanthemum, eaten before it blooms. The tough stems are discarded and only the top, tender stems and leaves are eaten. It is available at Oriental grocers.

125 g (4 oz) minced pork
freshly ground black pepper
2 tablespoons plus 1 teaspoon fish sauce*
1 brown shallot, peeled and finely chopped
6 cups chicken stock
500 g (1 lb) chrysanthemum choy
2 green shallots, cut into 5 cm (2 inch) lengths

METHOD: Put the pork in a bowl with a pinch of black pepper, 1 teaspoon fish sauce and the brown shallot. Mix well, then leave to stand for about 15 minutes. Shape the mixture into about 24 small balls, using about 1 teaspoonful for each.

Put the stock in a pan and bring to the boil. Add the pork balls and boil for 12 minutes, then add the remaining fish sauce and black pepper to taste.

Put the chrysanthemum choy and green shallots in a warmed large soup tureen. Pour over the boiling stock and meatballs. Serve hot with rice and fish sauce.
SERVES 4

VIT XAO MANG
DUCK SOUP WITH DRIED BAMBOO SHOOT
VIETNAM

At some stage during the New Year celebrations, every Vietnamese home will serve a dish containing dried bamboo shoots*. This soup is substantial enough to be served as a complete meal.

1 duck, weighing 1.5-2 kg (3-4 lb)
1 tablespoon salt
¼ teaspoon freshly ground black pepper
5 brown shallots, peeled and finely chopped
30 g (1 oz) dried bamboo shoot*, soaked in hot water for 2 hours
1 tablespoon raw sugar
4 tablespoons fish sauce*
250 g (8 oz) medium rice vermicelli*
about 8 cups boiling water
To serve:
1 tablespoon chopped green shallot, green part only
1 tablespoon chopped coriander leaves*
Nuoc Cham (see page 54)

METHOD: Sprinkle the duck with the salt and pepper, then rub all over with the finely chopped brown shallots. Leave to marinate for 1 hour.

Pour 5 cups water into a large pan and bring to the boil. Add the duck and bamboo shoot, bring back to the boil and simmer for 15 minutes, skimming frequently until no further scum is formed.

Add the sugar, cover and simmer for 1 hour. Add the fish sauce, cover and simmer for 30 minutes, or until the bamboo shoot is tender; it should have a chewy texture.

Meanwhile, cook the rice vermicelli in the boiling water for 5 minutes, then drain and rinse under cold running water.

Cut the duck into 8 pieces. Divide the vermicelli between 8 individual warmed soup bowls. Place a piece of duck and a few pieces of bamboo shoot on top, then cover with the hot soup. Sprinkle with the green shallot and coriander. Serve hot with the Nuoc Cham as an accompaniment.
SERVES 8

MIEN GA
CHICKEN NOODLE SOUP
VIETNAM

Not unlike good Chinese chicken noodle soup but, many say, lighter and with a more subtle flavour that changes between sips.

60 g (2 oz) cellophane noodles*
4 Chinese dried mushrooms*
6 cups chicken stock
4 half breasts of chicken
1 tablespoon vegetable oil
1 small white onion, peeled and halved lengthwise then cut in slivers
2 teaspoons fish sauce*
¼ teaspoon white pepper
4 green shallots, shredded diagonally
6 sprigs coriander*

METHOD: Soak the cellophane noodles and mushrooms separately in cold water to cover for 30 minutes, drain. Using a sharp knife or cleaver cut noodles into 5 cm (2 inch) lengths. Cut away and discard stems from mushrooms and slice caps into strips.

Bring chicken stock to the boil, add chicken breasts, reduce heat and simmer for 5 to 6 minutes. Remove chicken and when cool enough to handle remove skin and bones and discard. Shred meat into strips about 4 cm (1½ inches) long and 1 cm (½ inch) wide.

In a frying pan or wok heat the oil, add the onion and stir-fry for 1 to 2 minutes, without letting the onions brown. Add the chicken and mushrooms and cook a minute longer. Add to the simmering stock, stir in the fish sauce, pepper and noodles, and simmer for 5 minutes. Just before serving, sprinkle the soup with green shallots and coriander leaves.
SERVES 6

△ *Chrysanthemum Soup with Minced Pork (above); Crabmeat and Tapioca Pearl Soup; Duck Soup with Dried Bamboo Shoot*

CHA CUA

CRAB ROLLS
VIETNAM

Not unlike the Chinese spring roll, pork and crab is one of the favourite Vietnamese fillings for this crisp delicacy. Serve with a bowl of Nuoc Cham (see page 54).

Filling:

60 g (2 oz) cellophane noodles*, soaked in water for 10 minutes, then cut into 2.5 cm (1 inch) pieces
6 Chinese dried mushrooms*, soaked in warm water for 30 minutes, then stems removed and caps sliced
1 tablespoon vegetable oil
500 g (1 lb) lean minced pork
8-10 green shallots, finely chopped
375 g (12 oz) crabmeat, canned or fresh
4 egg yolks, lightly beaten
1 teaspoon salt
½ teaspoon white pepper
Wrappers:
4 eggs, beaten
16 dried rice papers*
2 cups vegetable oil
To garnish:
shredded green shallots

METHOD: To make the filling, drain the cellophane noodles and combine with the mushrooms. Heat a wok or frying pan, add the tablespoon oil, heat, then add the pork, mashing it constantly with the back of a spoon to break up any lumps. Cook for about 2 minutes. Off the heat add the chopped shallots, crabmeat, noodles and mushrooms, stirring constantly, then the egg yolks and seasonings. Mix well. Divide into 16 portions and pat each into the shape of a cylinder, about a finger's length.

To assemble each crab roll, brush the beaten egg over the entire surface of the rice paper. Leave a few seconds until soft and flexible. Place stuffing diagonally across the wrapper, roll over once, fold over the sides and roll once. Brush exposed wrapper with lightly beaten egg and roll into a neat package. The beaten egg will seal the wrapper and keep the roll intact. Place crab rolls on a plate. Refrigerate rolls, covered with plastic wrap if liked, until ready to fry.

Heat a wok, add the oil and heat – or use a deep-fat fryer. Deep-fry the crab rolls 3 or 4 at a time, turning them with a slotted spoon, for about 4 or 5 minutes or until they are golden brown and crispy. Drain on kitchen paper towels and keep warm while frying remaining rolls. Serve the crab rolls hot, garnished with a few shredded green shallots.

MAKES 16 ROLLS

TOM NUONG BANH HOI

BARBECUED PRAWNS
VIETNAM

500 g (1 lb) uncooked large prawns, unpeeled
185 g (6 oz) very thin rice vermicelli*
about 9 cups boiling water
2 teaspoons vegetable oil
3 green shallots, chopped
20 Roasted Peanuts (see page 78)
To serve:
few lemon slices, quartered
coriander leaves*
Nuoc Cham (see page 54)

METHOD: Cook the prawns over charcoal for about 7 minutes, turning once. Alternatively, bake them in a preheated moderately hot oven (200°C/400°F) for 10 minutes. Peel the prawns, then cut each one in half and set aside.

Add the rice vermicelli to the boiling water and boil for 2 minutes, then drain and rinse under cold running water. Drain again.

Heat the oil in a wok or frying pan, add the green shallots and fry gently until softened.

Arrange the rice vermicelli on a warmed serving plate, top with prawns, then sprinkle with green shallots and peanuts. Garnish with lemon slices and coriander. Serve hot with Nuoc Cham.

SERVES 4

CA KHO THOM
SIMMERED FISH WITH PINEAPPLE
VIETNAM

2 tablespoons vegetable oil
500 g (1 lb) fish steaks (snapper, sea bream, jewfish)
1 brown shallot, peeled and sliced
1 cup fresh pineapple, cut into 2.5 cm (1 inch) squares about 5 mm (¼ inch) thick
6 tablespoons fish sauce*
4 tablespoons sugar
1 tablespoon Caramelized Sugar (see right)
freshly ground black pepper

METHOD: Heat 1 tablespoon of the oil in a frying pan. Add the fish and fry gently until lightly browned on both sides, turning once.

Heat the remaining oil in a separate pan, add the shallot and fry gently until lightly browned. Add the pineapple and fry for about 3 minutes, then remove from the pan, using a slotted spoon. Discard the liquid.

Put half the fried pineapple and shallot in a small flameproof casserole. Place the fish steaks on top, then cover with the remaining pineapple and shallot. Add the remaining ingredients, cover with a tight-fitting lid and simmer for about 20 to 30 minutes until there is about ½ cup liquid remaining in the pan. Serve hot with rice.

SERVES 4

MANG TAY NAN CUA
CRAB AND ASPARAGUS SOUP
VIETNAM

Canned crabmeat and white asparagus may be used in place of fresh ingredients in this delicate soup. Salted duck egg is optional but gives a characteristic finish.

5 Chinese dried mushrooms*
6 cups chicken stock
1 small onion, peeled, halved and cut lengthwise into strips
500 g (1 lb) fresh asparagus, cooked, or large can white asparagus
500 g (1 lb) crabmeat, fresh or canned
2 teaspoons cornflour
1 Chinese salted duck egg yolk* (optional)
2 green shallots, cut in 2.5 cm (1 inch) lengths

METHOD: Cover the dried mushrooms with water and allow to soak for 30 minutes. Drain them and save the water, then discard the stems and slice the caps into strips.

In a saucepan combine the stock, mushroom water and onion, bring to the boil. Meanwhile cut the asparagus into 4 cm (1½ inch) lengths. Pick over crabmeat, removing bits of shell and cartilage. Add mushroom, asparagus and crabmeat to soup and bring to the boil again. Reduce heat, slake the cornflour with a little water and add to soup, stirring until soup thickens and is clear.

Just before serving crumble the salted egg yolk into small bits, if using, and sprinkle, with the shallots, on top of the crab and asparagus soup.

SERVES 6

CARAMELIZED SUGAR

Put 2 tablespoons sugar in a small frying pan with 4 tablespoons water. Stir well, then cook over high heat until the mixture turns brown, stirring constantly; remove from the heat when it turns a very dark brown colour and steam forms. Stir well and add 4 tablespoons water. Return to a high heat and cook for about 5 minutes, stirring all the time, then add a squeeze of lemon juice. Stir rapidly, remove from heat and leave to cool. Store in a screwtop jar until required.

▽ *Crab Rolls; Simmered Fish with Pineapple, served with rice and Nuoc Cham (see page 54)*

△ Chicken Spring Rolls served with Nuoc Cham

NUOC CHAM
VIETNAM

No Vietnamese meal is served without Nuoc Cham – a hot, tangy sauce which is sprinkled on food as desired and incorporated into many recipes.

If you do not possess a pestle and mortar, mash the ingredients with the back of a spoon.

Nuoc Cham can be made in larger quantities and stored in the refrigerator for up to 1 week. Keep in a small glass jar with a well-fitting lid.

2 garlic cloves, peeled
4 dried red chillis, or 1 fresh red chilli
5 teaspoons sugar
juice and pulp of ¼ lime
4 tablespoons fish sauce*
5 tablespoons water

METHOD: Pound the garlic, chillis and sugar using a pestle and mortar. Add the lime juice and pulp, then the fish sauce and water. Mix well to combine the ingredients. Use as required.
SERVES 4

CHA GIO GA
CHICKEN SPRING ROLLS
VIETNAM

Cha Gio Ga is the most popular dish in Vietnamese cuisine, for both rich and poor. It is usually filled with pork and crab, but a combination of any meat or seafood may be used. Serve as an appetizer with a bowl of Nuoc Cham (see left) or as a main course accompanied by a Vegetable Platter (see left) with Nuoc Cham served separately as a dip.

Cooked spring rolls can be frozen, then reheated in a moderate oven (180°C/350°F). Alternatively they can be partially cooked, refrigerated for 1 day, then completed the following day.

Filling:
60 g (2 oz) cellophane noodles*, soaked in water for 10 minutes, then cut into 2.5 cm (1 inch) pieces
500 g (1 lb) chicken breast meat, skinned and cut into thin strips
2 tablespoons dried wood ears*, soaked in warm water for 20 minutes, then finely chopped
3 garlic cloves, peeled and finely chopped
3 brown shallots, finely chopped
250 g (8 oz) crabmeat, canned or frozen
½ teaspoon freshly ground black pepper
Wrappers:
4 eggs, beaten
20 dried rice papers*
2 cups vegetable oil
To garnish:
shredded green shallot

METHOD: To make the filling, put all the ingredients in a bowl and mix well, using the hands. Divide the mixture into 20 portions and shape into small cylinders.

Brush beaten egg over the entire surface of each piece of rice paper. Leave for a few seconds until soft and flexible. Place the prepared filling along the curved edge of the paper, roll once, then fold over the sides to enclose the filling and continue rolling. (The beaten egg not only makes the wrapper flexible, it also holds it together.)

Pour the oil into a 30 cm (12 inch) frying pan and when oil is hot, add about one third of the spring rolls. Fry over moderate heat until golden brown, then remove with a slotted spoon and drain on absorbent kitchen paper towels. Fry the remaining spring rolls in the same way. Serve hot or at room temperature, garnished with shredded green shallot.
MAKES 20

GA XAO BUN TAU
CHICKEN WITH CELLOPHANE NOODLES
VIETNAM

This light dish is traditionally accompanied by a salad of sliced tomatoes and onions dressed with a little white vinegar, a sprinkling of sugar, salt and pepper.

2 whole chicken breasts
4 chicken thighs
2 tablespoons oil
2 green shallots, sliced
2 tablespoons fish sauce*
1 tablespoon light soy sauce
freshly ground black pepper
½ cup water
125 g (4 oz) cellophane noodles*, soaked in hot water for 30 minutes

METHOD: Remove skin and bones from breasts and thighs of chicken and cut flesh into 2.5 cm (1 inch) pieces.

Heat a wok or frying pan, add the oil and swirl to coat the surface. Add the chicken pieces and shallots, and stir-fry for 2 to 3 minutes. Add the fish and soy sauces, a grinding of black pepper and the water. Bring to the boil and simmer for a few minutes. Add the drained noodles, return to the boil and cook for a further 3 minutes.
SERVES 4-6

NAM DONG CO TIEM GA
STEAMED CHICKEN WITH MUSHROOMS
VIETNAM

A Chinese wok and bamboo steamer are the ideal utensils for this dish; an inexpensive Chinese noodle bowl can be used to hold the chicken. Serve with rice.

2 whole chicken breasts
4 chicken thighs
6 Chinese dried mushrooms*, soaked in warm water for 30 minutes, then stems removed and caps sliced
5 cm (2 inch) piece fresh ginger*, shredded
4 green shallots, sliced diagonally
¼ teaspoon ground pepper
2 teaspoons fish sauce*
1 garlic clove, peeled and crushed
¼ teaspoon salt
1 teaspoon sesame oil
2-3 cups water

METHOD: Remove bones from chicken breasts and thighs and cut the meat into 2.5 cm (1 inch) pieces. Put into a heatproof bowl. Add mushrooms to chicken along with the ginger, green shallots, pepper, fish sauce, garlic, salt and sesame oil. Mix lightly.

Bring the water to the boil in a wok or saucepan, set the bowl of chicken in the water, cover the bowl loosely with foil, cover and steam for 20 to 25 minutes or until the chicken is cooked. If the water boils away add more boiling water.
SERVES 4

GA XAO SA NUOC DUA
FRIED CHICKEN WITH COCONUT MILK AND LEMON GRASS
VIETNAM

4 chicken thighs, or 2 legs and 2 thighs, chopped into small pieces
2 garlic cloves, peeled and chopped
1 brown shallot, peeled and chopped
½ teaspoon sugar
¼ teaspoon salt
pinch of freshly ground black pepper
½ teaspoon curry powder
pinch of crushed dried red chillis, or more to taste
1 tablespoon fish sauce*
1 tablespoon vegetable oil
1 stalk lemon grass*, very finely chopped
1 cup coconut milk*
To garnish:
2 tablespoons Chopped Roasted Peanuts (see page 78)
1 green shallot, cut into 5 cm (2 inch) pieces
4 lime slices, halved (optional)

METHOD: Put the chicken in a bowl with half the garlic, the brown shallot, sugar, salt, black pepper, curry powder, crushed chillis and fish sauce. Stir well, then leave to marinate for 30 minutes.

Heat the oil in a wok or deep frying pan. Add the remaining garlic and the lemon grass, stir-fry for a few seconds, then add the chicken. Stir-fry for about 10 minutes until the chicken is lightly browned, then add the coconut milk to the wok. Simmer, uncovered, for 15 minutes or until the chicken is tender and the liquid is reduced to a thick sauce.

Place the chicken on a warmed serving plate. Top with the peanuts and green shallot. Arrange lime slices around the edge of the plate, if liked. Serve hot with rice.
SERVES 4

BARBECUED BEEF WITH LIME JUICE
VIETNAM

The literal translation of the name of this dish is 'Beef Barbecued on a Steel Griddle'. The dish is usually served in restaurants, where each diner is given a very small charcoal burner, a small steel griddle and a portion of food to cook for himself at the table. At home, use an electric frying pan, or ordinary frying pan or griddle over an electric hotplate or gas burner.

500 g (1 lb) slice rump or scotch fillet topside, about 2.5 cm (1 inch) thick
2 tablespoons vegetable oil
1 tablespoon fish sauce*
freshly ground black pepper
1 onion, peeled and thinly sliced into rings
To serve:
12 dried rice papers*
Vegetable Platter (see right)
few lime wedges
Nuoc Cham (see page 54)

METHOD: Slice the beef thinly against the grain, then arrange in overlapping circles on a serving dish. Sprinkle with 1 tablespoon of the oil, the fish sauce and pepper to taste, then arrange the onion slices on top.

To serve, each diner should place a rice paper on an individual serving plate and brush the surface with water. Leave for about 1 minute until the rice paper is soft and flexible, then place a lettuce leaf, a few pieces of cucumber and a sprig each of coriander and mint on the paper.

Meanwhile, heat the frying pan at the table and, when very hot, add the remaining oil. Let each person put in a few slices of beef and a slice of onion. Cook for a few seconds, then turn over and squeeze a little lime juice on to the meat.

Transfer the meat and onion to the top of the salad vegetables, then fold over the sides of the rice paper to enclose the food and roll up. Serve Nuoc Cham in individual bowls as a dip. Continue with the remaining ingredients until all are used up, eating the food as soon as it is cooked.
SERVES 4

VEGETABLE PLATTER

A platter of raw vegetables is an important part of almost every Laotian, Cambodian or Vietnamese meal. In South-East Asia, a variety of vegetables and different herbs are used. A satisfactory vegetable platter can be made with fewer ingredients.

soft lettuce leaves
mint leaves
coriander leaves*
cucumber, partially peeled and thinly sliced into half-moon shapes

METHOD: Pile the lettuce in a mound in the centre of a serving dish, then place the mint and coriander around the lettuce in separate mounds. Arrange the cucumber slices overlapping around the rim of the dish. Serve cold.
SERVES 4

BEEF WITH SESAME SAUCE
VIETNAM

If liked, other vegetables may be used in this dish, bamboo shoots, shredded Chinese cabbage or green peppers.

375 g (12 oz) rump steak
1 tablespoon soy sauce
3 tablespoons vegetable oil
1 garlic clove, peeled and crushed
1 cup bean sprouts, topped and tailed
½ cup beef stock
2 tablespoons cornflour
2 tablespoons cold water
2 teaspoons sesame paste
1-2 teaspoons Chinese chilli sauce*

METHOD: Trim beef of fat and sinews and shred into thin strips. Sprinkle with soy sauce and mix well. Leave to stand for 15 minutes.

Heat a wok, then add the oil and stir-fry the meat and garlic until the meat changes colour. Add the bean sprouts and continue to stir-fry for about 2 minutes. Add the stock and bring to the boil. Slake the cornflour with the cold water, then add to the beef, stirring until it comes to the boil. Add the sesame paste and chilli sauce. Serve with boiled rice.
SERVES 4

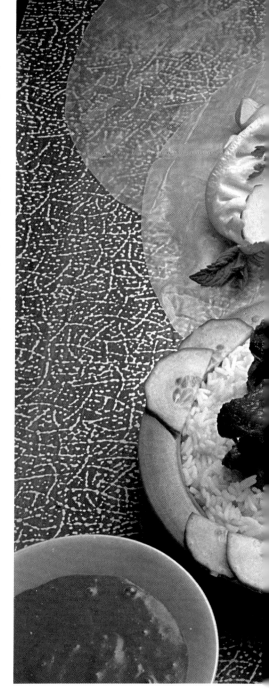

△ *Barbecued Beef with Lime Juice (above), served with Vegetable Platter (see left); Barbecued Spareribs, served with Nuoc Cham (see page 54)*

COM CHIEN THAP CAM
VIETNAMESE FRIED RICE
VIETNAM

A light and delicate variation of fried rice.

1½ cups medium grain white rice
2½ cups water
¼ cup plus 1 tablespoon vegetable oil
1 onion, peeled, halved lengthwise, then sliced lengthwise
6 Chinese dried mushrooms*, soaked in warm water for 30 minutes, then stems removed and caps sliced
1 tablespoon fish sauce*
250 g (8 oz) raw prawns, shelled, deveined and halved
2 Chinese sausages, fried lightly for 5-8 minutes
250 g (8 oz) crabmeat, fresh or canned
2 eggs
4 green shallots, cut into 2.5 cm (1 inch) pieces, then cut into 4 lengthwise

METHOD: Cook rice at least 2 hours or more ahead: wash rice well, drain and place in a pan with the water, bring to the boil, stirring once or twice, then lower the heat and simmer uncovered until the water has been absorbed into the rice. Lower heat, cover with tight-fitting lid and cook very gently for about 10 minutes. Fluff up with a fork, then spread on to a large tray lined with greaseproof paper. Allow to cool for at least 2 hours. If liked this can be stored, covered, overnight in a refrigerator.

Heat ¼ cup oil in a wok or frying pan, drop in the onion and stir-fry for about 2 minutes. Add the mushroom strips. Add the rice and stir-fry until the rice is heated through. Stir in the fish sauce.

Push rice to edge of the pan, add the remaining tablespoon oil to centre of pan, then add prawns without disturbing rice and cook until they turn pink. Slice the cooked sausage and add with crabmeat and mix well together with the rice. Cook over moderate heat, tossing, for about 5 minutes, then break in the eggs one at a time, stirring well after each addition.

Mix in the green shallots and a little more fish sauce if the rice seems too bland.
SERVES 4-6

SUON NUONG
BARBECUED SPARERIBS
VIETNAM

In Vietnam, this dish is barbecued over charcoal, but it can be roasted successfully in the oven. It is always served on a bed of plain boiled rice, as a one-dish meal.

5 brown shallots or ½ onion, peeled and sliced
2 garlic cloves, peeled
2 tablespoons sugar
4 tablespoons fish sauce*
¼ teaspoon freshly ground black pepper
750 g (1½ lb) pork spareribs
To serve:
plain boiled rice
Nuoc Cham (see page 54)
few cucumber slices

METHOD: Work the shallots, garlic and sugar to a paste, using a pestle and mortar or blender. Add the fish sauce and black pepper and stir well. Place the spareribs in a roasting pan and pour the mixture over them. Turn to coat thoroughly. Leave to marinate for at least 1 hour.

Roast in a preheated moderate oven (180°C/350°F) for 45 minutes until the spareribs are well browned. Cut the ribs into separate pieces.

Put the rice in a serving dish, arrange the spareribs on top and sprinkle with a little Nuoc Cham. Arrange cucumber slices around the edge of the dish. Serve hot, with a bowl of Nuoc Cham handed separately.
SERVES 4

MON SNGOR
CHICKEN SOUP
KAMPUCHEA

1 chicken, weighing 1-1.25 kg (2-2½ lb)
8 cups water
3 tablespoons fish sauce*
1 teaspoon sugar
juice of 1 lime
2 green shallots, chopped
4 tablespoons shredded culantro* or coriander leaves*
1 red chilli, sliced

METHOD: Put the chicken and water in a large pan and bring to the boil. Reduce heat and simmer for 30 minutes or until the chicken is cooked. Remove the chicken from the pan and tear the meat from the bones in bite-sized pieces. Return the meat and bones to the pan and bring back to the boil. Reduce heat and simmer for 5 minutes, then remove from the heat.

Put the fish sauce, sugar, and lime juice in a warmed soup tureen. Pour the hot soup into the tureen and stir well, then sprinkle over the green shallots, culantro and chilli. Serve hot with rice.
SERVES 4

SACH MON CHHA KHNHEI
STIR-FRIED CHICKEN WITH GINGER
KAMPUCHEA

2.5 cm (1 inch) piece of fresh ginger*, peeled and shredded
salt
2 tablespoons pork fat or vegetable oil
2 garlic cloves, peeled and chopped
6 chicken thighs, chopped into 2.5 cm (1 inch) squares
1 tablespoon fish sauce*
1 teaspoon sugar
1 tablespoon water
2 green shallots, cut into 5 cm (2 inch) pieces
coriander leaves* or parsley sprigs to garnish

METHOD: Sprinkle the ginger with a little salt, leave to stand for a few minutes, then squeeze and discard the liquid. Rinse the ginger with water and squeeze out the liquid again.

Heat the pork fat or oil in a frying pan. Add the garlic and stir-fry until lightly browned. Add the ginger and stir-fry for 1 minute, then add the chicken. Stir in the remaining ingredients, except the green shallots, then cover and cook over moderate heat for 10 minutes or until the chicken is completely cooked. Stir in the green shallots.

Transfer to a serving dish and garnish with coriander leaves or parsley sprigs. Serve hot with steamed rice as part of a family dinner.
SERVES 4

SOMLAR MOCHU SACHKO
SOUR BEEF STEW
KAMPUCHEA

2 stalks lemon grass*, thinly sliced
3 garlic cloves, peeled
5 fresh or dried lime leaves*, shredded
4 tablespoons tamarind paste*
1 tablespoon turmeric powder
2 tablespoons dried galingale*, soaked in hot water for 1 hour
1 red chilli
2 tablespoons fish paste*
2 tablespoons pork fat or vegetable oil
2 tablespoons fish sauce*

◁ *Stir-Fried Chicken with Ginger; Fried Pork Spareribs; Sour Beef Stew*

NUM BANH CHOC
RICE NOODLE FISH SOUP
KAMPUCHEA

This soup is usually served at breakfast in Kampuchea. Khcheay (white turmeric) is available in dried powdered form at Oriental grocers.

5 cups water
1 fish, mackerel, sea bream, gemfish, weighing 1.5 kg (3-3½ lb)
3 tablespoons khcheay (optional)
2 garlic cloves, peeled
5 lemon grass leaves*, thinly sliced
1 teaspoon turmeric powder
2 tablespoons fish paste*
2 tablespoons fish sauce*
1 teaspoon salt
1 teaspoon sugar
1 cup coconut milk*
To serve:
250 g (½ lb) medium rice vermicelli*
¾ cup fresh bean sprouts
½ cup shredded cucumber
½ cup shredded green pawpaw
2 tablespoons chopped dill
¾ cup shredded cabbage
½ cup fresh or canned banana blossoms, shredded (optional)

METHOD: Bring the water to the boil in a large pan. Add the fish and bring back to the boil, then simmer for about 15 minutes or until the fish flakes easily. Remove the fish and reserve the cooking liquid.

Remove all the flesh from the fish and discard the skin and bones. Put the khcheay (if using), garlic, lemon grass and turmeric in a blender or mortar and work to a paste. Add the fish and work again to a smooth paste.

Bring the reserved cooking liquid to the boil. Add the fish paste, fish sauce, salt, sugar and coconut milk. Bring back to the boil, add the pounded fish mixture, then boil for 10 to 15 minutes.

Boil the rice vermicelli in about 8 cups water for 5 minutes, then drain and rinse under cold running water. Drain again.

Pour the hot soup into a warmed soup tureen. Divide the rice vermicelli between 4 individual warmed soup bowls, add the remaining ingredients and ladle the soup over the top. Serve hot.
SERVES 4

---

1 kg (2 lb) stewing beef, cut into 2.5 cm (1 inch) cubes
½ cup water
To garnish:
2 tablespoons chopped green shallot, green part only

METHOD: Put all the ingredients except the beef, fish sauce, paste and pork fat in a blender or mortar and work to a paste.

Work the fish paste through a sieve and discard the pulp remaining in the seive.

Heat the pork fat or oil in a pan. Add the fish paste, stir-fry for a few seconds, then add the blended ingredients. Stir again, then add the fish sauce. Stir in the meat and water. Bring to the boil and simmer, uncovered, for 15 minutes.

Add more water as necessary to ensure the meat is just covered with liquid. Cover and simmer for 1 hour or until the meat is tender, adding more water if necessary during cooking.

Transfer to a serving dish and garnish with green shallot. Serve hot with rice as a main dish for a family dinner.
SERVES 6

CHOEENG CHOMNI CHROUC CHEAN
FRIED PORK SPARERIBS
KAMPUCHEA

1 kg (2 lb) pork spareribs, cut into separate pieces
2 tablespoons fish sauce*
1 tablespoon sugar
3 garlic cloves, peeled and chopped
pinch of freshly ground black pepper
3 tablespoons pork fat or vegetable oil
To garnish (optional):
thinly pared strip of chilli
parsley sprig

METHOD: Put the spareribs in a bowl, cover with the remaining ingredients except the fat or oil; marinate for 30 minutes.

Heat the pork fat or oil in a frying pan. Add the spareribs and fry gently for about 10 minutes on each side until golden brown and cooked through.

Drain the spareribs and arrange on a serving dish. Garnish with red chilli and parsley, if liked, arranged to resemble a flower head. Serve hot with rice.
SERVES 4

LAP KAY
CHICKEN LAP
LAOS

A dish of Lap Kay, a bowl of chicken soup, a bamboo steamer containing glutinous rice* and a Vegetable Platter (see page 56) – all of these are placed in the centre of the table. (In Laos, this would be a straw mat on the floor.)

Each diner is given a plate and a spoon. He then picks up about 1 tablespoon rice, squeezes it into a ball, presses it against the mound of Lap Kay, then eats the rice and the food that adheres to it. A spoonful of soup is eaten after each mouthful, followed by a few pieces of vegetable from the platter.

250 g (8 oz) boned chicken meat, skinned and finely diced
125 g (4 oz) chicken livers, finely diced
125 g (4 oz) chicken gizzards, finely diced (optional)
2 teaspoons anchovy sauce
2 teaspoons fish sauce*
1 tablespoon whole dried red chillis
2 tablespoons dried galingale*, soaked in hot water for 1 hour and finely chopped
1 tablespoon lime juice
¼ teaspoon salt
¼ teaspoon freshly ground black pepper
To garnish:
2 tablespoons chopped green shallot, green part only
coriander leaves*

METHOD: Mix together the chicken, livers and gizzards, if using. Place in a 20 cm (8 inch) square baking tin and press the mixture down firmly until about 1 cm (½ inch) thick. Bake in a preheated moderate oven (180°C/350°F) for 20 minutes.

Allow to cool slightly, then add the remaining ingredients and work into the mixture, with the hands, squeezing out all the excess liquid.

Arrange on a warmed serving dish and garnish with the green shallot and coriander. Serve hot or allow to cool before serving.
SERVES 4

OCKLAM
BARBECUED PORK WITH MUSHROOMS AND BEANS
LAOS

This is the national dish of Laos. Beef or chicken may be substituted for the pork used here. Fresh pork skin is obtainable at Chinese butchers' shops while dried pork skin can be obtained sometimes at Vietnamese grocery stores – it should be soaked in warm water for 30 minutes before use.

250 g (8 oz) pork, sliced into strips 2.5 cm (1 inch) wide and 5 mm (¼ inch) thick
250 g (8 oz) glutinous rice*
7½ cups water
2 tablespoons fish sauce*
½ teaspoon salt
1 eggplant, weighing about 500 g (1 lb)
1 tablespoon whole dried red chillis
125 g (4 oz) beans or Chinese green long beans, cut into 2.5 cm (1 inch) pieces
8 large Chinese dried mushrooms*, soaked in warm water for 30 minutes and shredded
3 bay leaves
10 cm (4 inch) square piece of fresh or dried pork skin, shredded into thin strips
To garnish:
few lemon slices
thinly pared strip of chilli
2.5 cm (1 inch) piece of green shallot

METHOD: Roast the pork in a preheated moderate oven (180°C/350°F) for 15 minutes. Meanwhile, put the glutinous rice in a mortar, add just enough water to cover, then crush with a pestle or blend lightly.

Pour 7½ cups water into a pan and bring to the boil. Add the fish sauce and salt, then the roast pork, eggplant and chillis. Boil for 10 minutes or until the eggplant is soft, then remove from the pan together with the chillis.

Work the eggplant and chillis, using a pestle and mortar or blender, then return to the pan. Add the beans, mushrooms and bay leaves. Bring to the boil, then add the glutinous rice with its soaking liquid and the pork skin. Boil for 20 minutes or until the glutinous rice is cooked. Remove the bay leaves.

Transfer to a serving dish and garnish with lemon slices, chilli and green shallot, coiling the chilli around the shallot to resemble a flower head. Serve hot with boiled rice and a Vegetable Platter (see page 56).
SERVES 4

△ *Chicken Lap, served with Chicken Soup, Glutinous Rice (see below) and Vegetable Platter (see page 56)*

GLUTINOUS RICE*

In Laos, rice is always served in the bamboo basket in which it has been steamed. In the West, however, it can be steamed by putting a layer of cheesecloth on one of the layers of an oriental steamer, and placing the soaked glutinous rice* on the cheesecloth. For this method of cooking rice, no measurements are necessary: every cup of glutinous rice* doubles in volume when cooked.

Soak the rice in water to cover for at least 6 hours, then drain. Bring water to the boil in the lower level of a steamer, making sure that the water does not touch the steaming level. Place the rack containing the rice on top of the boiling water, then cover and steam for about 15 minutes until the rice looks clear and is soft to the touch. The longer the soaking period, the shorter the cooking time.

KEN KAY
CHICKEN SOUP
LAOS

This is always served as an accompaniment to Lap Kay (see left).

1 tablespoon dried tamarind pulp*
750 g (1½ lb) chicken, chopped into 5 cm (2 inch) pieces, with the bones
7 cups water
2 tomatoes, cut into wedges
6 lime leaves*
2 tablespoons fish sauce*
½ teaspoon salt
pinch of freshly ground black pepper
To garnish:
2 tablespoons chopped green shallot, green part only
2 tablespoons chopped coriander leaves*

METHOD: Soak the tamarind pulp in ½ cup hot water for 10 minutes, then knead to extract the flavour. Strain the liquid, discarding the pulp.

Put the chicken, water, tomatoes, tamarind water and lime leaves in a pan and bring to the boil. Skim, then lower the heat and simmer, uncovered, for 20 minutes or until the chicken is tender. Add the fish sauce, salt and pepper.

Pour the hot soup into a warmed tureen and garnish with the green shallot and coriander. Serve hot.
SERVES 4

SHIN NGOA LAP
SPICY BEEF
LAOS

3 tablespoons glutinous rice*
500 g (1 lb) topside or rump steak, cut into 3 pieces
1 tablespoon fish sauce*
2 teaspoons anchovy paste
1 tablespoon dried galingale*, soaked in hot water for 1 hour and finely chopped
1 tablespoon chopped coriander leaves*
1 tablespoon chopped green shallot, green part only
To finish:
1 red chilli, sliced into rings
juice of ½ lime

METHOD: Fry the glutinous rice in a hot, dry frying pan until brown, then pound to a powder in a mortar or electric blender.

Roast the beef in a preheated moderately hot oven (200°C/400°F) for 15 minutes. Leave until cool enough to handle, then shred into thin strips and mix with the powdered rice.

Combine the fish sauce and anchovy paste in a pan, then cook over moderate heat until smooth. Add to the beef with the galingale, coriander and green shallot, stir well.

Arrange the meat mixture on a warmed serving dish and garnish with the chilli. Sprinkle with the lime juice just before serving. Serve hot, or at room temperature.
SERVES 4

TAM SOM
SOUR CARROT
LAOS

Tam Som appears as an appetizer at all social occasions. It has an amalgam of flavours – sour, salty, sweet and very hot.

250 g (8 oz) pork tripe
5 garlic cloves, peeled
5 dried red chillis
2 tomatoes
2 tablespoons fish sauce*
3 medium carrots, peeled and shredded

METHOD: Put the pork tripe in a pan, cover with water and boil for about 30 minutes.

Meanwhile, work the garlic, chillis and tomatoes in a mortar or blender. Stir in the fish sauce.

Place the shredded carrot on a serving dish and pour over the sauce. Drain the pork tripe, slice thinly and arrange on top of the salad. Mix well with chopsticks just before serving. Serve cold.
SERVES 4

KANG RON

TRANSPARENT VERMICELLI SOUP
THAILAND

Dried squid is an acquired taste. If you do not like its rubbery texture, omit it from this recipe. It is available from Chinese food stores.

125 g (4 oz) wun sen*, soaked in water for 10 minutes
2 coriander roots*, finely chopped
2 garlic cloves, peeled and chopped
1 teaspoon freshly ground black pepper
125 g (4 oz) pork, minced
5 cups water
125 g (4 oz) prawns, peeled and deveined
30 g (1 oz) dried prawns* (optional)
30 g (1 oz) dried squid, sliced (optional)
½ onion, peeled and sliced
2 tablespoons dried jelly mushrooms*, soaked in warm water for 20 minutes
pinch of monosodium glutamate*
1 egg
few green shallots, finely chopped, to garnish

METHOD: Drain the wun sen, then cut into 5 cm (2 inch) lengths. Put the coriander roots, garlic and pepper in a mortar and pound to a paste. Add the pork and continue pounding to a smooth paste. Shape the mixture into 10 to 12 inch balls, about 1 cm (½ inch) in diameter.

Bring the water to the boil in a pan, then drop in the pork balls and cook for 5 minutes. Add the fresh prawns and skim off any scum that comes to the surface with a slotted spoon. Simmer for a few minutes, stirring constantly.

Add the dried prawns and squid, if using, the onion, mushrooms, monosodium glutamate and the drained wun sen. Simmer for a few minutes, then stir the egg slowly into the soup and remove from the heat.

Pour into a warmed tureen and sprinkle with the green shallots. Serve hot.
SERVES 4

KOW TOM KAI

CHICKEN RICE PORRIDGE
THAILAND

This dish is popular for breakfast or as a late supper, and is often served with chilli pickle. If possible, make the stock with pork bones. If these are not available, however, use chicken stock cubes instead.

5 cups stock
2 half breasts of chicken, skinned, boned and cut into 1 cm (½ inch) cubes
125 g (4 oz) boned pork loin, cut into 1 cm (½ inch) cubes
1½ cups rice, cooked
2 celery sticks, with leaves, chopped into 1 cm (½ inch) lengths
2 green shallots, chopped
nam pla* (fish sauce), to taste
freshly ground black pepper

To garnish:

1 tablespoon vegetable oil
4 garlic cloves, peeled and finely chopped
125 g (4 oz) bacon, derinded and cut into 1 cm (½ inch) squares

METHOD: Bring the stock to the boil in a pan, then add the chicken and pork. Cook until the meat turns white, then add the rice. Remove from the heat, add the celery and green shallots, then add nam pla and pepper to taste. Set aside.

Heat the oil in a frying pan, add the garlic and fry until golden brown. Remove from the pan with a slotted spoon and set aside. Add the bacon to the pan and fry until brown and crisp.

Pour the soup into 4 warmed individual bowls and sprinkle with the garlic and bacon. Serve hot.
SERVES 4

▷ *Transparent Vermicelli Soup; Prawns and Squid Hot Soup*

KAENG TOM YAM KUNG

SHRIMP SOUP

THAILAND

A light and fragrant soup served hot in bowls – if liked, less chilli strips can be added to the soup, or additional chilli can be passed around for those who like this soup hotter still.

750 g (1½ lb) uncooked prawns, shelled and deveined
9 cups water
6 small makrut leaves*
1 tablespoon shredded takrai* (lemon grass)
2 teaspoons nam pla* (fish sauce)
⅓ cup fresh lime juice
4 tablespoons sliced coriander leaves*
3 tablespoons sliced green shallots
1 red chilli, seeded and sliced into 2.5 cm (1 inch) strips

METHOD: Wash prawns under running water, pat dry with absorbent kitchen paper towels. Bring water to the boil, add makrut and takrai and simmer for about 10 minutes or until the leaves become pale yellow. Add the nam pla and cook for a further 5 minutes. Reduce the heat, add the prawns and lime juice and cook gently until the prawns turn firm and a pale pink. Add the coriander, shallots and red chilli strips.
SERVES 6

TOM YUM KUNG LAE PLA MUK

PRAWNS AND SQUID HOT SOUP

THAILAND

Ideally, the stock for this soup should be made with pork bones. If these are not available, however, use chicken stock cubes instead.

250 g (8 oz) squid
7 cups stock
3 lime leaves*
1 stalk lemon grass*, crushed
250 g (8 oz) prawns, peeled and deveined
nam pla* (fish sauce), to taste
2-4 fresh chillis, sliced into rounds
2 garlic cloves, peeled and crushed
juice of 1 lime or lemon, or to taste
chopped coriander leaves* to garnish

METHOD: Clean the squid, cut off and chop the tentacles; cut the body into rings.
Put the stock, lime leaves and lemon grass in a pan, bring to the boil, then lower the heat and simmer for 5 minutes. Add the prawns, squid and nam pla. Cook until the prawns turn pink, then add the chillis.
Pour the soup into 4 warmed individual bowls. Mix together the garlic and lime or lemon juice to taste, then stir into the soup. Sprinkle with coriander. Serve hot.
SERVES 4

PAD MEE KROB
DEEP-FRIED RICE VERMICELLI WITH SAUCE
THAILAND

vegetable oil for deep-frying
185 g (6 oz) rice vermicelli*, broken into pieces
Sauce:
1 tablespoon vegetable oil
1 onion, peeled and finely chopped
2 garlic cloves, peeled and finely chopped
250 g (8 oz) prawns, peeled and deveined
90 g (3 oz) crabmeat
2 teaspoons brown sugar
2 tablespoons tamarind water*
1 teaspoon salt
1 tablespoon soy sauce
To garnish:
2 teaspoons finely grated orange rind
2 red chillis, shredded
chopped coriander leaves*
125 g (4 oz) fresh bean sprouts

METHOD: Heat the oil in a deep-fat fryer and fry the rice vermicelli in batches, for about 30 seconds until the strands swell and float. Drain and set aside.

To make the sauce, heat the oil in a wok or deep frying pan, add the onion and garlic and fry until lightly brown. Add the prawns and crab and cook until pink.

Stir in the remaining ingredients, with the fried vermicelli. Taste and adjust the seasoning. Heat through, then transfer to a warmed serving dish.

Garnish with the orange rind, chillis and coriander, and arrange the bean sprouts around the edge of the dish. Serve hot.
SERVES 4

PLA PRIO WAN
FRIED MACKEREL WITH TAMARIND SAUCE
THAILAND

4 medium mackerel or mullet
2 tablespoons vegetable oil
3 garlic cloves, peeled and finely chopped
2 tablespoons shredded fresh ginger*
3 tablespoons water
1 teaspoon sugar
3 tablespoons tamarind water*
To serve:
few green shallots, chopped
1 cucumber, skinned and sliced

METHOD: Clean the fish, but do not remove the skin. Wrap the fish together in well-buttered foil, then bake in a preheated cool oven (150°C/300°F) for 45 minutes or until tender. Unwrap the fish, then leave until cool and dry.

Heat the oil in a wok or deep frying pan, add the fish and fry gently until golden brown. Remove from the pan carefully and drain. Transfer to a warmed serving dish and keep hot.

To make the sauce, add the garlic to the pan in which the fish was fried and fry over high heat until light brown. Add the ginger and fry for a further 1 minute. Stir in the water, sugar and tamarind water. Heat through, then pour over the fish.

Sprinkle with the green shallots. Serve the fried mackerel hot, with the cucumber as a side dish.
SERVES 4

TOD MUN PLA
FRIED HOT FISH BALLS
THAILAND

4 garlic cloves, peeled and chopped
20 peppercorns
4 coriander roots*, finely chopped
pinch of sugar
3 dried chillis
750 g (1½ lb) fish fillets, skinned
1 tablespoon plain flour
1 tablespoon soy sauce
5 tablespoons vegetable oil
To serve:
½ cucumber, peeled and thinly sliced
1 teaspoon distilled vinegar
2 tablespoons water
1 teaspoon sugar
2 green shallots, peeled and finely chopped
1 small carrot, peeled and grated

METHOD: Put the garlic, peppercorns, coriander, sugar and chillis in a mortar or food processor and work to a paste. Add the fish a little at a time and continue working to a smooth paste. Add the flour and soy sauce, and then shape into 20 to 25 balls, about 2.5 cm (1 inch) in diameter.

Heat the oil in a wok or deep frying pan and fry the fish balls, a few at a time, until golden brown all over. Remove from the pan with a slotted spoon, drain and arrange on a serving dish. Keep hot while frying the remainder.

Arrange the cucumber slices in a separate serving dish. Mix together the vinegar, water, sugar, shallots and carrot. Sprinkle over the cucumber. Serve the fish balls hot, with the cucumber salad as a side dish.
SERVES 4

THAI CURRY PASTE (RED AND GREEN)

This paste can be made red or green. The recipe below is for red curry paste. For green curry paste use 6 green chillis instead of red and omit the paprika.

6 dried red or green chillis
3 tablespoons chopped green shallots
1 tablespoon chopped garlic
1 tablespoon paprika
1 tablespoon powdered takrai* (lemon grass)
1 tablespoon kapi* (shrimp paste)
1 teaspoon ground laos*
1 teaspoon caraway seeds
2 teaspoons coriander seeds
1 teaspoon finely grated lemon peel
1 teaspoon salt

METHOD: Wash chillis under running water. Remove stems from chillis and slit through, brush out any seeds.

Combine chillis and remaining ingredients in an electric blender and blend at high speed for 20 to 30 seconds. Turn off the machine, scrape down the sides with a rubber spatula and blend again until the mixture is a smooth paste.

Store in a small screwtop jar in refrigerator for 3 to 4 weeks. Use as described in Thai curry recipes.
MAKES ABOUT ½ CUP

KAENG KEAO WAN KUNG
PRAWN CURRY
THAILAND

Serve this delicious curry, freshly made, with a big bowl of steaming hot rice.

750 g (1½ lb) uncooked prawns, shelled and deveined
3 cups coconut milk*
2 tablespoons green Curry Paste (see left)
2 teaspoons ground laos*
2 tablespoons nam pla* (fish sauce)
1 tablespoon fresh green chilli, cut into 2.5 cm (1 inch) strips
4 fresh basil leaves

METHOD: Wash prawns under running water, pat dry and set aside. Chill coconut milk in refrigerator for an hour or so. The thick milk will rise to the surface, scoop 1 cup off the top and place in a heavy saucepan. Reserve the remaining coconut milk.

Bring the coconut milk to the boil and simmer uncovered, stirring occasionally until the coconut oil begins to bubble to the surface and the liquid has been reduced to about ¼ cup. Add the curry paste and laos and bring to the boil. Continue to cook the mixture until most of the liquid in the pan has evaporated.

Add the prawns and cook, turning them with a spoon, for about 3 to 4 minutes or until they are firm and pink. Stir in the remaining coconut milk and nam pla, stirring occasionally, and simmer for 6 to 8 minutes. Serve in a bowl, garnished with chilli strips and basil leaves cut into strips.
SERVES 4-6

◁ *Deep Fried Vermicelli with Sauce; Fried Mackerel with Tamarind Sauce*

KAI TOD KARB KRATIEM
FRIED CHICKEN WITH GARLIC
THAILAND

4 chicken breasts, skinned and boned
3 garlic cloves, peeled and crushed
1 tablespoon freshly ground black pepper
2 tablespoons soy sauce
1 teaspoon sugar
1 teaspoon salt
1 teaspoon sesame seed oil*
vegetable oil for shallow-frying

METHOD: Slit the surface of the chicken breasts on both sides, using a very sharp knife. Put the remaining ingredients in a bowl, mix well, then rub into the chicken breasts. Leave to marinate for 2 hours.

Heat about 5 tablespoons vegetable oil in a wok or frying pan. Add 2 chicken breasts and fry over moderate heat for about 4 minutes on each side until golden brown. Remove from the pan and drain. Fry the remaining chicken in the same way, adding more oil to the pan if necessary.

Cut each chicken breast in half, return to the pan and fry until the cut edges of the meat are no longer pink. Serve hot.
SERVES 4

MOO TOD
FRIED PORK BALLS
THAILAND

2 coriander roots*, finely chopped
2 teaspoons freshly ground black pepper
4 garlic cloves, peeled
pinch of sugar
500 g (1 lb) minced pork
2 tablespoons nam pla* (fish sauce)
flour for coating
4-5 tablespoons vegetable oil
coriander leaves* to garnish

METHOD: Put the coriander roots, pepper, garlic and sugar in a mortar or blender and work to a smooth paste.

Add the pork and pound to a pulp, then transfer to a bowl and add the nam pla. Stir well, then form into about 20 balls, approximately 2.5 cm (1 inch) in diameter, and coat lightly with flour.

Heat the oil in a wok or deep frying pan. Add about 5 pork balls and fry over moderate heat for 2 to 3 minutes, or until no liquid is released from the balls when pierced with a sharp knife. Remove from the pan; keep hot while frying the rest.

Pile the balls in a warmed serving dish and garnish with the coriander. Serve hot.
SERVES 4

PAD KING KAI
CHICKEN GINGER WITH HONEY
THAILAND

The flavour of this dish is greatly improved if it is cooked the day before it is required, then reheated just before serving.

5 green shallots, cut into 1 cm (½ inch) pieces
60 g (2 oz) fresh ginger*, shredded
2 tablespoons vegetable oil
3 chicken breasts, skinned, boned and cut into small pieces
3 chicken livers, chopped
1 onion, peeled and sliced
3 garlic cloves, peeled and chopped
2 tablespoons dried jelly mushrooms*, soaked in warm water for 20 minutes
2 tablespoons soy sauce
1 tablespoon honey

METHOD: Put the green shallots in a bowl, cover with cold water and leave to soak.

Mix the ginger with a little cold water, then drain and squeeze to reduce the hot taste. Rinse under cold running water, then drain well.

Heat the oil in a wok or frying pan, add the chicken and liver pieces and fry for 5 minutes. Remove from the pan with a slotted spoon and set aside.

Add the onion to the pan and fry gently until soft, then add the garlic and mushrooms and stir-fry for 1 minute. Return the chicken pieces to the pan.

Mix the soy sauce and honey together, pour over the chicken and stir well. Add the ginger and stir-fry for 2 to 3 minutes, then add the drained shallots.

Transfer the mixture to a bowl, cover and leave overnight. Reheat when required. Serve hot.
SERVES 4

KAI P'ANANG
DRY CHICKEN CURRY
THAILAND

150 g (5 oz) creamed coconut*, roughly chopped
⅔ cup water
2-3 large chicken breasts, skinned, boned and cut into serving pieces
Curry paste:
½ teaspoon caraway seeds
2 large chillis, seeded and chopped
½ teaspoon coriander seeds
2 teaspoons shredded takrai* (lemon grass)
3 brown shallots, peeled
1 teaspoon finely chopped coriander root*
5 garlic cloves, peeled
3 slices kha*
½ teaspoon makrut peel*, grated
½ teaspoon kapi* (shrimp paste)

METHOD: Put the creamed coconut in a large pan, add the water and heat gently until the coconut has melted, stirring frequently.

Add the chicken to the coconut and cook for about 10 minutes until almost tender. Remove the chicken from the pan. Boil the liquid for a few minutes until it becomes oily.

Meanwhile, make the curry paste: work the caraway seeds in a mortar or electric blender. Add the remaining ingredients one at a time, pounding between each addition, to obtain a smooth paste. Add the paste to the coconut liquid and heat gently, stirring constantly. Return the chicken to the pan and reheat, turning to coat with the sauce. Transfer to a warmed serving dish. Serve hot.

SERVES 4

△ *Chicken Ginger with Honey; Fried Pork Balls*

NUA NAM TOAK
BEEF WITH HOT SALAD
THAILAND

Round or topside steak can be used instead of fillet steak for a more economical meal; after slicing the meat treat it with meat tenderizer, then leave for about 10 minutes before cooking. In Thailand, paw-paw peel is used to make the meat tender.

The flavour of this dish is greatly improved if the onion, chillis and beef are grilled over glowing charcoals rather than using a conventional grill.

500 g (1 lb) fillet steak
1 large onion, peeled and sliced into rings
2 fresh chillis
2 garlic cloves, peeled and crushed
½ teaspoon sugar
1 teaspoon salt
½ teaspoon soy sauce
juice of 1 lime or lemon
1 teaspoon chopped mint
To serve:
fresh green seasonal vegetables (cucumber, tomatoes, Chinese cabbage, bean sprouts, etc.), chopped

METHOD: Cut the beef along the grain into strips about 6 cm (2½ inches) long, 2.5 cm (1 inch) wide and 1 cm (½ inch) thick. Put the onion rings and chillis on a skewer and grill until soft. Remove from the skewer, then mash together.

Grill the beef until just cooked to taste, then mix with the mashed onion and chillis. Add the remaining ingredients and mix.

Arrange the chopped vegetables around the edge of a warmed serving dish, then pile the beef mixture in the centre. Alternatively, toss the vegetables quickly with the beef and pile into a warmed serving dish. Serve hot.
SERVES 4

◁ *Beef with Hot Salad; Fried Beef and Horapa*

KAI LOOK KOEI
SON-IN-LAW EGGS
THAILAND

2 tablespoons vegetable oil
5 brown shallots or ½ onion, peeled and finely chopped
4 hard-boiled eggs, quartered
2 tablespoons tamarind water*
1 tablespoon water
2 teaspoons brown sugar
nam pla* (fish sauce), to taste

METHOD: Heat the oil in a wok or deep frying pan. Add the shallots or onions and fry until brown. Remove from the pan with a slotted spoon and set aside.

Add the eggs to the pan and fry until crisp and blistered on the outside, then remove from the pan and set aside.

Add the remaining ingredients to the pan and cook for 5 minutes, stirring constantly. Return the eggs to the pan and heat gently for 2 minutes, stirring carefully. Transfer to a warmed serving dish and garnish with the fried shallots or onions. Serve hot.
SERVES 4

PAD HO-RA-PA KUB NUA
FRIED BEEF AND HORAPA
THAILAND

2 tablespoons plus 1 teaspoon vegetable oil
750 g (1½ lb) rump steak, thinly sliced
2 onions, peeled and sliced
3 garlic cloves, peeled and finely chopped
3 tablespoons freshly chopped horapa leaves*
3 fresh chillis, sliced
nam pla* (fish sauce), to taste
few chopped green shallots to garnish

METHOD: Heat 1 teaspoon of the oil in a wok or frying pan, add the beef and fry until the juices are extracted from the meat. Stir twice and cook for about 3 minutes, then remove from the pan and set aside.

Heat the remaining oil in the pan, add the onions and garlic and fry over brisk heat until brown. Stir in the horapa, then return the beef to the pan. Add the chillis, fry for a further 1 minute, then add nam pla. Serve hot, garnished with the shallots.
SERVES 4

KAI YAD SAI
STUFFED PANCAKES
THAILAND

250 g (8 oz) minced pork
2 tablespoons tung chai*
1 teaspoon sugar
2 tablespoons soy sauce
2 onions, peeled and finely chopped
2 tablespoons vegetable oil
6 eggs, beaten
coriander leaves* to garnish

METHOD: Put the pork, tung chai, sugar, soy sauce and onions in a bowl and mix well. Heat 1 tablespoon oil in a wok or frying pan, add the pork mixture and fry gently for 3 minutes. Remove from the pan and set aside.

Add the remaining oil to the cleaned pan and tilt to coat the entire surface with oil. Pour off any excess oil, then heat the pan until smoking. Pour in half the beaten eggs to make a thin omelet. Spoon half the pork mixture into the centre, then fold over the edges. Turn the omelet over and cook quickly on the underside until lightly browned.

Remove from the pan and keep hot while cooking the remaining eggs and pork in the same way. Cut the pancakes into slices and arrange in a serving dish. Garnish with coriander. Serve immediately.
SERVES 4

SOM TUM
THAI SALAD

In Thailand, pawpaw is normally used in this salad, together with vegetables such as tomatoes and lettuce, so vary the salad with the vegetables on hand. It is a good side dish to serve with Fried Pork Balls and Fried Chicken with Garlic (see page 66).

2 cups shredded cabbage
1 cup shredded carrots
3 tablespoons Roasted Peanuts, crushed (see page 78)
1/3 cup dried shrimps*, ground
Dressing:
1 tablespoon nam pla* (fish sauce)
2 teaspoons sugar
freshly ground black pepper
2 garlic cloves, peeled and crushed
2 tablespoons lime or lemon juice

METHOD: Put all the salad ingredients in a bowl and stir well. Mix together the dressing ingredients, pour over salad and toss well to coat. Serve cold.
SERVES 4

KOW NEO TUA DOM
STICKY RICE WITH BLACK BEANS
THAILAND

In Thailand, this dish is cooked and sold in hollow sticks of green bamboo which have been cooked over charcoal. This recipe has been adapted for a domestic oven. Dried black beans are available at Chinese, Indian and Italian supermarkets.

150 g (5 oz) creamed coconut*, roughly chopped
2 1/2 cups water
1/2 cup dried black beans, soaked in cold water for 12 hours
1/4 cup glutinous rice*
2 tablespoons coconut sugar*

METHOD: Put the creamed coconut and water in a pan and heat gently, stirring frequently.

Drain the beans, then mix with the rice, sugar and coconut milk. Pour into a baking dish, cover and bake in a preheated very cool oven (120°C/250°F) for about 3 hours, stirring after 2 hours. Serve hot.
SERVES 4

KANG MASAMAN
MASAMAN CURRY
THAILAND

This is an unusual Thai curry in that it contains peanuts and tamarind water and there are many variations. It is equally good prepared with chicken, rather than beef.*

King Rama VI said in one of his poems, 'A lady who makes a good masaman will never be short of suitors.'

1 kg (2 lb) chuck steak, cut into 2.5 cm (1 inch) squares
5 cups water
200 g (7 oz) creamed coconut*, roughly chopped
1 cup Roasted Peanuts (see page 78)
nam pla* (fish sauce), to taste
3 tablespoons tamarind water*
coconut sugar*, to taste
Curry paste:
7 dried chillis, deseeded and finely chopped
1/2 teaspoon freshly ground black pepper
2 tablespoons coriander seeds
2 tablespoons cumin seeds
1 tablespoon shredded takrai* (lemon grass)
1 cinnamon stick
5 cardamom seeds
1/4 whole nutmeg, grated
1 teaspoon salt
7 brown shallots or 1 onion, peeled and chopped
5 garlic cloves, peeled
1/2 teaspoon kapi* (dried shrimp paste)

METHOD: Put the steak and water in a pan and bring to the boil. Lower the heat, cover and simmer for about 1 hour or until the meat is tender.

To make the curry paste: put the chillis in a pan with the pepper, coriander, cumin, takrai, cinnamon, cardamom and nutmeg. Cook over low heat until the mixture browns, stirring constantly. Transfer to an electric blender or mortar and work to a smooth paste. Add the remaining ingredients and work the mixture until smooth.

Remove the meat from the pan with a slotted spoon and set aside. Add the coconut cream to the liquid in the pan and heat gently, stirring frequently. Add the peanuts and a little nam pla. Boil the liquid until reduced in volume by one third. Add the prepared curry paste and simmer for about 5 minutes, stirring constantly.

Return the meat to the pan and cover with a tight-fitting lid. Bring back to the boil and continue cooking until the meat is very tender. Add the tamarind water with coconut sugar and nam pla to taste. Serve hot.
SERVES 6

△ *Masaman Curry (above); Thai Salad; Soya Bean and Coconut Dip*

MALED KHANUN
SWEET MUNG BEANS WITH COCONUT
THAILAND

1 cup mung beans*
150 g (5 oz) creamed coconut*, roughly chopped
2 cups water
1 cup sugar
4 egg yolks, beaten

METHOD: Crush the beans, using a blender or pestle and mortar, then leave to soak in cold water overnight.

Drain the beans and wash to remove the green skins. Put the beans in a pan, add enough water to cover, then simmer, covered, for about 20 minutes or until soft. Drain, then return to the cleaned pan and heat gently until the beans are dry and completely cooked, stirring occasionally. Mash to a smooth paste.

Put the creamed coconut in a pan, add 2/3 cup of the water and heat gently until melted, stirring frequently.

Add 3/4 cup of the sugar to the coconut liquid, then stir in the mashed beans. Bring to the boil, then boil, uncovered for about 30 minutes until the mixture is thick, stirring frequently with a wooden spoon. Remove

the pan from the heat and leave until completely cold.

Form the paste into about 50 small balls, approximately 1 cm (½ inch) in diameter. Put the remaining sugar and water in a pan. Heat gently until the sugar has dissolved, then boil until a thin syrup is formed.

Dip each ball into beaten egg yolk to coat, then immerse in the hot syrup and cook for about 30 seconds. Remove with a slotted spoon and arrange in a single layer on a serving dish, taking care that the balls are not touching or they will stick together. Chill in the refrigerator for at least 3 hours before serving. Serve very cold.

SERVES 4

KOW NEO SANG KAYA
STICKY RICE AND CUSTARD
THAILAND

Custard:
150 g (5 oz) creamed coconut*, roughly chopped
1¼ cups water
rose water, to taste
2 tablespoons brown sugar
4 eggs, beaten
Sticky rice:
1 cup glutinous rice*
125 g (4 oz) creamed coconut*, roughly chopped
1¼ cups water
1 teaspoon salt
1 tablespoon sugar
To decorate:
lime slices

METHOD: To make the custard: place creamed coconut in a pan, add the water and heat gently until the coconut has melted, stirring frequently.

Add rose water and sugar to the coconut milk. Stir well, then beat in the eggs. Strain into a heatproof bowl and steam for about 1½ hours or until the custard has set. Alternatively, place the bowl in a baking dish of water and bake in a preheated cool oven (140°C/275°F).

Meanwhile, make the sticky rice: put the rice in a bowl in the top of a steamer or double boiler. Place creamed coconut in a pan, add the water and heat gently until the coconut has melted, stirring frequently. Mix the coconut milk with the salt and sugar, then pour over the rice. Steam for 30 minutes or until the rice is cooked.

To serve: place the cooked custard on top of the rice and decorate with lime slices. Serve hot or cold.

SERVES 4

TAO CHIEW LON
SOYA BEAN AND COCONUT DIP
THAILAND

Serve this dip with a salad of chopped fresh vegetables according to availability.

125 g (4 oz) creamed coconut*, roughly chopped
1¼ cups water
3 tablespoons tao chiew*
1 tablespoon finely chopped brown shallots or onion
60 g (2 oz) cooked peeled prawns
¼ cup mashed potato
2 chillis, finely chopped
1 teaspoon brown sugar
3 tablespoons tamarind water*
chillis to garnish

METHOD: Place the creamed coconut in a pan with the water and heat gently until the coconut has melted, stirring frequently. Work the tao chiew and shallots or onion to a paste, using an electric blender or a pestle and mortar, then add to the coconut liquid with the prawns and potato.

Cook until the fat from the coconut floats to the surface of the sauce, stirring constantly to prevent sticking. Stir in the remaining ingredients and bring to the boil.

Transfer to a serving dish and garnish with chillis. Serve hot, with a crisp salad.

SERVES 4

HIN-NU-NWE HIN-GYO
SOUP WITH FRESH GREENS
BURMA

This is an everyday soup which is quick and very easy to make. The dried shrimps can be pounded at home or bought ready-powdered, and the soup can be varied from day to day by adding different fresh green vegetables: watercress, sorrel, spinach, cabbage, pea leaves or mustard leaves.

5 cups water
1 medium onion, peeled and sliced
3 garlic cloves, peeled and sliced
3 tablespoons pounded dried shrimps*
½ teaspoon shrimp paste* (optional)
2 teaspoons soy sauce
1 teaspoon salt
250 g (8 oz) fresh green leaves, washed

METHOD: Put the water, onion and garlic in a pan and bring to the boil. Lower the heat, then add the shrimps, shrimp paste, if using, soy sauce and salt. Stir well, then add the green leaves.

Boil for 5 minutes, taste and adjust the seasoning, then pour into a warmed soup tureen. Serve hot.
SERVES 4

HIN-GYO YO-YO
CLEAR SOUP
BURMA

This soup is usually served with rather oily dishes such as Wet-thani (see right). Its base is pork stock, made by boiling pork bones in water, but a stock made from chicken carcass can be used instead.

The soup can be made more substantial by adding cabbage, cauliflower, carrots, bean sprouts or noodles, and simmering the soup for 5 to 10 minutes longer than the time given below.

375 g (12 oz) pork bones
5 peppercorns, crushed
3 garlic cloves, peeled and crushed
2 teaspoons soy sauce
5 cups water
salt
freshly ground black pepper
To garnish:
2 tablespoons finely chopped celery (optional)
3 tablespoons finely chopped green shallots, including green tops

METHOD: Put the pork bones, peppercorns, garlic, soy sauce and water in a large pan. Bring to the boil, partly cover, then lower the heat and simmer for about 30 minutes.

Remove the bones from the soup with a slotted spoon. Add salt and pepper to taste, then transfer to a warmed soup tureen and sprinkle with the celery, if using, and green shallots. Serve hot.
SERVES 4

WET-THANI
RED PORK
BURMA

This dish is called 'Red or Golden Pork' because the oil in the dish is coloured by the chilli powder.

The Burmese like to use fatty pork – either shoulder or belly – for this recipe, but if this is not to your taste, then pork fillet may be used instead.

1 kg (2-2¼ lb) boned pork, cut into 2.5 cm (1 inch) cubes
3 tablespoons soy sauce
1 teaspoon freshly ground black pepper
5 cm (2 inch) piece of fresh ginger*, peeled
3 medium onions, peeled and pounded
3 garlic cloves, peeled and crushed
1 cup boiling water
1 teaspoon chilli powder
5 tablespoons vegetable oil

METHOD: Put the pork in a bowl with 2 tablespoons soy sauce and the pepper; mix well.

Pound half the ginger, then mix with the onions and garlic. Stir in all but 1 tablespoon of the boiling water, this can all be done in a blender, then strain the mixture and retain both the liquid and the pounded ingredients.

Stir the chilli powder into the reserved boiling water. Cut the remaining ginger into thin strips. Heat the oil in a large, heavy pan, add the ginger and fry until just sizzling, then add the pork and stir-fry until brown.

Add the liquid reserved from the pounded ingredients, cover the pan and simmer for about 10 minutes or until the liquid has almost all been absorbed. Add the chilli water, the remaining soy sauce and the reserved pounded ginger, onion and garlic mixture.

Cover and cook over low heat for about 40 minutes or until the pork is tender, stirring occasionally to prevent sticking. (If lean pork has been used, it may be necessary to add a little water during cooking.) Serve hot.
SERVES 4-6

MON-LA-U HIN-GYO
RADISH AND FISH SOUP
BURMA

This is a fairly rich soup, with a distinctive flavour which is imparted by the tamarind. It is usually made with long white radishes, but it can alternatively be made with spinach or sorrel leaves, or with sliced eggplant or okra.

250 g (8 oz) filleted white fish (bream, gemfish, etc.), cut into chunks
1 teaspoon salt
½ teaspoon ground turmeric
2 tablespoons vegetable oil
1 medium onion, peeled and pounded

3 garlic cloves, peeled and crushed
1 cm (½ inch) piece of fresh ginger*, peeled and pounded
½ teaspoon chilli powder
4 tomatoes, chopped
½ teaspoon shrimp paste* (optional)
1 tablespoon shrimp-flavoured soy sauce*
5 sprigs coriander leaves*
2 tablespoons dried tamarind pulp*
375 g (12 oz) long white radish*, including green tops, peeled and thinly sliced

METHOD: Put the fish in a bowl and rub with the salt and turmeric. Set aside.

Heat the oil in a large pan. Mix together the onion, garlic, ginger and chilli powder. Add to the pan and fry gently until lightly coloured, then add the fish. Stir-fry for a few minutes, then add the tomatoes, shrimp paste, if using, soy sauce, 5 cups cold water and the coriander. Bring to the boil, then lower the heat and simmer for 15 minutes.

Meanwhile, put the tamarind in a bowl, pour over 6 tablespoons hot water, then knead to extract the flavour. Strain the liquid, discarding the tamarind pulp.

Add the tamarind liquid and radish to the pan and simmer for 15 minutes or until the radish is clear and tender. Taste and adjust the seasoning, then leave to stand for about 30 minutes to allow the full flavour to develop.

Reheat, then pour into a warmed soup tureen. Serve hot.
SERVES 4-6

▽ *Clear Soup; Soup with Fresh Greens*

NGA-BAUNG-DOK
STEAMED FISH PARCELS
BURMA

In Burma, this subtly flavoured dish is steamed in banana leaves (as illustrated), but in the West, foil may be substituted. If liked, spinach or lettuce may be used instead of the Chinese cabbage suggested here.

575 g (1¼ lb) thick white fish fillets (bream, gemfish, etc.), cut into 7.5 × 3.5 cm (3 × 1½ inch) pieces
2 teaspoons salt
½ teaspoon ground turmeric
3 small onions, peeled
2 garlic cloves, peeled and crushed
2.5 cm (1 inch) piece of fresh ginger*, peeled and pounded
½ teaspoon chilli powder
1 tablespoon rice flour*
60 g (2 oz) creamed coconut*, roughly chopped (optional)
5 tablespoons boiling water
2 teaspoons vegetable oil
½ teaspoon powdered lemon grass*
10 Chinese cabbage leaves, washed and cut in half

METHOD: Put the fish in a bowl and rub lightly with half the salt and turmeric. Set aside.

Thinly slice 1 onion, then pound the remaining onions. Mix the pounded onions to a paste with the remaining salt and turmeric, the garlic, ginger, chilli powder and rice flour. This can be done in a blender.

If using creamed coconut, place in a bowl, add the water and stir until the coconut melts. Add to the onion paste with the oil, sliced onion and the lemon grass. Mix well.

Cut ten 18 cm (7 inch) squares of foil. Place 1 piece of Chinese cabbage on each foil square, then top with a little of the paste mixture. Place a piece of fish and a little more paste mixture on top of this, then cover with another piece of bok choy. Fold the foil, enclosing the filling, to form parcels. Fold the edges together to seal.

Steam the parcels for 20 minutes or until the fish is cooked through. Serve hot.
MAKES 10

PAZUN HIN
PRAWN CURRY WITH TOMATOES
BURMA

In Burma, large prawns are used to make this dish. If possible, try to use king prawns, but if these are not obtainable, then ordinary prawns may be used instead.

625 g (1¼ lb) peeled prawns
2 tablespoons shrimp-flavoured soy sauce*
½ teaspoon salt
½ teaspoon turmeric powder
4 tablespoons vegetable oil
1 large onion, peeled and chopped finely
4 garlic cloves, peeled and crushed
1 cm (½ inch) piece of fresh ginger*, peeled and pounded
½ teaspoon chilli powder
3 tomatoes, roughly chopped
2 tablespoons chopped coriander leaves*
4 tablespoons water
coriander leaves* to garnish

METHOD: Put the prawns in a bowl with the soy sauce, salt and turmeric. Mix well, then set aside.

Heat the oil in a pan, add the onion, garlic, ginger and chilli powder and stir-fry until fragrant but not dry.

Add the prawns, tomatoes and coriander, increase the heat slightly, then cover the pan and cook for 5 minutes. Stir in the water, lower the heat, cover and simmer for 10 minutes until the prawns are cooked and the water has been absorbed.

Transfer to a warmed serving dish and garnish with coriander leaves. Serve hot.
SERVES 4

NGA-GYAW
SPICED FRIED FISH WITH ONIONS
BURMA

750 g (1½ lb) white fish fillets (bream, ling, gemfish, etc.), cut into 10 cm (4 inch) squares
½ teaspoon ground turmeric
1 tablespoon shrimp-flavoured soy sauce*
2 tablespoons dried tamarind pulp*
6 tablespoons hot water
7 tablespoons vegetable oil
2 medium onions, peeled and sliced
1½ teaspoons chilli powder

METHOD: Put the fish in a bowl; rub lightly with the turmeric and soy sauce. Set aside.

Put the tamarind in a bowl, cover with the hot water, then knead to extract the flavour. Strain the liquid, discarding the pulp.

Heat the oil in a large frying pan, add the onions and fry over brisk heat until golden and crisp. Remove from the pan with a slotted spoon and drain the onions on kitchen paper towels.

Pour off half the oil from the pan, then add the chilli powder. Increase the heat slightly, add the fish and fry quickly for 1 minute.

Add the tamarind liquid, cover and simmer for about 15-20 minutes until the fish is cooked and the liquid has almost all been absorbed. (If necessary, add a little more oil during cooking, to prevent sticking.)

Transfer to a warmed serving dish and sprinkle the fried onions over. Serve hot.

SERVES 4

CHET-THA HSI-BYAN
BURMESE CHICKEN CURRY

This is a typical Burmese curry, cooked in such a way that the 'oil returns' (hsibyan in Burmese) to the top of the dish at the end of cooking. For the best flavour, chop the chicken into small pieces across the joints, as in Chinese cooking.

1 chicken, weighing 1.5 kg (3 lb), chopped into pieces
2 tablespoons soy sauce
1 teaspoon salt
½ teaspoon ground turmeric
3 medium onions, peeled
4 garlic cloves, peeled
2.5 cm (1 inch) piece of fresh ginger*, peeled and pounded
1-2 teaspoons chilli powder, to taste
5 tablespoons vegetable oil
3 bay leaves
1 piece of cinnamon stick

METHOD: Put the chicken in a bowl with the soy sauce, salt and turmeric; mix well.

Pound or blend 1 onion and 3 garlic cloves, mix with the ginger and chilli powder, then rub into the chicken.

Slice the remaining onions and garlic thinly. Heat the oil in a large pan, add the onions and garlic and fry gently for 5 to 10 minutes until soft and fragrant. Add the chicken and any remaining pounded mixture. Fry for 10 minutes until the chicken is brown on all sides, stirring occasionally.

Add the bay leaves and cinnamon and enough water to just cover the chicken (about 2½ cups). Increase the heat and bring to the boil, then cover and simmer for about 35 minutes until the oil has risen to the surface, leaving a thick curry sauce underneath. If there is too much liquid towards the end of the cooking time, increase the heat and boil, uncovered, until reduced and thickened. Serve hot with Coconut Rice (see page 80).

SERVES 4

△ *Prawn Curry with Tomatoes; Steamed Fish Parcels; Fried Spiced Fish with Onions*

UN-NO KAUK-SWE
CHICKEN WITH NOODLES AND COCONUT
BURMA

This is probably the most famous of all Burmese dishes. It is something of a feast, but it is not too difficult to prepare at home. Try to use the special split pea and lentil flours, as these give the dish its authentic Burmese flavour. Chick pea (garbanzo) flour may be substituted for the split pea flour, if this is more easily obtainable.

In Burma, the dish is served in wide soup bowls or plates – the noodles are placed in the bottom of the bowls, then a little of each of the accompaniments is sprinkled on top, followed by the hot chicken mixture. Each diner squeezes lemon juice over his serving just before eating.

1 chicken, weighing 1.5 kg (3 lb), cut into large pieces
salt
½ teaspoon ground turmeric
12 cups water
5 tablespoons vegetable oil
4 medium onions, peeled and pounded
4 garlic cloves, peeled and crushed
2.5 cm (1 inch) piece of fresh ginger*, peeled and pounded
2 teaspoons chilli powder
4 tablespoons split pea flour*
4 tablespoons lentil flour*
150 g (5 oz) creamed coconut*, roughly chopped
500 g (1 lb) fresh or dried egg noodles
To serve:
5 tablespoons oil
12 garlic cloves, peeled and sliced crossways
3 hard-boiled eggs, quartered
2 onions, peeled and sliced
5 green shallots, including green tops, finely chopped
1 tablespoon chilli powder (optional)
2 lemons, quartered

METHOD: Rub the chicken with 1 tablespoon salt and the turmeric, then place in a very large pan. Add the water, bring to the boil, then lower the heat and simmer for about 25 minutes until the chicken is just cooked, but still firm. Remove the chicken from the pan, leave the cooking liquid to simmer gently over low heat.

Remove the skin and bones from the chicken and add them to the simmering cooking liquid. (For maximum flavour the chicken bones should be cracked, but this is not essential.) Cut the chicken meat into bite-sized chunks.

Meanwhile, heat the oil in a large pan,

add the onions, garlic, ginger and chilli powder and stir-fry for 5 minutes. Add the chicken meat and stir-fry for 5 to 10 minutes. Turn off the heat.

Mix the flours to a paste with about 1 cup cooking liquid and set aside. Strain the remaining cooking liquid into the pan containing the chicken meat.

Stir in the flour paste and bring to the boil. Lower the heat, add the creamed coconut and simmer for about 20 minutes until the mixture has the consistency of thick pea soup, stirring frequently. If the mixture becomes too thick, add a little more water: if it is too thin, add a little more lentil flour paste. Turn off the heat, taste and adjust the seasoning, then cover the pan and set aside.

Cook the noodles in boiling salted water for about 7 minutes; drain and keep hot.

To serve, heat the oil in a small frying pan, add a handful of the boiled noodles and fry over brisk heat until crisp. Remove from the pan with a slotted spoon and drain on kitchen paper towels, then place in a serving bowl. Repeat until all the noodles are cooked.

Add the garlic to the pan, fry over brisk heat until golden and crisp, then transfer to a small serving bowl.

Reheat the chicken mixture, then pile into a warmed serving dish. Serve the remaining ingredients in separate small bowls as accompaniments to the chicken and noodles. Serve hot.
SERVES 6-8

△ *Chicken with Noodles and Coconut*

Mix together the onions, garlic, ginger and chilli powder. Heat the oil in a large, heavy pan, add the pounded mixture and stir-fry for 10 minutes or until the mixture begins to brown.

Add the beef, bay leaves, cinnamon and peppercorns and enough water to half cover the beef. Cover and simmer over low heat for about 45 minutes or until the meat is tender; stir in a little water if necessary during cooking.

Taste and adjust the seasoning towards the end of the cooking time, adding a little salt according to taste. Serve this Burmese beef curry hot.

SERVES 4-6

HIN-THI YWET HIN-TAMYO
VEGETABLE CURRY
BURMA

The proportion of vegetables can be varied to suit individual tastes and availability.

3 medium potatoes, peeled and cut into 3.5 cm (1½ inch) cubes
1 medium eggplant, cut into 2.5 cm (1 inch) slices
4 carrots, peeled and diced
1 medium cauliflower, divided into florets
250 g (8 oz) okra, cut into 2.5 cm (1 inch) lengths (optional)
4 tablespoons vegetable oil
1 medium onion, peeled and pounded
3 garlic cloves, peeled and crushed
1 cm (½ inch) piece of fresh ginger*, peeled and pounded
1 teaspoon chilli powder
½ teaspoon turmeric powder
90 g (3 oz) dried salt fish*, roughly sliced (optional)
3 tomatoes, roughly chopped
3 tablespoons chopped coriander leaves*
1 fresh green chilli (optional)

METHOD: Put the potatoes, eggplant, carrots, cauliflower and okra in a bowl. Cover with cold water and set aside.

Heat the oil in a large pan, add the onion, garlic, ginger, chilli powder and turmeric and stir-fry until fragrant.

Add the salt fish, if using, stir-fry for 2 minutes, then stir in one third of the tomatoes and the coriander. Add the potatoes and just enough water to cover. (Add a little salt if salt fish is not used.) Bring to the boil, then lower the heat and simmer for 10 minutes.

Add the eggplant and carrots, simmer for 5 minutes, then add the cauliflower and a little more water, if necessary. Bring back to the boil, add the remaining tomatoes and the chilli, if using. Simmer for 5 minutes, then add the okra, if using.

Lower the heat and simmer for 5 minutes or until the vegetables are cooked, but still firm, and most of the liquid has been absorbed. Discard the chilli, if used. Serve the vegetable curry hot.

SERVES 4-6

THANAT-SON-THOK
ASSORTED VEGETABLE SALAD
BURMA

Although called a salad, the vegetables in this dish are blanched or quickly cooked first. The choice of vegetables can be varied according to taste and availability.

3 carrots, scraped
salt
1½ cups green beans, topped and tailed
1 cup okra
2 cups fresh bean sprouts
2 large cauliflower florets
1 cup bamboo shoot (optional)
5 tablespoons sesame seeds*
2 tablespoons vegetable oil
1 medium onion, peeled and sliced

METHOD: Cook the carrots in boiling salted water for about 7 minutes, then remove from the pan and leave to cool.

Cook the remaining vegetables separately in boiling salted water, allowing about 3 minutes for each vegetable – they should remain crunchy. Leave to cool.

Put the sesame seeds in a small, heavy frying pan and fry over dry heat until 'toasted' golden brown, shaking the pan constantly. Remove from the pan and set aside.

Add the oil to the pan, heat gently, then add the onion. Fry over brisk heat until golden and crisp, then remove from the pan with a slotted spoon and drain on kitchen paper towels. Reserve 1 tablespoon of the oil.

Slice the carrots into thin matchstick strips. Slice the beans and okra diagonally into 1 cm (½ inch) pieces. Arrange the vegetables in separate piles on a long serving dish.

Stir a pinch of salt into the reserved oil, drizzle over the vegetables, then sprinkle with the sesame seeds and fried onion. Serve cold or chilled.

SERVES 6-8

AME-THA HIN
BEEF CURRY
BURMA

The beef in this recipe needs to be marinated for at least 4 hours, preferably overnight. It is then cooked slowly with very little liquid, so it is best cooked in a heavy-based pan. Adjust the cooking time according to the quality of the meat.

1 kg (2 lb) chuck steak, cut into 2.5 cm (1 inch) cubes
1 tablespoon shrimp-flavoured soy sauce*
½ teaspoon ground turmeric
1 tablespoon malt vinegar
2 medium onions, peeled and pounded
4 garlic cloves, peeled and crushed
2.5 cm (1 inch) piece of fresh ginger*, peeled and pounded
1 teaspoon chilli powder
3 tablespoons vegetable oil
3 bay leaves
2 pieces of cinnamon stick
5 peppercorns
salt

METHOD: Put the meat in a bowl with the soy sauce, turmeric and vinegar. Mix well, then leave to marinate for at least 4 hours, preferably overnight.

NGAPI-GYAW
BURMESE BALACHAUNG SHRIMP CONDIMENT

Every household in Burma has its own special recipe for making this spicy shrimp condiment, which is eaten as an accompaniment to most meals. It may also be eaten as an unusual sandwich filling. A word of warning – Ngapi-gyaw smells strongly during cooking! It will keep for up to 6 months in a screwtop jar in the refrigerator.

1 tablespoon dried tamarind pulp* (optional)
1 cup vegetable oil
1 medium onion, peeled and sliced
8 garlic cloves, peeled and sliced crossways
2.5 cm (1 inch) piece of fresh ginger*, peeled and sliced into strips
1 teaspoon chilli powder
1 teaspoon turmeric powder
200 g (7 oz) dried shrimp powder
2 teaspoons shrimp paste*

METHOD: If using tamarind, place in a bowl, cover with 3 tablespoons hot water, then knead to extract the flavour. Strain the liquid, discarding the tamarind pulp.

Heat the oil in a wok or deep frying pan, then fry the onion, garlic and ginger separately over brisk heat until golden and crisp. Remove from the pan with a slotted spoon and drain on kitchen paper towels.

Add the chilli powder to the pan and fry for 30 seconds, then add the turmeric and shrimp powder. Stir-fry until the shrimp powder has absorbed most of the oil, then remove from the pan and drain off any excess oil.

Add the shrimp paste to the pan with the tamarind liquid, if using. Fry over low heat for about 3 minutes, stirring constantly to prevent burning. Return the shrimp powder to the pan, mix quickly together, then remove from the heat and stir in the onions, garlic and ginger. Allow to cool.

Serve cold in individual dishes, as an accompaniment.
MAKES 2 CUPS

THANHAT
CUCUMBER SALAD
BURMA

This salad can also be made with carrots, cauliflower, green beans or fresh bean sprouts.

2 medium cucumbers, peeled, seeded and cut into 7.5 cm (3 inch) long strips
3 tablespoons vinegar
1 teaspoon salt
4 tablespoons vegetable oil
2 medium onions, peeled and sliced
8 garlic cloves, peeled and sliced
½ teaspoon ground turmeric
1 teaspoon sugar
2 tablespoons sesame seeds*

METHOD: Put the cucumber in a pan with 2 tablespoons of the vinegar and just enough water to cover. Bring to the boil, then lower the heat and simmer for about 4 minutes until the cucumber becomes transparent. Drain, sprinkle with ½ teaspoon salt, then leave to cool.

Heat the oil in a frying pan, add the onions and fry over brisk heat until golden and crisp. Remove from the pan with a slotted spoon and drain on kitchen paper towels. Add the garlic to the pan, fry until golden, then remove and drain.

Add the turmeric, sugar and remaining salt to the pan, stir, then add half the sesame seeds. Stir-fry for 1 to 2 minutes, remove from the heat and leave to cool in the pan.

Stir the remaining vinegar into the mixture in the pan, then add the cucumber and toss well. Drain off the excess oil and vinegar, then pile the cucumber into a pyramid shape on a serving plate. Sprinkle with the onion, garlic and remaining sesame seeds. Serve cold or chilled.
SERVES 4

△ *Tomato Salad; Cucumber Salad*

CHOPPED ROASTED PEANUTS

Heat a small frying pan until very hot, then add shelled red-skinned peanuts. Fry over dry heat until the skins turn black, stirring constantly, then transfer to a colander. Leave to cool for about 3 minutes, then rub between the hands to loosen the skins. Discard the skins. Chop the peanuts coarsely using a pestle and mortar or electric blender, if required.

FRIED EGGPLANT
BURMA

This vegetable dish can be served as a side dish to a main meal of curry and rice, or eaten on its own. The eggplant can be baked in advance.

1 large eggplant
2 tablespoons vegetable oil
1 medium onion, peeled and sliced
1 garlic clove, peeled and crushed
1.2 cm (½ inch) piece of fresh ginger*, peeled and pounded
½ teaspoon salt
2 green shallots, including green tops, finely chopped, to garnish

METHOD: Put the eggplant on a lightly oiled baking tray and bake in a preheated hot oven (220°C/425°F) for about 1 hour or until soft to the touch, turning occasionally. Remove from the oven and leave to cool.

Heat the oil in a frying pan, and fry the onion and garlic until beginning to brown.

Meanwhile, peel off the eggplant skin, scoop out the flesh and mash with a fork. Add to the pan with the ginger and salt, then stir-fry for 5 to 10 minutes. Transfer to a warmed serving dish and garnish with the green shallots. Serve hot or cold.
SERVES 4-6

HKAYAN-CHIN-THI LET-THOK
TOMATO SALAD
BURMA

This salad is best made with under-ripe tomatoes.

4 tablespoons vegetable oil
1 medium onion, peeled and sliced
4 medium tomatoes, thinly sliced
1 tablespoon Roasted Peanuts (see left), pounded
3 tablespoons chopped coriander leaves*
1 teaspoon shrimp-flavoured soy sauce*
juice of ½ lemon
coriander leaves* to garnish

METHOD: Heat 3 tablespoons of the oil in a small frying pan, add the onion and fry over brisk heat until golden and crisp. Remove from the pan with a slotted spoon and drain on kitchen paper towels.

Put the tomatoes in a bowl, then add the peanuts, coriander, soy sauce and remaining oil and toss lightly to mix.

Arrange the tomato mixture on a serving plate, sprinkle with the lemon juice and top with the onion. Garnish with coriander. Serve cold or chilled.
SERVES 4

KYAUK-KYAW
SEAWEED JELLY
BURMA

This is a very firm jelly with an unusual coconut flavour. It sets in two layers – a creamy layer on top, with a cloudy layer underneath.

25 g (1 oz) dried agar-agar*
125 g (4 oz) creamed coconut*, roughly chopped
1 cup granulated sugar

METHOD: Put the agar-agar in a bowl, add just enough cold water to cover and leave to soak for 2 to 3 hours.

Strain the agar-agar, discarding the water, then measure the agar-agar. For each measure of agar-agar, use double the amount of fresh water; 25 g (1 oz) soaked agar-agar should fill a 2½ cup measure, so the required amount of water will be about 5 cups.

Put one quarter of the creamed coconut in a small bowl, bring 7 tablespoons of the measured water to the boil, pour over the coconut and stir until melted. Set aside.

Put the remaining creamed coconut in a pan with the agar-agar and sugar. Bring the remaining water to the boil, add to the pan and simmer gently for about 10 minutes, until the mixture is smooth, stirring occasionally.

Pour the mixture into a shallow square dish. Leave to cool slightly, then pour over the reserved coconut. Leave in a cool place for about 1 hour until set, then cut into diamond shapes and arrange on a serving plate.

SERVES 6-8

THA-GU MON
TAPIOCA PUDDING
BURMA

In Burma, palm sugar is used in this pudding. Brown or black sugar can be used instead – black sugar is sold in health food shops.

1⅓ cups tapioca
1 cup brown sugar, firmly packed
½ teaspoon salt
3¾ cups water
1⅓ cups desiccated or freshly grated coconut
2 teaspoons caster sugar

METHOD: Put the tapioca, brown sugar, salt and water in a pan and bring to the boil. Lower the heat and simmer for about 10 minutes until the tapioca becomes soft and transparent and the mixture is thick, stirring constantly.

Remove from the heat, pour into a greased shallow dish and leave until cold.

Scoop out the mixture in tablespoonfuls, then roll in the coconut and caster sugar. Arrange on a serving plate.

SERVES 6-8

ON HTAMIN
COCONUT RICE
BURMA

Coconut rice makes a pleasant change from plain boiled rice as an accompaniment to a main course. It goes particularly well with Burmese Chicken Curry (see page 75). For a variation, add 1 piece of cinnamon stick, 1 bay leaf, 2 cloves and 2 cardamom pods – these will give the rice a delicious, slightly spicy flavour.

2½ cups long-grain rice, washed thoroughly
5 cups water
90 g (3 oz) creamed coconut*, roughly chopped
1 medium onion, peeled and quartered
½ teaspoon salt
1 teaspoon vegetable oil

METHOD: Put the rice in a large pan and add the water. Add the remaining ingredients and bring to the boil over high heat. Cover the pan, lower the heat to a minimum and cook for about 20 minutes, until the rice is tender.

Remove the lid and stir the rice once – the liquid should have been absorbed completely and the rice grains should be fluffy. Serve hot.

SERVES 6

SANWIN-MAKIN
SESAME SEMOLINA PUDDING
BURMA

The secret of the flavour of this pudding is the dry cooking of the semolina.

1½ cups semolina
1 cup dark brown sugar
½ teaspoon salt
185 g (6 oz) creamed coconut*, roughly chopped
5 cups boiling water
60 g (2 oz) butter or margarine
2 teaspoons vegetable oil
2 medium eggs, beaten
½ cup seeded raisins
4 tablespoons sesame seeds* or poppy seeds

METHOD: Put the semolina in a large, heavy pan and cook over low heat for about 10 minutes, stirring occasionally. The semolina should become scorched or 'toasted', but not burnt.

Remove from the heat and stir in the brown sugar, salt, creamed coconut and water. Leave to stand for at least 30 minutes, then cook over low heat for about 15 minutes or until quite thick, stirring occasionally.

Remove from the heat, add the butter or margarine and stir until melted. Stir in the oil, leave to cool slightly, then stir in the eggs.

Return to the heat and cook gently for 5 minutes, stirring constantly. Stir in the raisins and cook for 5 to 10 minutes until the mixture is thick, but not solid.

Pour into a greased, shallow, ovenproof square dish and sprinkle with the sesame or poppy seeds. Bake in a preheated moderately hot oven (200°C/400°F) for about 1½ hours until the pudding has begun to shrink away from the sides of the dish and the seeds are brown.

Leave until cold, then cut into squares or diamond shapes to serve.
SERVES 6-8

▷ *Sesame Semolina Pudding (above); Tapioca Pudding; Seaweed Jelly*

Chinese dishes are cooked without the use of exotic ingredients. Instead good quality fresh ingredients are combined to produce a dish of contrasting tastes but at the same time retaining the texture and colour of the individual ingredients.

The vast expanse of China has a far greater range of climates than all of the countries of Europe have. In the northernmost reaches of Manchuria sub-arctic conditions prevail. The ground stays frozen for eight months of the year while the southern provinces of Fukien, Kwangtung, Yunnan and Kwangi enjoy year round tropical temperatures and plentiful rain, allowing for good cultivation of the land. Such harsh and varied conditions inevitably shaped the Chinese attitude towards food. Contrary to what one might expect, these conditions have not dampened the Chinese interest in food. Indeed Chinese cooking is superlative and the Chinese cuisine is a triumphant blending of inventiveness, flavour and refinement. Many believe Chinese cuisine is better than any other in the world, and those holding this view include devotees of French food.

The preparation of Chinese food takes great care and in most cases a longer time than the actual cooking. The technique of cutting is of prime importance. When cut in uniform size and shape, many dissimilar ingredients blend into surprising harmony.

Pork is the primary meat of China. Duck and chicken are also important. Buddhism not only held the cow sacrosanct but respected all living things. This gave impetus to the excellent vegetarian cookery of China. However, lamb and beef are now appearing in more dishes.

Noodles are often very long – a symbol of longevity – and have been a basic of the Chinese cuisine for thousands of years; from a noodle dough many delicious dumplings which may be steamed and fried are made.

Soup is another dish in which the Chinese take great delight, often serving a light and fragrant soup between courses to contrast with a previously served salty or dry dish.

Rice in China is not only the staple food, but the symbol of life and fertility. Hence at Chinese weddings as well as our own the custom of showering the bride and groom with rice is symbolic of long life and many children.

There is really no mystery about the art of Chinese cooking: once you have learnt a few basic facts, you will discover that authentic Chinese food can be cooked even without using unusual and exotic ingredients. Essentially, there are three fundamental principles in Chinese cooking: flavour, texture and colour.

Flavour

The essential elements for seasoning and bringing out subtle flavours are: soy sauce, rice wine* (medium or dry sherry is an excellent substitute), sugar, vinegar, fresh root ginger* and green shallots. Garlic, peppers and chillis are also used occasionally, but discreetly, for their purpose is to enhance the flavour of the food

rather than overpower it. Cornflour is used in moderation for thickening sauces and for coating meat, particularly when this is finely sliced and shredded, as it helps to preserve flavour and tenderness. Cornflour should never be used to excess, however, otherwise the food will look unappetizing and taste starchy.

The practice of blending different flavours in one dish is quite common in China. The idea is to give the dish contrasting tastes as well as promote an exchange of flavours between ingredients. Each item in the dish acts as a seasoning agent, imparting a little flavour to the other ingredients. It is therefore important to choose the ingredients to be blended with care, with the emphasis on harmonized contrast.

Above all else, the Chinese believe in the freshness of their food: vegetables should be dawn-picked, or ideally picked just before they are cooked; meats are never hung except perhaps Peking Duck, which is air dried to help make the skin crispy when fried or roasted; poultry and fish are always bought still alive! The Chinese claim that loss of freshness is loss of flavour.

Texture and colour

Every dish in a Chinese meal should include two or more of the following textures: tenderness, crispness, crunchiness, smoothness and softness. Ingredients should also be chosen to complement each other in colour.

Ingredients are therefore chosen to obtain a harmony of flavours, colours and textures. For example, the main ingredient in Jiecai Chao Jiding (see page 101) is chicken, which is white and tender. Mushrooms (soft and black) and celery (crisp and pale green) are used as the subsidiary ingredients to give the dish a harmonized texture. A colourful red pepper is also added for contrast and bamboo shoot (smooth in texture) for extra flavour. This combination, with the addition of salt, egg white, cornflour, fresh ginger, spring onions (green shallots), soy sauce and sherry makes the dish a unique experience for the palate. Apart from the Chinese dried mushrooms*, which can be substituted by fresh mushrooms, nothing out of the ordinary is used in the way of ingredients and everything can easily be obtained in any quality grocer or supermarket.

Preparation of ingredients is the secret of Chinese cooking. They are cut finely to ensure short cooking times, thereby retaining the crispness of the vegetables and even cooking of the meat.

Cooking techniques and preparation

Chinese cooking techniques are quite simple, and the most important aspect is the preparation before cooking.

Cutting: Most Chinese foods are cut into very small pieces before cooking; therefore only a short cooking time is required and this helps to preserve the natural flavours. The Chinese attach great importance to the various methods of cutting.

Slicing: The ingredients are cut into thin slices, normally not much larger than a postage stamp, and as thin as cardboard. When slicing meat, always cut across the grain, which makes it more tender when cooked. Vegetables, such as carrots, are often cut on the slant so that the slices have a larger surface area to absorb flavourings.

Shredding: The ingredients are first sliced, then stacked like a pack of cards and cut into thin strips about the size of matchsticks.

Dicing: The ingredients are first cut into strips as wide as they are thick, then cut at right angles to the same width to make cubes, usually about 1 cm (½ inch).

Mincing: The ingredients are very finely chopped in a mincer.

Diagonal cutting: This method is normally used for cutting vegetables, such as carrots and celery. A diagonal cut is made straight down, then the vegetable is rolled a half-turn and sliced diagonally again, in order to obtain a diamond-shaped piece.

Chopping: A heavy cleaver is used to cut through the bones and flesh of a chicken or duck. The normal method of cutting up a chicken is as follows: (1) Chop off the 'parson's nose' and either discard or, if it is to be served, split in half. (2) Disjoint the two wings. (3) Remove the legs and thighs. (4) Turn the body on its side, then separate the breast from the backbone. (5) Divide the breast into two sections, then cut each half crossways into three or four pieces. (6) Cut each wing into three pieces, and each leg and thigh into five.

Marinating: After cutting, the next step is to prepare the meat for cooking by marinating it. Salt, egg white and cornflour are normally used for chicken and fish; soy sauce, sugar, sherry and cornflour are used for meat.

Cooking methods

The various cooking methods can be divided into four basic categories:
Water cooking: boiling and simmering.
Oil cooking: frying and braising.
Fire cooking: roasting and barbecuing.
Steam cooking: steaming.

The most important factor in cooking Chinese food is the degree of heat. The actual timing, although important, is governed by the heat. It is therefore very difficult for most Chinese recipes to give a precise cooking time as so much depends on the size of the ingredients and the type of stove and utensils used. For this reason, cooking times for the recipes in this chapter are intended as a guide, rather than a rule.

Cooking equipment

The Chinese wok is a most useful utensil. It is cone-shaped with a rounded bottom and is normally made of iron, which keeps an intense, steady heat throughout cooking. The main advantage of the wok is its shape, which enables the heat to spread evenly so only a short cooking time is required. The shape of the wok also encourages ingredients to return to the centre, however vigorously you stir them.

A wok will fit on most gas burners. Electric cookers are generally less suitable because the heat cannot usually be controlled as easily – a metal ring to fit under a wok and lift it off the heat source can be used on both gas burners and electric plates. If a wok is not available, a deep, heavy frying pan can be used.

A range of basic equipment used for preparing and cooking Chinese dishes.

A wok is ideal for stir-frying, the cooking method most commonly used in China. First heat the wok over high heat, then add a small amount of vegetable oil or lard; never use butter or dripping. Heat until the oil or fat is very hot and smoking, then toss in the ingredients and stir and turn them constantly for a short time. Timing is of the utmost importance. Correctly cooked, Chinese food is crisp and wholesome. Very little water – or none at all – is added, since the high heat will extract sufficient juices from the meat and vegetables to moisten, particularly if they are fresh. In most cases when two or more ingredients are combined in one dish, each ingredient is partially cooked separately and then mixed together for the final stage of cooking.

After cooking, the wok must always be rinsed thoroughly in very hot water to prevent it retaining flavours. Iron woks should be dried immediately to prevent rusting.

Regional cooking styles

China is a vast country, about the same size as the United States, and its climate and food products are as varied. Each region of China has its own specialities and different methods of cooking. Although many of these different schools have merged into each other in recent years, most regions still retain strong individual characteristics. There are four broadly defined schools of cuisine:

Eastern School. This school is also known as the Jiangsi Fujian style of cooking. It includes the lower Yangtse basin, Shanghai and the provinces of Jiangsi (Kiangsi) and Fujian (Fukien), although the latter is often linked with the southern school. This is one of the most fertile parts of China, known as the 'Land of Fish and Rice'. Besides being famous for its various noodles and dumplings the main characteristics of its style can be summarized as subtle in flavour, sweet in taste and exquisite in appearance.

Southern School. Guangdong, with its capital Guangshau (Canton), is the southern school, although it is possible to pick out several different regional styles. Here the climate is subtropical and the land extremely fertile. It can undoubtedly be described as the jewel of Chinese cuisine, although its reputation has unfortunately been damaged outside China by the so-called 'chop suey house'. Cantonese cuisine prides itself on being able to bring out the best of the natural flavours of any food.

Western School. Sichuan (Szechuan), in contrast, is the western school of richly flavoured and piquant food. It is a comparatively recent discovery in the West and is sadly less well known than the other styles of cooking. The neighbouring province of Hunan, with its peppery food, is generally associated with this school.

Northern School. This consists of the Beijing (Peking), Shandong and Henan cuisines. Although the northern school may not be the best, it is certainly the oldest of Chinese culinary art, as its origin lies on the basin of the Yellow River – the cradle of Chinese civilization. Because Peking has been the capital of China for many centuries, it has accumulated the best dishes from each region to become the culinary centre of China while, at the same time, developing a cuisine of its own.

Serving

Harmony is the most important aspect of Chinese food. When planning a menu, it is most important to choose a selection of dishes which complement each other, but give contrast in flavour, texture and colour. A meal composed of three main dishes and one soup will provide adequate contrast and will be sufficient for four to six people. The more people eating a meal, the more variety can be achieved for – not only is the quantity of food increased – a wider selection of dishes can be offered.

The Chinese seldom serve only one dish at a meal, as it offers little variety. If you are dining alone, you should have at least two cooked dishes to provide contrast, or choose one dish with two different ingredients. The cooked dish or dishes form one part of a meal; rice or wheat – cooked either as dumplings or noodles – forms the other part. These cereals are the staple food for most Chinese. The art of Chinese cooking lies in selecting the cooked dishes to accompany the staple food.

Do not serve tea with a Chinese meal – have either soup or wine. Tea is seldom drunk during the meal, it is more frequently served as an aperitif or as a digestif, and is frequently taken at other times of the day but not with food. There is no reason why wine cannot be drunk with Chinese food; let your personal taste be your guide.

The recipes in this chapter do not give the number of servings for each dish, for the reasons given above. It is really a number of dishes that go together to make a whole meal.

Bon appetit! or Chin-chin as they say in Chinese.

CAIHUA GENG
CAULIFLOWER GRUEL

Do not be put off by the term 'gruel'; this is in fact a delicious thick soup and a very colourful dish.

1 small cauliflower, finely chopped
125 g (4 oz) chicken meat, coarsely chopped
4 cups chicken stock
2 eggs, beaten
1 teaspoon salt
60 g (2 oz) lean ham, finely chopped
chopped coriander leaves* to garnish

METHOD: Put the cauliflower, chicken and stock in a pan and cook gently for 15 to 20 minutes. Pour the eggs into the soup, then stir in the salt. Add the ham, pour into a warmed soup tureen and sprinkle with coriander. Serve hot.

YAGU BAICAI TANG
DUCK AND CABBAGE SOUP

1 duck carcass, with giblets
2 slices fresh ginger*, peeled
500 g (1 lb) Chinese cabbage, sliced
salt
freshly ground black pepper

METHOD: Break up the carcass, then place in large pan. Add the giblets and any other meat left over from the duck.

Cover with water, add the ginger, then bring to the boil. Skim, then lower the heat and simmer gently for at least 30 minutes.

Add the cabbage and season to taste. Continue cooking for about 20 minutes.

Discard the duck carcass and ginger, taste and adjust the seasoning. Pour into a warmed soup tureen. Serve hot.

NIUROU DANHUA TANG
BEEF AND EGG-FLOWER SOUP

5 cups hot chicken stock or water
125 g (4 oz) lean beef steak, coarsely chopped
2 teaspoons salt
1 celery stick, coarsely chopped
1 egg, beaten
freshly ground black pepper
few green shallots, finely sliced, to garnish

METHOD: Bring the stock or water to the boil in a pan, then add the beef, salt and celery. Bring back to the boil, then add the egg, a little at a time, stirring vigorously to achieve the 'egg-flower' effect. Add pepper to taste.

Sprinkle with green shallots before serving. Serve hot.

ROUWAN TANG
MEATBALLS IN SOUP

250 g (8 oz) boned lean pork, finely minced
2½ teaspoons salt
1 slice fresh ginger*, peeled and finely chopped
½ egg, beaten
2 tablespoons cornflour
6 cups hot chicken stock
15 g (½ oz) dried wood ears*, soaked in warm water for 20 minutes
½ cucumber, cut into diamond-shaped chunks
1 tablespoon medium or dry sherry
freshly ground black pepper

METHOD: Mix the pork with ½ teaspoon of the salt, the ginger, egg and cornflour. Form the mixture into about 20 small meatballs with your hands.

Bring the stock to the boil in a pan. Add the meatballs, wood ears and the remaining salt, then add the cucumber and sherry. Simmer until the meatballs float to the surface. Pour into a warmed soup tureen and sprinkle with pepper to taste. Serve the soup hot.

DONGGU DUN JI
CHICKEN AND MUSHROOM SOUP

This soup can be eaten as a complete meal because the chicken is served whole in its cooking liquid. The meat should be very tender so that it can easily be torn into pieces with chopsticks or a soup spoon.

30 g (1 oz) Chinese dried mushrooms*, soaked in warm water for 30 minutes
1 chicken, weighing 1 kg (2 lb)
1 tablespoon rice wine* or sherry
1 green shallot
1 slice fresh ginger*, peeled
1½ teaspoons salt

METHOD: Drain the mushrooms, then squeeze dry, reserving the soaking liquid. Discard the mushroom stalks.

Put the chicken in a large pan of boiling water. Boil rapidly for 2 to 3 minutes, then remove the chicken and rinse thoroughly under cold running water.

Put the chicken and mushrooms in a pan or casserole with a tight-fitting lid. Add just enough water to cover the chicken, then add the wine, shallot, ginger and reserved soaking liquid from the mushrooms.

Bring to the boil, then lower the heat, cover and simmer gently for at least 2 hours.

Just before serving, remove any impurities that float to the surface of the soup and discard the shallot and ginger if wished. Stir in the salt and pour into a warmed soup tureen. Serve hot.

ROUSI TANGMIAN
SHREDDED PORK AND NOODLES IN SOUP

3-4 Chinese dried mushrooms*, soaked in warm water for 30 minutes
250 g (8 oz) boned lean pork, shredded
1 tablespoon soy sauce
1 tablespoon rice wine* or sherry
1 teaspoon sugar
2 teaspoons cornflour
375 g (12 oz) egg noodles
3 tablespoons vegetable oil
2 green shallots, cut into 2.5 cm (1 inch) lengths
125 g (4 oz) bamboo shoots, shredded
salt
2½ cups boiling chicken stock

METHOD: Drain the mushrooms, then squeeze dry, reserving the soaking liquid. Discard the hard stalks, then slice the caps into thin strips.

Put the pork in a bowl with the soy sauce, wine, sugar and cornflour. Stir well, then leave to marinate for about 20 minutes.

Cook the noodles in boiling water for about 5 minutes, then drain.

Heat half the oil in a wok or frying pan, add the pork and stir-fry until it changes colour. Remove from the pan with a slotted spoon and drain.

Heat the remaining oil in the pan, add the shallots, then the mushrooms and bamboo shoot. Stir, then add a little salt. Return the pork to the pan together with the soaking liquid from the mushrooms.

Place the noodles in a large serving bowl, pour over the boiling stock, then add the pork and vegetables. Serve hot.

◁ *Duck and Cabbage Soup (above); Shredded Pork and Noodles in Soup; Cauliflower Gruel*

ZHACAI ROUPIAN TANG
SLICED PORK AND SZECHUAN PRESERVED VEGETABLE SOUP

250 g (8 oz) boned lean pork, very thinly sliced
1 teaspoon soy sauce
1 teaspoon rice wine* or sherry
1 tablespoon cornflour
45 g (1½ oz) transparent noodles*, soaked in water for 10 minutes
1 tablespoon vegetable oil
6 cups hot chicken stock
½ cucumber, sliced into thin strips
1 teaspoon salt
freshly ground black pepper
60 g (2 oz) Szechuan preserved vegetable*, thinly sliced

METHOD: Put the pork in a bowl with the soy sauce, sherry and cornflour. Stir well, then leave the meat to marinate for about 20 minutes.

Meanwhile, cut the noodles into manageable lengths with scissors.

Heat the oil in a wok or frying pan. Add the pork and stir-fry until it changes colour.

Bring the stock to a rolling boil in a separate pan. Add the cucumber, salt and pepper to taste. Return to the boil, then add the pork, preserved vegetable and noodles. Boil for a few seconds, then pour into a warmed soup tureen. Serve hot.

▷ *Stir-Fried Squid with Mixed Vegetables (above); Crab Omelet*

XIEROU CHAO DAN
CRAB OMELET

| 2 green shallots |
| 4 eggs, beaten |
| salt |
| 3 tablespoons vegetable oil |
| 2 slices fresh ginger*, peeled and shredded |
| 185 g (6 oz) crabmeat, fresh, frozen or canned |
| 1 tablespoon rice wine* or sherry |
| 1 tablespoon soy sauce |
| 2 teaspoons sugar |
| *To garnish:* |
| shredded lettuce |
| tomato and grape (optional) |

METHOD: Cut the white part of the shallots into 2.5 cm (1 inch) lengths. Chop the green parts finely and beat into the eggs, with salt to taste.

Heat the oil in a wok or frying pan. Add the white part of the shallots and the ginger, then the crab and wine.

Stir-fry for a few seconds, then add the soy sauce and sugar. Lower the heat, pour in the egg mixture and cook for a further 30 seconds.

Transfer to a serving plate and garnish with shredded lettuce. To finish, place a serrated-cut tomato half and a grape in the centre to resemble a flower head, if liked. Serve immediately.

LUOPU ROUPIAN TANG
SLICED CARROT AND PORK SOUP

| 125 g (4 oz) boned lean pork, very thinly sliced |
| 1 tablespoon soy sauce |
| 1 tablespoon sesame seed oil* |
| 1 teaspoon cornflour |
| 250 g (8 oz) carrots, scraped and sliced |
| 5 cups chicken stock |
| 2 teaspoons salt |
| chopped coriander leaves* to garnish |

METHOD: Put the pork in a bowl with the soy sauce, oil and cornflour. Stir well, then leave to marinate for 10 minutes.

Meanwhile, place the carrots, stock and salt in a pan, bring to the boil and simmer for 5 minutes. Add the pork and simmer for 8 to 10 minutes until the pork and carrots are tender.

Pour into a warmed soup tureen and sprinkle with coriander. Serve hot.

ZAJIN CHAO XIANYOU
STIR-FRIED SQUID WITH MIXED VEGETABLES

Do not overcook the squid or it will be tough and chewy.

| 400 g (14 oz) squid |
| 2 slices fresh ginger*, peeled and finely chopped |
| 1 tablespoon rice wine* or sherry |
| 1 tablespoon cornflour |
| 15 g (½ oz) dried wood ears*, soaked in warm water for 20 minutes |
| 4 tablespoons vegetable oil |
| 2 green shallots, cut into 2.5 cm (1 inch) lengths |
| 250 g (8 oz) cauliflower or broccoli, divided into florets |
| 2 medium carrots, peeled and cut into diamond-shaped chunks |
| 1 teaspoon salt |
| 1 teaspoon sugar |
| 1 teaspoon sesame seed oil* |

METHOD: Clean the squid, discarding the head, transparent backbone and ink bag. Cut the flesh into thin slices or rings. Place in a bowl with half the ginger, the wine and cornflour. Mix well, then leave to marinate for about 20 minutes.

Meanwhile, drain the wood ears and break into small pieces, discarding the hard bits.

Heat 2 tablespoons of the oil in a wok or frying pan. Add the shallots and remaining ginger, then the cauliflower or broccoli, carrots and wood ears. Stir, then add the salt and sugar and continue cooking until the vegetables are tender, adding a little water if necessary. Remove from the pan with a slotted spoon and drain.

Heat the remaining oil in the pan, add the squid and stir-fry for about 1 minute. Return the vegetables to the pan, add the sesame seed oil and mix all the ingredients well together. Serve hot.

FANQIE ROUPIAN TANG
PORK AND TOMATO SOUP

| 125 g (4 oz) boned lean pork, very thinly sliced |
| 1 teaspoon soy sauce |
| 1 teaspoon rice wine* or sherry |
| 2 tablespoons vegetable oil |
| 1 small onion, peeled and chopped |
| 2 tomatoes, chopped |
| 5 cups chicken stock |
| 1 teaspoon salt |
| freshly ground black pepper |
| 1 egg, beaten |
| chopped coriander leaves* to garnish |

METHOD: Put the pork in a bowl with the soy sauce and wine. Stir well, then leave to marinate for about 20 minutes.

Heat the oil in a wok or frying pan, add the onion and pork and stir-fry for 2 minutes. Add the tomatoes and stock and bring to the boil. Add salt and pepper to taste and simmer for a few minutes.

Stir in the egg, then immediately pour into a warmed soup tureen and sprinkle with coriander. Serve hot.

BOCAI DOUGU TANG
BEAN CURD AND SPINACH SOUP

| 300 g block bean curd* |
| 3 cups chicken stock |
| 125 g (4 oz) fresh spinach leaves, torn into pieces |
| 1 green shallot, chopped (optional) |
| 2 teaspoons salt |
| ¼ teaspoon monosodium glutamate* (optional) |
| freshly ground black pepper |

METHOD: Cut the bean curd into 1 cm (½ inch) cubes. Bring the stock to the boil in a saucepan, add the spinach and shallot if using. Simmer for 5 minutes, then add the bean curd and simmer for 2 to 3 minutes.

Skim the soup, then add the salt, monosodium glutamate, if using, and pepper to taste. Pour into a warmed soup tureen. Serve hot.

ZHENG JIDAN
STEAMED EGGS

Dry the spinach leaves thoroughly after rinsing them.

6 eggs, beaten
1 cup hot water
1 teaspoon salt
2 teaspoons rice wine* or sherry
60 g (2 oz) fresh spinach leaves
60 g (2 oz) cooked ham, chopped
60 g (2 oz) peeled prawns
To garnish:
1 tablespoon soy sauce
1 teaspoon sesame seed oil*

METHOD: Put the eggs in a heatproof bowl, add the water, salt and wine and stir well.

Arrange the spinach, ham and prawns on top of the egg mixture, then lower the uncovered bowl into a large pan of boiling water.

Cover the pan, lower the heat so the water in the pan is just simmering and steam the eggs gently for 20 minutes. Sprinkle with the soy sauce and sesame seed oil. Serve hot.

XIAREN SHAO DOUFU
BEAN CURD AND PRAWNS

6 × 300 g blocks bean curd*
60 g (2 oz) peeled prawns
3 tablespoons vegetable oil
½ teaspoon salt
1 teaspoon sugar
1 teaspoon rice wine* or sherry
2 tablespoons soy sauce
shredded green shallots to garnish

METHOD: Cut each bean curd block into 5 mm (¼ inch) thick slices, then cut each slice into 3 or 4 pieces. Cut any large prawns in half, leaving the small ones whole.

Heat the oil in a wok or frying pan. Add the bean curd and stir-fry until golden on all sides. Add the salt, sugar, wine and soy sauce and stir-fry for a few seconds.

Add the prawns, stir gently and cook for 1 to 2 minutes.

Serve hot, garnished with the shredded green shallots.

QINGDOU XIAREN
STIR-FRIED PRAWNS AND PEAS

If fresh peas are unobtainable, frozen ones may be used for this recipe, but they should be thawed first and stir-fried for 1 minute only.

250 g (8 oz) peeled prawns
1 egg white
2 teaspoons cornflour
3 tablespoons vegetable oil
2 green shallots, white part only, finely chopped
1 slice fresh ginger*, peeled and finely chopped
1½ cups shelled peas
1 teaspoon salt
1 tablespoon rice wine* or sherry

METHOD: Put the prawns in a bowl with the egg white and cornflour. Mix well, then leave to marinate in the refrigerator for about 20 minutes.

Heat the oil in a wok or frying pan, add the prawns and stir-fry over moderate heat for about 1 minute. Remove from the pan with a slotted spoon and drain.

Increase the heat, add the shallots, ginger, peas and salt and stir-fry for 2 minutes.

Return the prawns to the pan, add the wine and continue cooking for a further 1 minute. Serve hot.

▷ *Deep-Fried Prawns in Shells*

DEEP-FRIED PRAWNS IN SHELLS

500 g (1 lb) uncooked prawns, unshelled
2 slices fresh ginger*, peeled and finely chopped
1 teaspoon rice wine* or sherry
1½ teaspoons cornflour
2 cups vegetable oil for deep-frying
1 teaspoon salt
1 teaspoon chilli sauce (optional)
To garnish:
coriander leaves*
lemon peel (optional)

METHOD: Remove heads and place the unshelled prawns in a bowl with the ginger, wine and cornflour. Stir gently to mix, then leave to marinate in the refrigerator for about 20 minutes.

Heat the oil in a wok or deep-fat fryer to 180°C/350°F. Lower the heat, add the prawns and deep-fry for about 1 minute. Remove the prawns with a slotted spoon and drain.

Pour off the oil, then return the prawns to the pan. Add the salt and chilli sauce if using; mix well. Serve hot, garnished with coriander and lemon peel, if liked.

ABALONE IN OYSTER SAUCE

3 Chinese dried mushrooms*, soaked in warm water for 30 minutes
2 tablespoons vegetable oil
1 × 425 g can abalone, sliced
60 g (2 oz) bamboo shoot, sliced
1 teaspoon rice wine* or sherry
1 tablespoon oyster sauce*
1 teaspoon sugar
½ teaspoon salt
2 teaspoons cornflour, mixed to a paste with a little water
1 teaspoon sesame seed oil*

METHOD: Squeeze the mushrooms dry, discard the stalks, then slice the caps.

Heat the vegetable oil in a wok or frying pan. Add the abalone with the juice from the can, the mushrooms, bamboo shoot, wine, oyster sauce, sugar and salt. Stir-fry for about 2 minutes, then add the cornflour mixture and cook until the sauce thickens.

Add the sesame seed oil, then serve hot.

JAIN DOUBIAN YU

FISH STEAKS IN BEAN SAUCE

400 g (14 oz) fish steaks (jewfish or snapper)
1 tablespoon yellow bean sauce*
3 tablespoons soy sauce
1 tablespoon rice wine* or sherry
1 tablespoon sugar
1 teaspoon chilli sauce (optional)
3 tablespoons chicken stock or water
pinch of monosodium glutamate* (optional)
2 tablespoons vegetable oil

METHOD: Cut each fish steak into 2 or 3 pieces and remove any bones. Put the fish in a bowl, then add the remaining ingredients, except the oil. Toss gently to mix, then leave to marinate for 20 minutes.

Heat the oil in a wok or frying pan, add the fish and fry over moderate heat until golden on all sides. Add the marinade remaining in the bowl. Increase the heat and cook until almost all of the sauce has been absorbed. Serve hot.

JIELAN CHAO XIAQIU

PRAWN BALLS WITH BROCCOLI

Do not overcook the prawns or they will lose their delicate flavour.

250 g (8 oz) green king prawns, unshelled, heads removed
1 slice fresh ginger*, peeled and finely chopped
1 teaspoon rice wine* or sherry
1 egg white
1 tablespoon cornflour
3 tablespoons vegetable oil
2 green shallots, finely chopped
250 g (8 oz) broccoli, cut into small pieces
1 teaspoon salt
1 teaspoon sugar

METHOD: Wash the unshelled prawns, dry thoroughly with kitchen paper towels, then use a sharp knife to make a shallow incision down the back of the prawn and pull out the black intestinal vein. Split each prawn in half lengthwise, then cut into small

pieces so that they become little round balls when cooked.

Put the prawns in a bowl with the ginger, wine, egg white and cornflour. Stir well, then leave to marinate in the refrigerator for about 20 minutes.

Heat 1 tablespoon of the oil in a wok or frying pan, add the prawns and stir-fry over moderate heat until they change colour. Remove from the pan with a slotted spoon.

Heat the remaining oil in the pan, add the green shallots and broccoli, stir, then add the salt and sugar. Cook until the broccoli is just tender, then add the prawns, and stir well. Serve hot.

▽ *Prawn Balls with Broccoli; Carp with Sweet and Sour Sauce*

TANGCU LIYU
CARP WITH SWEET AND SOUR SAUCE

Carp is a symbol of good fortune, so it is served at New Year and other festivities. Snapper can be used.

15 g (½ oz) dried wood ears*, soaked in warm water for 20 minutes
1 carp weighing 750 g-1 kg (1½-2 lb)
2 teaspoons salt
3 tablespoons flour
4 tablespoons vegetable oil
2-3 green shallots, shredded
2 slices fresh ginger*, peeled and shredded
1 garlic clove, peeled and finely chopped
15 g (½ oz) bamboo shoot, thinly sliced
60 g (2 oz) water chestnuts*, thinly sliced
1 red pepper, cored, seeded and shredded
3 tablespoons wine vinegar
Sauce:
3 tablespoons sugar
2 tablespoons soy sauce
2 tablespoons rice wine* or sherry
2 teaspoons cornflour
⅔ cup chicken stock or water
1 teaspoon chilli sauce

METHOD: Drain the wood ears and slice very thinly, discarding the hard bits.

Clean the fish thoroughly and remove the fins and tail but leave the head on. Make diagonal slashes through to the bone along both sides of the fish at 5 mm (¼ inch) intervals. Dry thoroughly, then rub the fish inside and out with 1 teaspoon salt. Coat with the flour from head to tail.

Heat the oil in a large wok or frying pan until very hot. Lower the heat a little, add the fish and fry for about 4 to 5 minutes on each side until golden and crisp, turning the fish carefully. Drain, then transfer carefully to a warmed serving dish. Keep hot.

Mix the sauce ingredients together. Add the green shallots, ginger and garlic to the oil remaining in the pan. Stir in the wood ears, bamboo shoot, water chestnuts and red pepper, then the remaining salt and the vinegar. Add the sauce mixture and cook, stirring, until thickened. Pour over the fish. Serve immediately.

JIANGCONG SHAO YU
BRAISED FISH WITH GREEN SHALLOTS AND GINGER

The skin of a whole fish must be scored before cooking, to prevent it from bursting and to allow the heat to penetrate more quickly. It will also make it easier for the flesh to absorb the flavours of the seasoning and sauce.

1 fish (mullet, bream, etc) weighing 750 g (1½ lb)
1 teaspoon salt
2 tablespoons flour
3 tablespoons vegetable oil
3-4 green shallots, cut into 2.5 cm (1 inch) lengths
2-3 slices fresh ginger*, peeled and shredded
Sauce:
2 tablespoons soy sauce
2 tablespoons rice wine* or sherry
⅔ cup chicken stock or water
1 teaspoon cornflour
freshly ground black pepper
To garnish:
tomato halves
coriander leaves*
cherries (optional)

METHOD: Clean the fish thoroughly, leaving the fins, tail and head on. Slash both sides of the fish diagonally with a sharp knife at 5 mm (¼ inch) intervals as far as the bone. Rub the fish inside and out with the salt, then coat with the flour from head to tail.

Heat the oil in a large wok or frying pan until very hot. Lower the heat a little, add the fish and fry for about 3 minutes on each side or until golden and crisp, turning the fish carefully. Remove from the pan.

Mix the sauce ingredients together. Increase the heat and add the green shallots and ginger to the oil remaining in the pan. Stir-fry for a few seconds, then stir in the sauce mixture and return the fish to the pan. Simmer for a few minutes until the fish is cooked, then carefully transfer the fish to a warmed serving dish and pour over the sauce.

If liked, garnish the dish with tomato halves, trimmed with coriander leaves and cherries (if using). Serve hot.

YOULIN JI
OIL-BASTED CHICKEN

1 chicken, weighing 1.5 kg (3 lb)
2 tablespoons soy sauce
1 tablespoon rice wine* or sherry
5 cups vegetable oil for deep-frying
Sauce:
2 green shallots, finely chopped
2 slices fresh ginger*, peeled and finely chopped
1 garlic clove, peeled and finely chopped
2 tablespoons vinegar
1 tablespoon sugar
1 tablespoon yellow bean sauce*

METHOD: Wash and clean the chicken thoroughly, then plunge into a large pan of boiling water. Boil rapidly for 2 to 3 minutes, then remove and drain.

Mix together the soy sauce and wine, then brush over the chicken. Leave to marinate for about 20 minutes. Meanwhile, mix together the sauce ingredients in a small pan.

Heat the oil in a large wok or deep-fat fryer. Add the chicken and cook over moderate heat for 20 or 30 minutes until browned on all sides, basting constantly.

Remove the chicken from the pan, chop into small pieces, then arrange neatly on a warmed serving dish. Add any remaining marinade to the sauce mixture, heat through, then pour over the chicken. Serve hot.

HONGMEN JICHI
BRAISED CHICKEN WINGS

12 chicken wings
4 Chinese dried mushrooms*, soaked in warm water for 30 minutes
2 tablespoons vegetable oil
2 green shallots, finely chopped
2 slices fresh ginger*, peeled and finely chopped
2 tablespoons soy sauce
2 tablespoons rice wine* or sherry
1 tablespoon sugar
½ teaspoon five spice powder*
1½ cups water
185 g (6 oz) bamboo shoot, cut into chunks
2 teaspoons cornflour, mixed to a paste with a little water

METHOD: Trim and discard the tips of the chicken wings, then cut each wing into 2 pieces by breaking the joint.

Squeeze the mushrooms dry, discard the stalks, then cut the caps into small pieces.

Heat the oil in a wok or frying pan until it reaches smoking point. Add the green shallots and ginger, then the chicken wings. Stir-fry until the chicken changes colour, then add the soy sauce, wine, sugar, five spice powder and water.

Lower the heat and cook gently until the liquid has reduced by about half. Add the mushrooms and bamboo shoot and continue cooking until the juice has almost completely evaporated. Remove the bamboo shoot chunks, rinse, drain and arrange around the edge of a warmed serving dish.

Add the cornflour paste to the pan and cook, stirring constantly, until thickened. Place the chicken mixture on the centre of the bamboo shoot. Serve hot.

BAIQIE JI
WHITE-CUT CHICKEN

This famous Cantonese dish is very simple to cook. It is delicious hot or chilled and excellent for a picnic.

1 chicken, weighing 1.5 kg (3 lb)
Sauce:
2-3 green shallots, finely chopped
2 slices fresh ginger*, peeled and finely chopped
1 teaspoon salt
1 tablespoon soy sauce
1 tablespoon sesame seed oil*
freshly ground black pepper

METHOD: Put the chicken in a large pan, add cold water to cover, then cover the pan with a tight-fitting lid. Bring to the boil, then lower the heat and simmer for exactly 7 minutes. Turn off the heat and leave the chicken to cook in the hot water for at least 30 minutes without removing the lid.

About 1 hour before serving, remove the chicken from the water and chop it into small pieces, using a cleaver. Reassemble the chicken pieces on a serving dish.

Mix together the sauce ingredients and pour over the chicken. Serve warm or cover and leave in the refrigerator for at least 30 minutes before serving chilled.

JICHI HUI JIELAN
CHICKEN WINGS AND BROCCOLI ASSEMBLY

12 chicken wings
4 green shallots, finely chopped
2 slices fresh ginger*, peeled and finely chopped
1 tablespoon lemon juice
1 tablespoon soy sauce
1½ teaspoons salt
1 tablespoon rice wine* or dry sherry
4 tablespoons vegetable oil
250 g (8 oz) broccoli, divided into florets
60 g (2 oz) tomatoes, chopped
1 tablespoon cornflour, mixed to a paste with a little water

METHOD: Trim and discard the tips of the chicken wings, then cut each wing into 2 pieces by breaking the joint.

Put the chicken in a bowl with the green shallots, ginger, lemon juice, soy sauce, ½ teaspoon salt and the wine. Stir well, then leave to marinate for about 20 minutes.

Heat 2 tablespoons of the oil in a large wok or frying pan. Add the broccoli and remaining salt and stir-fry until tender but still crisp. Arrange the broccoli neatly around the edge of a warmed serving dish and keep hot.

Remove the chicken pieces, reserving the marinade. Heat the remaining oil in the pan, add the chicken and fry until golden. Remove from the pan with a slotted spoon and drain.

Add the tomatoes to the pan and stir-fry until reduced to a pulp. Return the chicken to the pan and add the marinade. Cook for about 2 minutes, then add the cornflour paste and cook, stirring constantly, until thickened. Spoon into the centre of the serving dish. Serve immediately.

◁ *Braised Chicken Wings; Chicken Wings and Broccoli Assembly*

ZINHUA YUSHU JI
GOLDEN FLOWER AND JADE TREE CHICKEN

This is a very colourful dish, as its name implies; 'Golden Flower' refers to the ham from King-hua, 'Jade' is the chicken, and 'Tree' is the greens. It can be served as a first course at formal dinners, or as a main course for an informal dinner.

1 chicken, weighing 1.5 kg (3 lb)
2 slices fresh ginger*, peeled
2 green shallots
3 tablespoons vegetable oil
500 g (1 lb) broccoli or other greens, divided into small florets or pieces
2 teaspoons salt
1 cup chicken stock
250 g (8 oz) cooked ham
1 tablespoon cornflour, mixed to a paste with a little water.

METHOD: Put the chicken in a large pan and cover with cold water. Add the ginger and green shallots, cover with a tight-fitting lid and bring to the boil. Lower the heat and simmer for exactly 3 minutes. Turn off the heat and leave the chicken to cook in the hot water for at least 3 hours, without removing the lid.

Heat the oil in a wok or frying pan. Add the broccoli or greens and 1 teaspoon salt and stir-fry for 3 to 4 minutes, until cooked to taste, moistening with a little of the stock if necessary. Remove from the pan and arrange around the edge of a large serving dish.

Remove the chicken from the pan, then carefully remove the meat from the bones, keeping the skin on the meat. Cut the chicken and ham into thin rectangular slices and arrange in alternating, overlapping layers in the centre of the broccoli.

Just before serving, heat the remaining stock with the remaining salt in a small pan. Add the cornflour paste and cook, stirring, until thickened. Pour over the chicken and ham to form a thin glaze, resembling jade. Serve hot.

DONGGU ZHENG ZIJI
STEAMED CHICKEN WITH CHINESE DRIED MUSHROOMS

500 g (1 lb) boned chicken (breasts and thighs), cut into small pieces
1 tablespoon soy sauce
1 tablespoon rice wine* or sherry
1 teaspoon sugar
1 teaspoon cornflour
4 Chinese dried mushrooms*, soaked in warm water for 30 minutes
1 tablespoon vegetable oil
2 slices fresh ginger*, peeled and shredded
freshly ground black pepper
1 teaspoon sesame seed oil*

METHOD: Put the chicken in a bowl with the soy sauce, wine, sugar and cornflour. Mix well, then leave to marinate for about 20 minutes.

Squeeze the mushrooms dry, discard the stalks, then cut the caps into pieces, roughly the same size as the chicken.

Brush a heatproof plate with the vegetable oil. Place the chicken pieces on the plate, top with the mushrooms, then sprinkle with the ginger, pepper to taste and the sesame seed oil.

Place in a steamer or over a pan of simmering water and cover the plate with a lid. Steam over high heat for 25 to 30 minutes. Serve hot.

YUXIANG JISI
SHREDDED CHICKEN WITH 'FISH SAUCE'

Fish is not used in this recipe, the sauce is normally used for cooking fish dishes, hence the name.

375 g (12 oz) chicken breast meat, skinned and shredded
½ teaspoon salt
½ egg white
1 teaspoon cornflour
4 tablespoons vegetable oil
2 green shallots, cut into 2.5 cm (1 inch) lengths
1 slice fresh ginger*, peeled and shredded
1 small green pepper, cored, seeded and cut into rings
1 small red pepper, cored, seeded and cut into rings
3 celery sticks, sliced
1 tablespoon soy sauce
1 teaspoon sugar
1 teaspoon vinegar
1 teaspoon chilli sauce (optional)

METHOD: Put the chicken in a bowl with the salt, egg white and cornflour. Mix well, then leave to stand for about 20 minutes.

Heat 2 tablespoons oil in a wok or frying pan, add the chicken and stir-fry over moderate heat for about 2 minutes. Remove from the pan with a slotted spoon and drain.

Heat remaining oil in the pan and add the shallots, ginger, peppers and celery. Stir in the soy sauce, sugar, vinegar and chilli sauce, if using. Return the chicken to the pan and combine all the ingredients together. Serve hot.

CHIYOU JI
SOY CHICKEN

This dish can be served hot as a main course, or cold as part of a buffet. Do not discard the cooking sauce; it can be stored in the refrigerator for future use.

1 chicken, weighing 1.5 kg (3 lb)
1 teaspoon freshly ground black pepper
2 teaspoons finely chopped fresh ginger*
4 tablespoons soy sauce
3 tablespoons rice wine* or sherry
1 tablespoon brown sugar
3 tablespoons vegetable oil
1¼ cups chicken stock or water
coriander leaves* to garnish

METHOD: Wash the chicken, dry thoroughly and rub inside and out with the pepper and ginger. Mix together the soy sauce, wine and sugar. Spoon over the chicken and leave to marinate for at least 3 hours, turning the chicken occasionally.

Heat the oil in a large pan, add the whole chicken and fry, turning, until lightly browned on all sides.

Dilute the marinade with the stock or water. Add to the pan, bring to the boil, then lower the heat. Cover and simmer for 45 minutes, turning the chicken several times during cooking and taking care to avoid breaking the skin.

Chop the chicken into small pieces. Arrange on a serving dish and baste with 2 tablespoons of the sauce. Garnish with coriander leaves. Serve hot or cold.

△ *Shredded Chicken with 'Fish Sauce';
Golden Flower and Jade Tree Chicken*

CHIJIAO CHAO JISI
SHREDDED CHICKEN WITH PEPPERS

This is a colourful dish with a piquant taste.

250 g (8 oz) chicken breast meat, skinned and shredded
½ teaspoon salt
1 tablespoon soy sauce
1 egg white
1 tablespoon cornflour
5 tablespoons vegetable oil
2 slices fresh ginger*, peeled and shredded
2-3 green shallots, shredded
1 hot chilli, shredded
1 green pepper, cored, seeded and shredded
1 red pepper, cored, seeded and shredded
2-3 celery sticks, shredded
2 tablespoons black bean sauce*

METHOD: Put the chicken in a bowl with the salt, soy sauce, egg white and cornflour and mix well.

Heat the oil in a wok or frying pan, add the chicken and stir-fry over moderate heat until half-cooked. Remove from the pan with a slotted spoon.

Increase the heat to high. When the oil starts to smoke, add the ginger to the pan with the green shallots, chilli, peppers and celery. Stir well, then add the black bean sauce and continue cooking for a few seconds.

Return the chicken to the pan, mix well, then stir-fry for about 1 to 1½ minutes until the meat is tender, but the vegetables are still crisp and crunchy. Serve hot.

FURONG JI
LOTUS-WHITE CHICKEN

5 egg whites
½ cup chicken stock
1 teaspoon salt
1 teaspoon rice wine* or sherry
2 teaspoons cornflour
125 g (4 oz) chicken breast meat, skinned and finely chopped
oil for deep-frying
To garnish:
1-2 tablespoons cooked green peas
30 g (1 oz) cooked ham, shredded

METHOD: Put the egg whites in a bowl. Stir in 3 tablespoons of the chicken stock, the salt, wine and half the cornflour. Add the chicken and mix well.

Heat the oil in a wok or deep-fat fryer to 180°C/350°F, then gently pour in about one third of the egg and chicken mixture. Deep-fry for 10 seconds until the mixture begins to rise to the surface, then carefully turn over. Deep-fry until golden, then remove from the pan with a slotted spoon, drain and place on a warmed serving dish. Keep hot while cooking the remainder.

Heat the remaining stock in a small pan. Mix the remaining cornflour to a paste with a little cold water, add to the stock and simmer, stirring, until thickened. Pour over the chicken. Garnish with the peas and ham. Serve hot.

YINXIANG BAO JI
CHICKEN IN SILVER FOIL

This is a variation of the traditional 'paper-wrapped chicken'. Prawns or other meat can be used instead of chicken.

500 g (1 lb) skinned chicken breast meat
3 green shallots, white part only
¼ teaspoon salt
1 tablespoon soy sauce
1 teaspoon sugar
1 teaspoon rice wine* or sherry
1 teaspoon sesame seed oil*
4 tablespoons vegetable oil
To garnish:
shredded green shallot
finely chopped red pepper

METHOD: Cut the chicken into 12 roughly equal-sized pieces. Cut each green shallot into 4 pieces. Combine the chicken and green shallots with the salt, soy sauce, sugar, wine and sesame seed oil in a bowl. Leave to marinate for about 20 minutes.

Cut 12 squares of foil large enough to wrap around the chicken pieces 4 times. Brush the pieces of foil with oil, then place a piece of chicken on each. Top with a slice of green shallot, then wrap the foil around the chicken to make a parcel, making sure that no meat is exposed.

Heat the oil in a wok or frying pan. Add the chicken parcels and fry over moderate heat for about 2 minutes on each side. Remove and leave to drain on a wok rack or in a strainer for a few minutes; turn off the heat.

Reheat the oil. When it is very hot, return the chicken parcels to the pan and fry for 1 minute only. Serve hot in the silver foil, garnished with shredded green shallot and red pepper.

ZHA JITUI
FRIED CHICKEN LEGS

6 chicken legs (drumsticks)
2 tablespoons soy sauce
1 tablespoon rice wine* or sherry
½ teaspoon freshly ground black pepper
2 tablespoons cornflour
1¼ cups vegetable oil
1 tablespoon finely chopped green shallot

METHOD: Chop each chicken leg into 2 or 3 pieces, then mix with the soy sauce, wine and pepper. Leave to marinate for about 20 minutes, turning occasionally.

Coat each piece of chicken with cornflour. Heat the oil in a wok or deep-fat fryer to 180°C/350°F. Lower the heat, add the chicken pieces and deep-fry until golden. Remove from the pan with a slotted spoon and drain.

Pour off all but 1 tablespoon oil, then add the green shallot to the pan with the drained chicken pieces. Stir-fry over moderate heat for about 2 minutes. Serve hot.

▷ *Chicken in Silver Foil (above); Fried Chicken Legs; Lotus-White Chicken*

BO BING
MANDARIN PANCAKES

4 cups plain flour
1¼ cups boiling water
little vegetable oil

METHOD: Sift the flour into a bowl. Mix the water with 1 teaspoon oil, then slowly stir into the flour, using chopsticks or a wooden spoon.

Knead the mixture into a firm dough, then divide into 3 equal portions. Roll each portion into a long 'sausage', then cut each sausage into 8 equal pieces.

Press each piece into a flat pancake with the palm of the hand. Brush one pancake with a little oil, then place another on top to form a 'sandwich', repeat with the remaining dough to make 12 sandwiches.

Flatten each 'sandwich' on a lightly floured surface with a rolling-pin into a 15 cm (6 inch) circle.

Place an ungreased frying pan over moderate heat. When it is very hot, fry the 'sandwiches', one at a time. Turn the pancakes as soon as air bubbles appear on the surface. Cook the other side until little brown spots appear underneath. Remove the 'sandwich' from the pan; peel the layers apart gently. Fold each into four.
MAKES 24 PANCAKES

CONGYOU YA
ONION DUCK

4 Chinese dried mushrooms*, soaked in warm water for 30 minutes
1 duckling, weighing 2 kg (4½ lb)
½ cup soy sauce
3 tablespoons sugar
125 g (4 oz) bamboo shoot, sliced
1 tablespoon lard or vegetable oil
3 green shallots, finely chopped

METHOD: Squeeze the mushrooms dry, then discard the stalks. Put the duckling in a large pan, cover with cold water and bring to the boil. Remove the duckling from the pan and rinse under cold running water. Skim the surface of the cooking water, then return the duckling to the pan. Add more fresh water to cover the duckling if necessary and bring back to the boil.

Add the soy sauce, sugar and mushrooms to the pan. Cover and cook gently for 2½ hours, turning the duckling halfway through cooking. Add the bamboo shoot and simmer for 30 minutes.

Transfer the duckling to a warmed serving dish. Drain the mushrooms and bamboo shoot and arrange around the hot duckling.

Heat the lard or oil in a separate pan, add the green shallots and fry for 1 to 2 minutes. Pour over the duckling and serve.

GANJIAN JIPU
PAN-FRIED CHICKEN BREAST

250 g (8 oz) chicken breast meat, skinned and boned
1-2 green shallots, chopped
1 slice fresh ginger*, peeled and finely chopped
1 tablespoon rice wine* or sherry
2 teaspoons salt
1 egg, beaten
2 teaspoons cornflour
3 tablespoons vegetable oil
1 small lettuce
Sauce:
1 tablespoon tomato paste
1 teaspoon sugar
1 teaspoon sesame seed oil*
1 tablespoon water

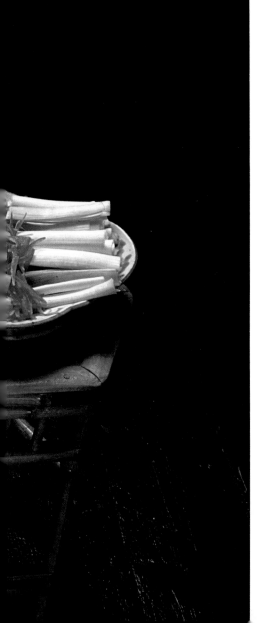

METHOD: Cut the chicken into thin rectangular slices and place in a bowl. Add the green shallots, ginger, wine and salt and mix well. Leave to marinate for about 20 minutes.

Stir the egg into the marinated chicken, then sprinkle with the cornflour and toss to coat thoroughly. Heat the oil in a wok or frying pan. Add the chicken mixture and fry until tender and golden on all sides. Remove from the pan with a slotted spoon and arrange on a bed of lettuce.

Mix together the sauce ingredients. Add to the pan in which the chicken was cooked and heat through, then either pour over the chicken, or serve as a dip. Serve hot.

JIECAI CHAO JIDING
DICED CHICKEN WITH CELERY

3-4 Chinese dried mushrooms*, soaked in warm water for 30 minutes
250 g (8 oz) chicken breast meat, skinned and diced
½ teaspoon salt
1 egg white
1 tablespoon cornflour
4 tablespoons vegetable oil
2 slices fresh ginger*, peeled and finely chopped
2-3 green shallots, finely chopped
1 small head celery, diced
125 g (4 oz) bamboo shoot, diced
1 red pepper, cored, seeded and diced
3 tablespoons soy sauce
1 teaspoon rice wine* or sherry
chopped coriander leaves* or parsley to garnish

METHOD: Squeeze the mushrooms dry, discard the stalks, then dice the caps.

Sprinkle the chicken with the salt, dip into the egg white, then coat with the cornflour.

Heat the oil in a wok or frying pan. Add the chicken and stir-fry over moderate heat until half-cooked, then remove with a slotted spoon.

Increase the heat to high and add the ginger and green shallots to the pan. Add the mushrooms and remaining vegetables and stir-fry for 1 minute.

Return the chicken to the pan, add the soy sauce and wine and cook for a further 1 minute until the liquid thickens, stirring constantly. Serve hot, garnished with chopped coriander or parsley.

◁ *Roast Duck Peking-Style, served with traditional accompaniments: Mandarin Pancakes, dipping sauce and raw vegetables*

BEIJING KAO YA
ROAST DUCK PEKING-STYLE

Peking-style duck is unique in Chinese cuisine, not only for the way in which it is cooked, but also for the specially reared species of duck used. The ducks are brought to exactly the right degree of plumpness and tenderness by several stages of force-feeding and care.

If liked, the sauce given here may be replaced by 6 tablespoons commercially prepared hoi sin sauce.

Spring onion or shallot flowers are the traditional garnish for Peking-style duck. To prepare these: make several cuts from top to bottom along each green shallot, without cutting right through the base. Leave in a bowl of iced water to open.

The traditional way to serve this dish is to arrange all the separate dishes of food on the table and allow the guests to help themselves.

1 duckling, weighing 1.5-1.75 kg (3-4¼ lb)
1 tablespoon sugar
1 teaspoon salt
1¼ cups water
Sauce:
3 tablespoons yellow bean sauce*
2 tablespoons sugar
1 tablespoon sesame seed oil*
To serve:
24 Mandarin Pancakes (see left)
10-12 green shallot flowers
4 small leeks or 8 green shallots cut into 7.5 cm (3 inch) strips
½ cucumber, cut into 7.5 cm (3 inch) strips
½ red pepper, cored, seeded and shredded

METHOD: Clean the duck and hang it up to dry thoroughly, preferably overnight in a cool, well-ventilated room

The next day, dissolve the sugar and salt in the water and rub all over the duck. Leave for several hours until dry.

Place the duck on a rack in a roasting pan and roast in the centre of a preheated moderately hot oven (200°C/400°F) for 1 hour.

Place the sauce ingredients in a pan and heat gently for 2 to 3 minutes, stirring constantly, then pour into a serving bowl.

Carve the duck into neat slices and arrange on a serving dish. Arrange the Mandarin pancakes on a separate dish and garnish both dishes with green shallot flowers. If the leeks are large, cut lengthwise in 2 or 4, put the leeks, cucumber and pepper on another dish.

To eat: spread each pancake with a little sauce, then place a little leek and cucumber in the middle. Top with 1 or 2 slices of duck. Roll up the pancake.

LU JIDAN ZHUROU
BRAISED EGGS WITH PORK

If you happen to have any sauce left over from Braised Tripe (see page 109) or Soy Chicken (see page 97), add it to the sauce with the pork and eggs, as it will greatly improve the flavour of this dish.

6 eggs
250 g (8 oz) boned lean pork, in one piece
Sauce:
4 tablespoons soy sauce
2 tablespoons sugar
1 teaspoon salt
1 teaspoon five spice powder*
2½ cups water

METHOD: Cook the unshelled eggs in boiling water for 5 minutes, plunge into cold water, then carefully remove the shells.

Add the pork to a pan of boiling water. Remove when it changes colour, drain and dry on kitchen paper towels.

To make the sauce: put all the ingredients in a pan, bring to the boil, stirring, then lower the heat and simmer for about 10 minutes. Add the pork and eggs and simmer for 15 minutes, then turn off the heat and leave the eggs and pork to cool in the sauce for at least 50 minutes.

Remove the eggs and pork from the sauce. Cut the eggs into halves or quarters and thinly slice the pork. Arrange the eggs around the edge of a serving plate and place the pork in the centre. Serve cold.

Note: Keep the sauce in the refrigerator for future use.

DOUYA CHAO ROUSI
BEAN SPROUTS WITH SHREDDED PORK

250 g (8 oz) fresh bean sprouts
375 g (12 oz) boned lean pork, shredded
2 tablespoons soy sauce
2 teaspoons rice wine* or sherry
2 teaspoons cornflour
3 tablespoons vegetable oil
2 green shallots, shredded
1 slice fresh ginger*, peeled and shredded
1 teaspoon salt
60 g (2 oz) leeks, shredded

METHOD: Rinse the bean sprouts in cold water, discarding any husks that float to the surface. Nip off any brown straggly tails.

Put the pork in a bowl. Sprinkle with the soy sauce, wine and cornflour. Mix well, then leave to marinate for about 20 minutes.

Heat 1 tablespoon of the oil in a wok or frying pan. Add the green shallots and ginger, then the pork. Stir-fry until the pork changes colour, then remove the pork from the pan with a slotted spoon and drain.

Heat the remaining oil in the pan. Add the salt, then the bean sprouts and leeks. Stir-fry for about 1 minute. Return the pork to the pan, stir well and cook for a further 1 minute. Serve hot.

CAIHUA CHAO ROUPIAN
PORK SLICES WITH CAULIFLOWER

4 Chinese dried mushrooms*, soaked in warm water for 30 minutes
250 g (8 oz) boned lean pork, sliced
2 tablespoons soy sauce
1 tablespoon rice wine* or sherry
1 tablespoon cornflour
1 medium cauliflower, divided into florets
salt
3 tablespoons vegetable oil
2 green shallots, cut into 2.5 cm (1 inch) lengths
1 slice fresh ginger*, peeled and cut into strips

METHOD: Squeeze the mushrooms dry, discard the stalks, then cut the mushroom caps into halves or quarters, according to size.

Put the pork in a bowl and sprinkle with the soy sauce, wine and 1 teaspoon of the cornflour. Mix well, then leave to marinate for about 20 minutes.

Meanwhile, blanch the cauliflower in boiling salted water for 1 to 2 minutes, then drain and set aside.

Heat the oil in a large wok or frying pan. Add the green shallots and ginger, then the pork. Stir-fry until the pork changes colour, then add the mushrooms and 1 teaspoon salt. Stir-fry for a further 1 minute, then add the cauliflower and stir well.

Mix the remaining cornflour to a paste with a little water, add to the pan and cook, stirring, until thickened.

Arrange the cauliflower around the edge of a serving dish and pile the pork mixture into the centre. Serve hot.

YASHAO YA
OIL-BRAISED DUCK

1 duckling, weighing 1.75-2 kg (4-4¾ lb)
4 tablespoons orange juice
2 tablespoons sugar
4 tablespoons soy sauce
4 teaspoons salt
4 tablespoons rice wine* or sherry
1 tablespoon vinegar
½ teaspoon five spice powder*
1 slice fresh ginger*, peeled
2½ cups chicken stock
5 cups vegetable oil

METHOD: Plunge the duckling into a pan of boiling water. Leave for a few minutes, then drain and place in a clean pan with all the remaining ingredients except the oil. Bring to the boil, then lower the heat. Cover with a tight-fitting lid and simmer gently for 45 minutes, turning the duckling at least twice during cooking. Remove the duckling from the pan, drain and thoroughly dry. Leave the cooking liquid simmering over low heat to reduce and thicken.

Heat the oil in a wok or deep-fat fryer. Add the duckling to the oil and cook over moderate heat until browned on all sides.

Return the duckling to the simmering liquid and turn it several times to coat with the sauce.

Remove from the pan and cut into small pieces. Rearrange the duckling on a warmed serving dish and pour the remaining sauce over the top. Serve hot.

△ *Pork Slices with Cauliflower (above); Bean Sprouts with Shredded Pork*

CHIZHI ZHENG PAIGU

STEAMED SPARERIBS IN BLACK BEAN SAUCE

500 g (1 lb) pork spareribs, chopped into small pieces
1 garlic clove, peeled and crushed
1 slice fresh ginger*, peeled and finely chopped
1 tablespoon vegetable oil
Sauce:
2 tablespoons black beans, rinsed and crushed
1 tablespoon soy sauce
1 teaspoon sugar
2 teaspoons rice wine* or sherry
1 teaspoon cornflour
To garnish:
1 small green or red pepper, cored, seeded and shredded
1 teaspoon sesame seed oil* (optional)

METHOD: Put the spareribs in a bowl with the garlic, ginger and sauce ingredients. Mix well, then leave to marinate for about 20 minutes.

Brush a heatproof plate with the vegetable oil, then put the sparerib mixture on the plate. Place in a steamer, or over a pan of boiling water and cover with a lid. Steam over a high heat for 30 minutes. Sprinkle with the green or red pepper and sesame seed oil, if using. Serve steamed spareribs in black bean sauce hot.

▷ *Red Cooked Pork Leg; Stir-Fried Pork with Bamboo Shoot*

HONGSHAO ROUWAN
BRAISED MEATBALLS

3 Chinese dried mushrooms*, soaked in warm water for 30 minutes
250 g (8 oz) boned pork, finely minced
1 egg white
2 tablespoons soy sauce
1 tablespoon rice wine* or sherry
1 teaspoon sugar
1 tablespoon cornflour
3 tablespoons vegetable oil
1 slice fresh ginger*, peeled and finely chopped
2 green shallots, white part only, finely chopped
250 g (8 oz) Chinese cabbage, shredded
1 teaspoon salt
2 cups chicken stock (approximately)
60 g (2 oz) cellophane noodles*, soaked in water for 10 minutes and drained

METHOD: Squeeze the mushrooms dry, then discard the hard stalks.

Mix the pork with the egg white, soy sauce, wine, sugar and cornflour. Form the mixture into about 8 meatballs.

Heat the oil in a pan, add the meatballs and fry until golden. Remove from the pan with a slotted spoon. Add the ginger and green shallots to the pan, then stir in the cabbage, mushrooms and salt. Return the meatballs to the pan and pour in just enough stock to cover. Bring to the boil, then lower the heat and simmer for 25 minutes.

Stir in the noodles and simmer for about 3 minutes. Serve hot.

DONGSUN CHAO ROUSI
STIR-FRIED PORK WITH BAMBOO SHOOT

250 g (8 oz) boned lean pork, thinly sliced
2 teaspoons rice wine* or sherry
2 tablespoons soy sauce
3 tablespoons vegetable oil
1 garlic clove, peeled and chopped
300 g (10 oz) bamboo shoot, thinly sliced
2 teaspoons vinegar
shredded green shallots and tomato to garnish

METHOD: Put the pork in a bowl with the wine and 2 teaspoons of the soy sauce. Mix well, then leave to marinate for about 20 minutes.

Heat the oil in a wok or frying pan, add the garlic and fry until golden brown.

Remove from the pan with a slotted spoon and discard.

Add the pork to the pan and stir-fry until it changes colour. Add the bamboo shoot, the remaining soy sauce and the vinegar. Stir-fry for about 30 seconds. Serve hot, garnished with shredded green shallot and tomato.

HONGSHAO ZHUTI
RED-COOKED PORK LEG OR SHOULDER

Red-cooked pork should be so tender that it can easily be pulled off the bone with chopsticks or a fork.

4 Chinese dried mushrooms*, soaked in warm water for 30 minutes
piece of leg or shoulder of pork, weighing 1.5 kg (3 lb)
1 garlic clove, peeled and crushed
5 tablespoons soy sauce
3 tablespoons rice wine* or sherry
3 tablespoons brown sugar
1 teaspoon five spice powder*
To garnish:
1 carrot, thinly sliced into rounds
shredded green shallots

METHOD: Squeeze the mushrooms dry, then discard the stalks.

Put the pork in a large pan of cold water. Bring to the boil, boil for a few minutes, then drain. Rinse the pork under cold running water, then drain again.

Return the pork to the cleaned pan. Add the mushrooms, garlic, soy sauce, sherry, sugar and five spice powder. Cover with a tight-fitting lid and bring to the boil.

Lower the heat and simmer gently for 2 to 3 hours, turning the pork several times during cooking. There should be very little liquid left at the end of the cooking time; if necessary, increase the heat and simmer, uncovered, until the liquid has reduced and thickened.

Serve the pork hot or cold, garnished with carrot slices and shredded green shallots.

CHA SHAO
PORK COOKED IN BARBECUE SAUCE

750 g (1½ lb) pork fillet, cut into thick strips
2 tablespoons rice wine* or sherry
3 tablespoons sugar
2 tablespoons soy sauce
½ teaspoon five spice powder*
1 teaspoon salt
3 tablespoons vegetable oil
2 green shallots, finely chopped
1 slice fresh ginger*, peeled and finely chopped
1 garlic clove, peeled and finely chopped

METHOD: Put the pork in a bowl with the wine, sugar, soy sauce, five spice powder and salt. Mix well, then leave to marinate for at least 2 hours, turning the pork occasionally.

Heat the oil in a wok or frying pan. Add the green shallots, ginger and garlic and stir-fry for a few seconds.

Drain the pork, reserving the marinade, then add to the pan and fry until brown. Remove the pork and vegetables from the pan, pour off the excess oil, then add the reserved marinade and heat through. Return the pork and vegetables to the pan and cook gently until almost all the juice has been absorbed.

Leave to cool, then cut the pork into thin slices. Serve cold.

CHAO MUXU ROU
MU-HSU PORK

Mu-Hsu is the Chinese for laurel, which has bright yellow fragrant flowers in autumn. This dish owes its name to the bright yellow colour of the scrambled eggs which is mixed with the pork.

Traditionally, this Mu-hsu Pork is often used as a filling for Mandarin Pancakes (see page 100).

30 g (1 oz) lily buds*, soaked in warm water for 20 minutes
15 g (½ oz) wood ears*, soaked in warm water for 20 minutes
4 eggs
salt
3 tablespoons vegetable oil
4 green shallots, shredded
250 g (8 oz) pork fillet, shredded
1 tablespoon soy sauce
2 teaspoons rice wine* or sherry
1 teaspoon sesame seed oil*

METHOD: Drain the lily buds and wood ears, discard any hard bits and shred finely.

Beat the eggs with a little salt. Heat 1 tablespoon of the oil in a wok or frying pan. Add the eggs and scramble lightly, removing them from the pan before they set too hard.

Heat the remaining oil in the same pan. Add the green shallots and pork and stir-fry until the pork changes colour. Add the lily buds and wood ears, 1 teaspoon salt, the soy sauce and wine. Stir-fry for about 2 minutes, then add the scrambled eggs and sesame seed oil. Mix all the ingredients well together. Serve hot.

▽ *Mu-Hsu Pork; 'Ants Climbing Trees'*

MAYI SHANGSHU
'ANTS CLIMBING TREES'

This strangely named dish is quite simply stir-fried minced pork mixed with cellophane noodles.

250 g (8 oz) boned pork, minced
2 tablespoons soy sauce
1 tablespoon sugar
1 teaspoon cornflour
½ teaspoon chilli sauce
3 tablespoons vegetable oil
1 small red chilli, chopped
2 green shallots, chopped
90 g (3 oz) cellophane noodles*, soaked in water for 30 minutes
½ cup chicken stock or water
shredded green shallots to garnish

METHOD: Put the pork in a bowl with the soy sauce, sugar, cornflour and chilli sauce. Mix well, then leave to marinate for about 20 minutes.

Heat the oil in a wok or frying pan, add the chilli and green shallots. Stir-fry for a few seconds, then add the pork. Stir-fry until the pork changes colour.

Drain the noodles, then add to the pan. Blend well, then add the stock or water and continue cooking until all the liquid has been absorbed.

Serve hot, garnished with shredded green shallots.

CHAO SANBAI
STIR-FRIED 'THREE WHITES'

125 g (4 oz) chicken breast meat, skinned and diced
125 g (4 oz) pork fillet, diced
1 teaspoon salt
1 egg white
1 tablespoon cornflour
3 tablespoons vegetable oil
2 green shallots, white part only, finely chopped
2 garlic cloves, peeled and finely chopped
125 g (4 oz) bamboo shoot, diced
1 tablespoon rice wine* or sherry
1 tablespoon yellow bean sauce*
little chicken stock or water (optional)

METHOD: Put the chicken and pork in separate bowls. Mix together the salt, egg white and cornflour; divide equally between the chicken and pork and mix well.

Heat 1 tablespoon oil in a wok or frying pan, add the chicken and stir-fry until half-cooked. Remove from the pan with a slotted spoon and drain. Add another tablespoon oil to the pan and stir-fry the pork until half-cooked. Remove and drain.

Increase the heat and add the remaining oil to the pan. Add the green shallots, garlic and bamboo shoot, then return the chicken and pork to the pan. Stir in the wine and bean sauce, then add a little stock or water to moisten if necessary.

Cook, stirring, until the meats and bamboo shoot are well coated with sauce and most of the liquid has been absorbed. Serve hot.

CHAO YAOHUA
STIR-FRIED KIDNEY FLOWERS

15 g (½ oz) wood ears*, soaked in warm water for 20 minutes
250 g (8 oz) pig's kidney
1½ teaspoons salt
2 teaspoons cornflour
6 tablespoons vegetable oil
1 garlic clove, peeled and crushed
1 slice fresh ginger*, peeled and finely chopped
1 green shallot, finely chopped
60 g (2 oz) water chestnuts*, sliced
60 g (2 oz) bamboo shoot, sliced
125 g (4 oz) seasonal green vegetables (lettuce, cabbage or spinach), blanched in boiling water and drained
1 tablespoon vinegar
1 tablespoon soy sauce

METHOD: Drain the wood ears and discard the hard parts. Split the kidneys in half lengthways and discard the fat and white core. Score the surface of the kidneys in a criss-cross pattern, then cut into pieces. Sprinkle with ½ teaspoon salt and 1 teaspoon cornflour.

Heat the oil in a pan until it is very hot. Add the kidneys and stir-fry until evenly browned. Remove from the pan with a slotted spoon and drain.

Pour off all but 2 tablespoons oil, then add the garlic, ginger and green shallot to the pan. Stir-fry for a few seconds, then add the wood ears, water chestnuts, bamboo shoot and green vegetables.

Stir in the vinegar and remaining salt, then return the kidneys to the pan. Mix the remaining cornflour with a little water, then add to the pan with the soy sauce and cook, stirring, for 1 minute. Serve hot.

BOCAI CHAO ZHUGAN
STIR-FRIED LIVER WITH SPINACH

Avoid overcooking the pig's liver or it will become tough.

375 g (12 oz) pig's liver, cut into thin triangular slices
2 tablespoons cornflour
4 tablespoons vegetable oil
500 g (1 lb) fresh spinach leaves, rinsed and drained thoroughly
1 teaspoon salt
2 slices fresh ginger*, peeled
1 tablespoon soy sauce
1 tablespoon rice wine* or sherry
shredded green shallot to garnish

METHOD: Blanch the liver for a few seconds in boiling water, then drain and coat the slices with the cornflour.

Heat 2 tablespoons of the oil in a wok or frying pan. Add the spinach and salt and stir-fry for 2 minutes. Remove from the pan, then arrange around the edge of a warmed serving dish and keep hot.

Heat the remaining oil in the pan until it is very hot. Add the ginger, liver, soy sauce and wine. Stir well, then pour over the spinach.

Serve immediately, garnished with shredded green shallot.

LU ZHUDU
BRAISED TRIPE

This dish can be served either cold as a first course, or hot as a main course. Reserve the cooking liquid from the tripe; it will keep in the refrigerator and can be used in other dishes, such as Braised Eggs with Pork (see page 102).

1 kg (2 lb) tripe
salt
2 tablespoons vegetable oil
2 slices fresh ginger*, peeled
2 green shallots
1 teaspoon five spice powder*
2 tablespoons rice wine* or sherry
4 tablespoons soy sauce
1 teaspoon sugar
4 cups chicken stock or water
To finish:
1 teaspoon sesame seed oil*
chopped coriander leaves*

METHOD: Wash the tripe thoroughly. Rub all over with salt, then rinse well. Put the tripe in a pan of boiling water. Lower the heat, cover and simmer for 20 minutes. Drain thoroughly.

Heat the vegetable oil in a heavy pan, add the tripe and brown lightly. Add the remaining ingredients and bring to the boil. Lower the heat, cover with a tight-fitting lid, then simmer gently for 2 hours.

Remove the tripe from the cooking liquid and cut into small slices. Arrange on a serving dish and sprinkle with the sesame seed oil. Serve hot or cold, garnished with chopped coriander.

YUXIANG QIEZI
EGGPLANT AND PORK IN HOT SAUCE

185 g (6 oz) boned lean pork, shredded
2 green shallots, finely chopped
1 slice fresh ginger*, peeled and finely chopped
1 garlic clove, peeled and finely chopped
1 tablespoon soy sauce
2 teaspoons rice wine* or sherry
1½ teaspoons cornflour
1¼ cups vegetable oil for deep-frying
250 g (8 oz) eggplant, cut into diamond-shaped chunks
1 tablespoon chilli sauce
3-4 tablespoons chicken stock or water
chopped green shallot to garnish

METHOD: Put the pork in a bowl with the green shallot, ginger, garlic, soy sauce, wine and cornflour. Mix well, then leave to marinate for about 20 minutes.

Heat the oil in a wok or deep-fat fryer to 180°C/350°F. Lower the heat, add the eggplant and deep-fry for about 1½ minutes. Remove from the pan with a slotted spoon and drain.

Pour off all but 1 tablespoon oil from the pan, then add the pork and stir-fry for about 1 minute. Add the eggplant and chilli sauce and cook for about 1½ minutes, then moisten with the stock or water. Simmer until the liquid has almost completely evaporated. Serve hot, garnished with chopped green shallot.

◁ *Eggplant and Pork with Hot Sauce (above); Stir-Fried Liver with Spinach*

JIELAN CHAO NIUROU
STIR-FRIED BEEF WITH BROCCOLI

250 g (8 oz) lean rump steak, thinly sliced
2 teaspoons salt
2 teaspoons rice wine* or sherry
1 tablespoon cornflour
4 tablespoons vegetable oil
250 g (8 oz) broccoli, divided into small florets
little chicken stock or water (optional)
2 green shallots, cut into 2.5 cm (1 inch) lengths
125 g (4 oz) button mushrooms, sliced
1 tablespoon soy sauce

METHOD: Cut the thinly sliced beef into narrow strips. Put in a bowl with ½ teaspoon salt, the wine and cornflour and mix well. Leave for 20 minutes.

Heat 2 tablespoons of the oil in a wok or frying pan. Add the broccoli and remaining salt and stir-fry for a few minutes, adding a little stock or water to moisten if necessary. Remove from the pan with a slotted spoon and drain.

Heat the remaining oil in the pan. Add the green shallots and fry for a few seconds. Add the steak and stir-fry until evenly browned. Stir in the mushrooms, soy sauce and broccoli. Serve hot.

LUOPU MEN NIUNAN
BEEF AND CARROT STEW

2 tablespoons vegetable oil
1 garlic clove, peeled and crushed
1 slice fresh ginger*, peeled and chopped
1 green shallot, chopped
750 g (1½ lb) stewing beef, cut into 1 cm (½ inch) squares
3 tablespoons soy sauce
1 tablespoon sugar
1 tablespoon rice wine* or sherry
½ teaspoon five spice powder*
500 g (1 lb) carrots, peeled

METHOD: Heat the oil in a heavy pan or flameproof casserole. Add the garlic, ginger and green shallot and fry until golden brown. Add the beef and the remaining ingredients, except the carrots. Add just enough cold water to cover. Bring to the boil, lower the heat and simmer for about 1½ hours.

Cut the carrots diagonally into diamond shapes. Add to the beef and simmer for 30 minutes or until tender. Serve hot.

XUEDO NIUROU
SNOW PEAS AND BEEF

250 g (8 oz) rump or round steak, thinly sliced
2 tablespoons oyster sauce*
1 tablespoon rice wine* or sherry
1 teaspoon cornflour
4 tablespoons vegetable oil
2 green shallots, cut into 2.5 cm (1 inch) lengths
1 slice fresh ginger*, peeled and cut into strips
250 g (8 oz) snow peas, topped and tailed
1 tablespoon salt
1 teaspoon sugar

METHOD: Cut the beef slices into narrow strips and put in a bowl with the oyster sauce, wine and cornflour. Mix well, then leave to marinate for about 20 minutes.

Heat half the oil in a wok or frying pan. Add the green shallots and ginger. Stir-fry for a few seconds, then add the beef. Stir-fry until evenly browned, then transfer the mixture to a warmed serving dish and keep hot.

Heat the remaining oil in the pan. Add the snow peas, salt and sugar and stir-fry for about 2 minutes. (Do not overcook, or the snow peas will lose their texture and colour.)

Add the snow peas to the beef and mix well. Serve hot.

QING JIAO NIUROU PIAN
STIR-FRIED BEEF AND GREEN PEPPERS

250 g (8 oz) rump or round steak, thinly sliced

2 teaspoons salt

2 teaspoons sugar

1 tablespoon rice wine* or sherry

1 tablespoon cornflour

½ teaspoon chilli sauce (optional)

freshly ground black pepper

3 tablespoons vegetable oil

1 large green pepper, cored, seeded and thinly sliced

1 large tomato, cut into 6 pieces

2 green shallots, chopped

1 slice fresh ginger*, peeled and finely chopped

1 tablespoon soy sauce

METHOD: Put the steak in a bowl with ½ teaspoon salt, the sugar, wine, cornflour, chilli sauce if using, and black pepper to taste. Mix well, then leave to marinate for about 20 minutes.

Heat 1 tablespoon of the oil in a wok or frying pan. Add the green pepper, tomato and remaining salt and stir-fry for a few seconds over high heat. Remove from the pan with a slotted spoon and drain.

Heat the remaining oil in the pan. Add the green shallots and ginger, then the meat. Stir-fry for a few seconds, then add the soy sauce. Return the green pepper and tomato mixture to the pan and stir well. Serve hot.

▽ *Beef and Carrot Stew (above); Snow Peas and Beef; Stir-Fried Beef with Broccoli*

△ *Kidney-Flower Salad; Bean Sprout Salad*

LIANGBAN YAOHUA

KIDNEY-FLOWER SALAD

The kidneys are scored and cut before cooking so that they will open up — hence the name kidney flowers.

375 g (12 oz) pigs' kidneys, skinned and split in half lengthways
1 small head celery, sliced diagonally
2 slices fresh ginger*, peeled and finely shredded
2 green shallots, finely chopped
Sauce:
2 tablespoons soy sauce
1 tablespoon vinegar
1 tablespoon sesame seed oil*
1 teaspoon chilli sauce
½ teaspoon sugar
To garnish: (optional)
pineapple chunks
radish slices
grapes

METHOD: Score the surface of the kidneys in a criss-cross pattern, then cut them into pieces. Cook the kidneys in boiling water for 2 minutes. Drain, rinse in cold water, then drain again and transfer to a serving plate. Arrange the celery around the cold kidneys.

Combine all the sauce ingredients together, then mix with half the ginger and the green shallots. Pour the sauce over the kidneys, then leave to marinate for about 30 minutes before serving.

Top with the remaining ginger. Garnish with pineapple, radish and grapes, if liked. Serve cold.

SHUA YANGROU
MONGOLIAN LAMB HOT POT

This is the famous Peking dish that ranks almost as high as Roast Duck.

If the meat is sliced when half-frozen, it will be much easier to obtain the very thin slices required.

The Hot Pot – sometimes known as a Mongolian fire pot or chafing pot – is placed in the centre of the table with the other ingredients arranged around it. A fondue set can be used instead.

1 boned shoulder, loin or leg of lamb, weighing 1.5 kg (3 lb)
500 g (1 lb) fresh spinach leaves, cut into large pieces
1 kg (2 lb) Chinese cabbage, cut into large pieces
3 × 300 g blocks bean curd*, each cut into 8-10 slices
125 g (4 oz) cellophane noodles*, soaked in water for 10 minutes and drained
Sauces:
3 tablespoons hoi sin sauce*
3 tablespoons chilli sauce
2 tablespoons soy sauce
1 tablespoon sesame seed oil*
2 tablespoons chopped green shallots
1 tablespoon chopped fresh ginger*
2-3 garlic cloves, peeled and finely chopped
To serve:
10 cups chicken stock or water

METHOD: Cut the lamb into fairly large, very thin slices and arrange on a serving plate. Arrange the spinach, cabbage, bean curd and noodles on another serving plate.

Put the hoi sin sauce and chilli sauce in separate bowls. Combine the soy sauce and sesame seed oil in a third bowl. Mix the green shallots, ginger and garlic in another.

Place the meat, vegetables and sauces on the table. Stand the Hot Pot in the middle and pour in the stock or water.

When the diners are seated, bring the stock to the boil. Meanwhile, allow guests to prepare their own sauces by mixing the different ingredients together.

When the stock is boiling vigorously, each guest should pick up a piece of lamb with chopsticks and cook it in the stock until just tender; this should take no longer than 20 or 30 seconds, depending on the thickness of the meat. The meat is then dipped into a sauce before eating.

The vegetables can be cooked and eaten in the same way, adding more stock or water to the Hot Pot as necessary. When all the meat is eaten, put the remaining vegetables and the noodles and, if needed, additional stock or water in the pot. Boil for a few minutes, then serve as a soup.

HONGSHAO NIUROU
RED-COOKED BEEF

750 g (1½ lb) stewing beef, in one piece
4 slices fresh ginger*, peeled
2 tablespoons rice wine* or sherry
2 tablespoons vegetable oil
4 tablespoons soy sauce
1 tablespoon sugar
1 tablespoon sesame seed oil* (optional)

METHOD: Put the beef, ginger and wine in a large pan. Add just enough water to cover and bring to the boil. Skim the surface, then lower the heat, cover and simmer gently for about 1 hour.

Remove the beef from the pan, reserving the cooking liquid, drain and cut into 2.5 cm (1 inch) chunks.

Heat the vegetable oil in a clean pan, add the beef and stir-fry for about 30 seconds, then add the soy sauce, sugar and reserved cooking liquid.

Cover and simmer for about 40 minutes or until the beef is tender. Sprinkle with the sesame seed oil if using. Serve hot.

LAINGBAN DOUYAR
BEAN SPROUT SALAD

500 g (1 lb) fresh bean sprouts
salt
2 eggs
1 tablespoon vegetable oil
125 g (4 oz) cooked ham, cut into thin strips
Sauce:
2 tablespoons soy sauce
2 tablespoons vinegar
1 tablespoon sesame seed oil*
freshly ground black pepper
To garnish:
thinly pared strip of red pepper
parsley sprig

METHOD: Wash and rinse the bean sprouts in cold water, discarding any husks that float to the surface. Cook in boiling salted water for 3 minutes. Drain, rinse in cold water, then drain again and set aside.

Beat the eggs with a little salt. Heat the oil in a frying pan over low heat. Add the eggs and cook to make a thin omelet. Remove from the pan, leave to cool, then cut into thin strips.

Mix all the sauce ingredients together, then add the bean sprouts. Transfer to a serving plate and arrange the ham and omelet strips on top. Garnish with the red pepper, coiled to resemble a flower head, with the parsley in the middle. Serve cold.

SHIJIN CHAOMIAN
TEN-VARIETY FRIED NOODLES (CHOW MEIN)

185 g (6 oz) boned lean pork, shredded
1 tablespoon soy sauce
1 teaspoon sugar
2 teaspoons cornflour
375 g (12 oz) egg noodles
2 eggs
salt
4 tablespoons vegetable oil
2 green shallots, cut into 2.5 cm (1 inch) lengths
125 g (4 oz) bamboo shoot, shredded
125 g (4 oz) fresh spinach leaves or other green vegetable, shredded
125 g (4 oz) peeled prawns
little chicken stock or water (optional)

METHOD: Put the pork in a bowl with the soy sauce, sugar and cornflour. Mix well, then leave the meat to marinate for about 20 minutes.

Cook the noodles in boiling water for about 5 minutes, drain and rinse under cold running water, then drain again.

Beat the eggs with a little salt. Heat a little of the oil in a frying pan over low heat. Add the eggs and cook to make a thin omelet. Remove from the pan and cut into thin strips.

Heat a little more oil in the pan, add the pork and stir-fry until it changes colour. Remove from the pan with a slotted spoon and drain.

Heat the remaining oil in the pan. Add the green shallots, then the bamboo shoot, spinach and a little salt. Stir, then add the prawns and return the pork to the pan with the egg strips.

Mix the ingredients thoroughly, adding a little chicken stock or water to moisten if necessary. Stir in the noodles, heat through and stir-fry until there is no liquid remaining in the pan. Serve hot.

SHIJIN CHAOFAN
TEN-VARIETY FRIED RICE

For best results cook the rice the day before it is required for this dish or cook some hours ahead. Spread cooled rice out on a tray and refrigerate until required.

1 cup long-grain rice
3 Chinese dried mushrooms*, soaked in warm water for 30 minutes
3 eggs
salt
3 tablespoons vegetable oil
4-5 green shallots, finely chopped
125 g (4 oz) peeled prawns
60 g (2 oz) cooked ham, diced
60 g (2 oz) cooked chicken or pork, diced
60 g (2 oz) bamboo shoot, diced
1/4 cup shelled peas
2 tablespoons soy sauce

METHOD: Prepare rice ahead: wash the rice in cold water once only, then place in a saucepan and cover with enough cold water to come about 2.5 cm (1 inch) above the surface of the rice.

Bring to the boil, then stir once with a spoon to prevent the rice sticking to the bottom of the pan during cooking. Cover with a tight-fitting lid, reduce the heat to as low as possible and cook for 15 to 20 minutes.

Squeeze the mushrooms dry, discard the hard stalks, then dice the caps.

Meanwhile, beat the eggs with a little salt. Heat 1 tablespoon of the oil in a frying pan over a low heat. Add the eggs and cook to make an omelet. Remove from the pan and leave to cool.

Heat the remaining oil in the pan, add the green shallots, then stir in the prawns, ham, chicken or pork, mushrooms, bamboo shoot and peas. Add the soy sauce and cooked rice. Cook, stirring, for about 1 minute. Break the omelet into pieces and fold into the rice mixture. Serve hot.

SAN BUZHAN
NON-STICK THREE WAYS

This dessert is so called because it should not stick to the pan, nor the chopsticks, nor the teeth!

5 egg yolks
3/4 cup sugar
2 tablespoons cornflour

2/3 cup water
4 tablespoons vegetable oil or lard

METHOD: Put the egg yolks in a bowl, add the sugar, cornflour and water and mix well.

Heat the oil or lard in a frying pan until it is very hot. Pour about half into a cup and reserve. Add the egg mixture to the pan, tilting the pan in order to hold the mixture together. Stir continuously for 2 minutes, adding the reserved oil or lard little by little around the edges. Cook until golden. Serve immediately.

MEIXUE ZHENGCHUN
PLUM-BLOSSOM AND SNOW COMPETING FOR SPRING

2 eating apples
2 bananas
juice of 1/2 lemon
2 eggs, separated
1/2 cup sugar
3 tablespoons milk
3 tablespoons water
3 tablespoons cornflour

METHOD: Peel and core the apples and slice thinly. Peel the bananas and slice thinly. Arrange the apple and banana slices in alternate layers on an ovenproof dish, sprinkling each layer with lemon juice.

Put the egg yolks in a pan with the sugar, milk, water and cornflour. Heat very gently, stirring, until smooth, then pour over the fruit.

Beat the egg whites until stiff, then spoon over the top. Bake in a preheated hot oven (220°C/425°F) for about 5 minutes until the top is crisp and golden. Serve hot or cold.

▷ *Sweet Bean Paste Pancakes, served hot with Chinese tea*

DOUSHA BAO
STEAMED DUMPLINGS WITH SWEET FILLING

If liked, you can make these dumplings with a cooked savoury filling.

Pastry:
1 tablespoon dried yeast
2½ teaspoons sugar
3 tablespoons lukewarm water
4 cups plain flour
1¼ cups lukewarm milk
Filling:
225 g (8 oz) can sweetened chestnut purée, or yellow bean sauce*

METHOD: To make the pastry, dissolve the yeast and sugar in the water. Sift the flour into a large bowl, then gradually stir in the

yeast mixture and the milk. Mix to form a firm dough.

Turn the dough out onto a lightly floured surface and knead well for at least 5 minutes. Transfer to a bowl, cover with a damp cloth and leave in a warm place for 1½ to 2 hours or until doubled in bulk.

To make the dumplings, knead the dough on a lightly floured surface for about 5 minutes, then roll into a long 'sausage' about 5 cm (2 inches) in diameter. Slice the 'sausage' with a sharp knife into 2.5 cm (1 inch) rounds. Flatten each round with the palm of the hand, then roll out until 10 cm (4 inches) in diameter.

Place 1 teaspoon chestnut purée or bean sauce in the centre of each round, then gather up the dough around the filling to meet at the top. Twist the top of the dough to enclose the filling tightly. Leave to rest for at least 20 minutes.

Place the dumplings on a damp cloth in the bottom of a steamer, leaving 2.5 cm (1 inch) space between each one. Steam for 15 to 20 minutes. Serve hot.

MAKES ABOUT 24 DUMPLINGS

DOUSHA SHAO BING
SWEET BEAN PASTE PANCAKES

Sweet red bean paste – also called a sweet soy bean paste – is a thick bean paste sold in cans in Chinese foodstores. It is often used as a base for sweet sauces.

1 cup plain flour
1 egg, beaten
⅔ cup water
6-8 tablespoons sweet red bean paste or finely chopped dates
vegetable oil for deep-frying

METHOD: Put the flour into a large bowl, make a well in the centre and add the egg. Add the water gradually, beating constantly, to make a smooth batter.

Lightly oil an 18 cm (7 inch) frying pan and place over moderate heat. When the pan is very hot, pour in just enough batter to cover the bottom thinly, tilting the pan to spread it evenly. Cook for 30 seconds or until the underside is just firm, then carefully remove from the pan. Repeat with the remaining batter.

Divide the sweet red bean paste or dates equally between the pancakes, placing it in the centre of the uncooked side of each one. Fold the bottom edge over the filling, then fold the sides towards the centre, to form an envelope. Brush the edge of the top flap with a little water, fold down and press the edges together firmly to seal.

Heat the oil in a deep-fat fryer and fry the pancakes for 1 minute or until crisp and golden. Remove and drain on kitchen paper towels.

Cut each pancake into 6 or 8 slices. Serve hot, with Chinese tea.

Korean food is unique. Despite its many different flavours, that range from chilli hot to delicately subtle, the overall impression is one of sweetness. The Koreans often combine fruit with meat and poultry and this bears more resemblance to Indonesian food than to Chinese or Japanese.

The name of Korea or Koryo means 'high and clear', and is symbolic of the country's rugged mountains, rushing shallow streams and clear blue skies which have earned it the nickname of the 'Switzerland of Asia'.

The Koreans are descended from several Mongol tribes dating back to prehistoric times. Despite the proximity to Japan and China and repeated invasions by these two countries, the Koreans have clung to one language, one culture and their own ancient traditions.

Korean food consists of staple grains, subsidiary dishes and special foods. The grains are rice, barley and millet, either prepared singly or mixed, but almost always cooked simply by boiling. Special foods are usually highly seasoned with red pepper, garlic, green shallots, fresh root ginger*, soy sauce, salt, sesame seed oil* and baked sesame seeds*, then served with plain boiled rice and subsidiary dishes such as the peppery-hot, fermented pickled cabbage called Kim Chee (see page 119). This is a unique Korean dish and one without which no Korean kitchen would be complete.

Korean food has many different flavours, from chilli-hot to delicately subtle, but the overall impression for the newcomer to the Korean table is one of sweetness, found in such dishes as Bulgogi (see page 124) and Thak Tuigim Jang (see page 125). The taste of Korean food is unique, but not so remote from Western dishes which combine sweet foods, such as fruit, with meat and poultry. This sweetness, or maybe the sheer satisfaction of eating Korean food, may be the reason why desserts as we know them do not feature in a Korean meal. In fact, Koreans will often eat fruit and rice cakes before a meal, and will finish with a plate of decoratively cut fruit.

With the advent of the smaller Western breakfast, dinner is fast becoming the main meal of the day. For dinner, each person has a bowl of rice and a bowl of soup; in addition, there are at least five different side dishes, plus soy sauce for dipping, and Kim Chee. At a special dinner, at least fifteen different dishes could be offered. The food is eaten with chopsticks and a spoon and in no specific order; soup may well appear on the table halfway through the meal, for example.

Cooking Equipment and Utensils

The basic items in a Korean kitchen are a rice kettle and a soup kettle, which are heavy lidded pots made of pig iron. Other cooking takes place in a *sot*, which is similar to the Chinese wok, curved at the bottom so that it sits in an aperture over the flame.

The Korean housewife would also have a Shin-Sol-Lo pot for special occasion cooking. She might also have a Bulgogi pan, although this is, in Korean terms, a fairly recent invention having only been around for about 60 years. These pans are available from many Oriental supply shops or Korean shops in major cities. Without a Bulgogi pan, the cook would use a special Bulgogi grill (see page 124).

Other basic utensils include a chopper and several extremely sharp knives.

Preparation and Cooking

In Korean cookery, great emphasis is placed on very fine cutting. This art, coupled with the decorative cutting of vegetables for garnish and fresh fruit for pure beauty, is the first element of cuisine learned by a Korean girl.

Often more time is spent in preparing ingredients (chopping, slicing and marinating), than cooking. In many cases, particularly vegetables, the ingredients are literally 'shown' to the pan and taken out again. The Koreans like to eat their vegetables almost raw and their meat and fish are usually so finely sliced that these too, take very little time to cook. Most cooking is over high heat for a short time, otherwise the dishes are steamed.

Ginseng

Wine or sake* can be drunk with Korean food, but it is more usual to serve the meal with Korean tea made from barley, often with a little Ginseng added. Ginseng, or *insam* as it is called in Korea, is the best known and most firmly credited of all Oriental herb medicines. It can be grown in any temperate climate, but Korean Ginseng is acknowledged as the finest one available.

A glass of Ginseng brandy at the end of your Korean meal will complement and complete a unique experience.

The Koreans have made an art out of garnishing their food and Korean girls are taught the importance of beautiful presentation from a very early age.

BINTATOK
KOREAN PIZZA

This dish is a cross between a pizza and a pancake. It should be made with dried halved mung beans with skins removed. If these are not available, use split peas instead.

250 g (8 oz) mung beans
3 tablespoons vegetable oil
1 large onion, peeled and finely chopped
4 green shallots, green part only, finely chopped
1 carrot, peeled and finely chopped
1 small red pepper, cored, seeded and thinly sliced
60 g (2 oz) minced beef
salt
freshly ground black pepper
Korean Soy Sauce (see right) to serve

METHOD: Put the beans in a bowl, cover with warm water and leave to soak for at least 3 hours, preferably overnight.

Transfer the beans and any remaining liquid to an electric blender and work to a thick, smooth batter. Alternatively, pound the mixture until smooth using a pestle and mortar.

Heat a quarter of the oil in a small omelet pan (about 15 cm (6 inches) in diameter). Add a quarter of the batter and tilt the pan with a circular motion to spread the batter evenly over the base.

Sprinkle a quarter of the remaining ingredients over the top of the bintatok and fry for at least 3 minutes until the edges begin to curl. Turn the bintatok over carefully and fry the other side for 3 minutes until golden brown underneath. Transfer to a warmed serving dish and keep hot while cooking the remaining ingredients in the same way to make 4 bintatoks.

Serve hot with Korean soy sauce handed separately as a dip.

SERVES 4

KOREAN SOY SAUCE

This is basic soy sauce which is enhanced by additional ingredients. It is served in individual bowls as a dip to accompany many of the Korean dishes in this chapter.

3 tablespoons soy sauce
1 tablespoon chopped green shallots
1 teaspoon sesame seeds*
1 teaspoon sesame seed oil*
1 teaspoon crushed garlic
½ teaspoon sugar
1 teaspoon vinegar
pinch of chilli powder

METHOD: Mix all the ingredients together, then divide equally between 4 individual shallow dishes.
SERVES 4

HOBAK CHUN
SAVOURY BATTERED ZUCCHINI

This delicate-tasting hors d'oeuvre can be eaten hot or cold.

400 g (14 oz) large zucchini, thinly sliced into rounds
salt
125 g (4 oz) bean curd* (optional)
125 g (4 oz) topside beef, minced
2 teaspoons sesame seeds*
2 teaspoons sesame seed oil*
1 tablespoon chopped green shallots
1 teaspoon crushed garlic
½ teaspoon freshly ground black pepper
1 cup plain flour
3 small eggs, beaten
4 tablespoons vegetable oil
To serve:
boo* (optional)
parsley sprig (optional)
Korean Soy Sauce (see opposite)

METHOD: Put the zucchini in a single layer on a plate, sprinkle with salt, then set aside.

Mash the bean curd, then squeeze out the water until the bean curd is dry. Place in a bowl with the beef, sesame seeds, sesame seed oil, green shallots, garlic, pepper and salt to taste. Mix well.

Dip one side of each zucchini slice in flour. Spread a little beef mixture on the floured side, pressing it down well and spreading it out to cover. Dip both sides of each zucchini slice in more flour, then in the egg.

Heat the oil in a frying pan, add the zucchini, meat side down, and fry for 2 to 3 minutes until brown. Turn the slices over and fry until the underside is golden. Remove with a slotted spoon and drain on kitchen paper towels.

Arrange on a serving dish. Garnish, if liked, with flower shapes, cut from boo, and parsley. Serve hot or cold with Korean soy sauce handed separately as a dip.
SERVES 4

KOON MANDOO
PAN-FRIED MEAT DUMPLINGS

These are not the type of dumplings normally found in stews — they look rather like miniature Cornish pasties and are wrapped in a very thin dough. The Koreans often pinch the wun tun skins* decoratively, or pull the edges of the crescent down and twist them together to form a shape like a hat with a brim. Serve hot as part of a main meal, or cold as part of an hors d'oeuvre.

250 g (8 oz) topside beef, minced
½ teaspoon sesame seeds*
1 teaspoon sesame seed oil
2 teaspoons chopped green shallots
1 teaspoon crushed garlic
½ teaspoon salt
30 wun tun skins*
4 tablespoons vegetable oil
To serve:
carrot (optional)
parsley sprig (optional)
Korean Soy Sauce (see opposite)

METHOD: Put all the ingredients in a bowl, except the wun tun skins and vegetable oil. Mix well, then put a small teaspoon of the mixture in the middle of each wun tun skin. Fold the skin over and pinch together to form a semi-circle or triangle.

Drop the dumplings into a pan of boiling water and boil for 3 minutes. Heat the vegetable oil in a frying pan. Remove the dumplings from the water with a slotted spoon, drain, then transfer to the oil. Fry until golden, turning constantly. Remove and drain.

Arrange on a serving dish. Garnish, if liked, with flower shapes, cut from carrot, and parsley. Serve hot or cold, with Korean soy sauce as a dip.
SERVES 4

KIM CHEE
PICKLED CHINESE CABBAGE

This famous hot pickled cabbage, made by the jarful, is something no self-respecting Korean would be without!

1 head Chinese cabbage, chopped
3 tablespoons salt
2 teaspoons hot chilli powder
2 teaspoons crushed garlic
4 green shallots, finely chopped
1 tablespoon sugar
1 hard pear, peeled, cored and grated

METHOD: Put the cabbage in a bowl, add the salt and leave overnight.

Remove the cabbage from the bowl and rinse under cold running water. Drain, then pat dry. Place in a large jar and stir in the remaining ingredients. Cover with a heavy weight; leave for 1 to 2 days before using.
MAKES ABOUT 1 KG/2 LB

△ *Pan-Fried Meat Dumplings; Savoury Battered Zucchini*

SHIN-SOL-LO
KOREAN CELEBRATION FIREPOT

Shin-Sol-Lo was once the dish of 'kings', because only the royal household could afford to eat it. Originally it would have been served in traditional Korean Royal Palace style in a Shin-Sol-Lo cook pot, and it would have contained crabs, prawns and many different meats. This recipe is a much simplified version, although it is still fairly time-consuming to make. Special Shin-Sol-Lo cook pots are difficult to obtain, but a fondue pot makes an acceptable substitute.

500 g (1 lb) boo*
2 tablespoons sesame seed oil*
4 medium onions, peeled and finely chopped
2 teaspoons crushed garlic
2 teaspoons sesame seeds*
185 g (6 oz) liver, thinly sliced
4 tablespoons vegetable oil
185 g (6 oz) gemfish or other firm white fish fillets, sliced
400 g (14 oz) minced beef
2 eggs, beaten
salt
freshly ground black pepper
4 cups beef stock, Tang (see right)
pinch of monosodium glutamate*
250 g (8 oz) cooked beef brisket or topside, cut into thin strips
1 medium cucumber, sliced diagonally
4 mushrooms, finely sliced
2 medium carrots, peeled and sliced diagonally
8 green shallots, shredded
90 g (3 oz) bamboo shoot
2 tablespoons pine nuts
Batter:
1 cup plain flour
2 eggs, well beaten
2 tablespoons water (approximately)

METHOD: Cook the boo in boiling water for 20 minutes, then drain and cut into small pieces. Heat the sesame seed oil in a frying pan, add the onion and fry gently until soft. Add the garlic and sesame seeds, then remove from the heat and mix with the boo.

To make the batter: put the flour and eggs in a bowl and beat thoroughly until smooth. Add the water gradually, stirring constantly until the batter is smooth.

Dip the liver slices in the batter. Heat 1 tablespoon of the vegetable oil in the frying pan, add the liver and fry for 5 minutes. Remove from the pan with a slotted spoon,

drain on kitchen paper towels and leave to cool. Meanwhile, dip the fish slices in the remaining batter. Heat another tablespoon of the oil in the pan, add the fish and fry for 5 minutes. Drain as for the liver.

Mix the minced beef and eggs together, then add salt and pepper to taste. Roll into 1 cm (½ inch) balls. Heat the remaining vegetable oil in the frying pan. Add the meatballs and fry for about 5 minutes, turning frequently, until evenly browned. Remove from the pan with a slotted spoon, then drain on kitchen paper towels.

Put the stock in a pan with 1 teaspoon of pepper and a pinch of monosodium glutamate. Bring to the boil, then lower the heat and simmer gently.

Meanwhile, arrange the ingredients in layers in individual Shin-Sol-Lo pots or a fondue pot. Put a layer of beef strips in the bottom, cover with boo mixture, then arrange the liver and fish slices on top in alternate layers.

Top with the cucumber, mushroom, carrot, green shallots, bamboo shoot and meatballs; arrange decoratively clockwise so that each third of the pan is filled in the same way.

Arrange the pine nuts around the funnel of the Shin-Sol-Lo pot or heap together in the centre of the fondue pot. Pour the stock gently over the ingredients, taking care not to disturb the arrangements.

If using Shin-Sol-Lo pots, put lighted charcoal into the centre, fan until the charcoal ignites, then heat for approximately 5 minutes. If using a fondue pot, bring gently to the boil over moderate heat. Serve hot.
SERVES 4-6

TANG
BEEF STOCK

This is the stock used in Korean soups and recipes where beef stock is called for.

1.5 kg (3 lb) beef rib bones
1 kg (2 lb) shin beef
4 large slices fresh ginger*
1 teaspoon salt

METHOD: Put bones and shin beef, ginger and salt in a large saucepan or stock pot and add sufficient cold water to cover. Bring slowly to the boil. Remove scum from surface, lower heat, cover and simmer gently on a low heat for 2 hours. Cool. Strain stock and chill in refrigerator. Before using remove fat from surface.

SHIKUMCHEE-TAENG-JANG-KUK
SPINACH SOUP WITH BEAN CURD AND SQUID

Despite its lengthy name, this soup is very easy to make.

| 2½ cups beef stock, Tang (see opposite) |
| 125 g (4 oz) bean curd*, diced |
| 60 g (2 oz) cleaned squid, cut into thin strips (optional) |
| 125 g (4 oz) fresh young spinach leaves, cut into thin strips |
| 2 teaspoons crushed garlic |
| 1 tablespoon soy bean paste* |
| 4 tablespoons sliced green shallots |
| salt |

METHOD: Put the stock in a pan and bring to the boil. Add the remaining ingredients and boil for 2 minutes. Serve hot in warmed individual soup bowls.
SERVES 4

YUK KE JANG
SPICY HOT BEEF SOUP WITH BEAN SPROUTS

| 3 tablespoons vegetable oil |
| 1 teaspoon chilli powder |
| 2 teaspoons crushed garlic |
| 1 teaspoon crushed fresh ginger* |
| 4 cups beef stock, Tang (see opposite) |
| 300 g (10 oz) cooked beef topside, thinly sliced |
| 2 tablespoons chopped green shallots |
| 125 g (4 oz) fresh bean sprouts |
| ¼-½ teaspoon salt |

METHOD: Heat the oil in a frying pan. Add the chilli powder, garlic and ginger and stir-fry over moderate heat for 1 minute. Remove from the heat.

Put the stock in a pan and bring to the boil. Add the chilli mixture and the remaining ingredients and simmer for 10 minutes. Serve hot.
SERVES 4

◁ *Korean Celebration Firepot, served in a traditional pot; Spinach Soup with Bean Curd and Squid*

OJINGO POKUM
SQUID WITH VEGETABLES IN CHILLI-HOT SWEET SAUCE

The squid should be scored crossways to help tenderize it during cooking.

500 g (1 lb) fresh squid
2 tablespoons vegetable oil
1 small green pepper, cored, seeded and thinly sliced into rings
1 small red pepper, cored, seeded and thinly sliced into rings
1 medium onion, peeled and finely chopped
2 teaspoons crushed garlic
2 teaspoons sugar
1 tablespoon kochujang*

METHOD: Clean the squid, discarding the head, transparent backbone and ink bag. Cut the flesh into 2.5 cm (1 inch) squares and score crossways.

Heat the oil in a frying pan. Add the vegetables and fry over brisk heat for 2 minutes, shaking the pan constantly. Remove from the heat, then add the squid, garlic and sugar.

Return to the heat and fry briskly for 2 minutes, stirring and shaking the pan constantly. Stir in the kochujang and fry for 1 minute over high heat, stirring all the time. Serve hot.
SERVES 4

MAEUM TANG
SPICED FISH SOUP

This is a dish for those who love spicy hot food.

750 g (1½ lb) fish fillets, skinned and cut into large chunks
2½ cups water
2 tablespoons vegetable oil
1 medium onion, peeled and finely chopped
2 tablespoons chopped green shallots
2 teaspoons crushed garlic
1 teaspoon crushed fresh ginger*
2-6 teaspoons chilli powder, according to taste
2-3 teaspoons salt
125 g (4 oz) zucchini, thinly sliced
1 medium green pepper, cored, seeded and finely sliced

METHOD: Put the fish in a pan with the water. Bring to the boil, then lower the heat and simmer gently for 5 minutes. Remove from the heat and set aside.

Heat the oil in a frying pan. Add the onion, green shallots, garlic, ginger, chilli powder and salt to taste. Stir-fry over moderate heat for 1 minute, then add the zucchini and pepper and stir-fry for 1 minute. Add the fish and simmer gently until heated through. Serve hot.
SERVES 4

▽ *Spiced Fish Soup*

SOLONG TANG
BEEF SOUP WITH NOODLES AND GINGER

This soup is a little time-consuming to make, but the end result is delicious and well worth the effort.

125 g (4 oz) fine noodles
375 g (12 oz) cooked beef brisket or topside
4 cups beef stock, Tang (see page 120)
½ cup finely chopped green shallots
2 teaspoons crushed fresh ginger*
1 teaspoon sugar
2 teaspoons freshly ground black pepper
2-3 teaspoons salt
pinch of monosodium glutamate*

METHOD: Cook the noodles in boiling water for 3 to 5 minutes, then drain and set aside.

Cut the meat into very thin slices, then cut each slice into strips, about 5 cm (2 inches) long and 1 cm (½ inch) wide.

Put all the ingredients in a pan, except the noodles and beef. Bring to the boil, then add the beef and simmer for 5 minutes. Hold the noodles in a sieve over the pan and spoon the liquid over them to reheat, allowing the liquid to strain through into the pan.

Divide the noodles equally between 4 warmed individual soup bowls, then pour over the soup, distributing the strips of beef evenly. Serve hot.

SERVES 4

NENG MYUN
COLD NOODLE SOUP

500 g (1 lb) fine noodles
250 g (8 oz) cooked beef brisket or topside
4 cups chicken stock
8 whole black peppercorns
5 cm (2 inch) piece of fresh ginger*, peeled
1-2 teaspoons salt
1 teaspoon soy sauce
4 dried chillis
To serve:
24 cucumber slices
1 large hard pear, peeled, cored and thinly sliced
2 hard-boiled eggs, halved lengthwise
prepared mustard and vinegar to taste (optional)

METHOD: Cook the noodles in boiling water for 3 to 5 minutes, then drain and leave to cool.

Cut the meat into very thin slices, then cut each slice into strips, about 5 cm (2 inches) long and 1 cm (½ inch) wide.

Put all the ingredients in a pan, except the noodles. Bring to the boil, then simmer for 5 minutes. Remove from the heat, leave until cold, then remove the peppercorns, ginger and chillis.

Divide the noodles between 4 to 6 individual soup bowls. Divide the cucumber and pear slices between the bowls, alternating the slices in layers on top of the noodles. Top each bowl with an egg half, then gently pour over the cold soup, taking care not to disturb the layers. Add a little mustard and vinegar before serving, if liked. Serve cold.

SERVES 4-6

BULGOGI
MARINATED SLICED BEEF IN SWEET SAUCE

Bulgogi is Korea's best-known dish. It is traditionally cooked and served in a special bulgogi pan, but it can equally well be made in a heavy frying pan.

Apart from the time it takes to marinate the meat, it is a very quick dish to make. If partially frozen beef is used, it will be easier to obtain very thin slices.

750 g (1½ lb) beef, lean rump, fillet or Scotch fillet
Marinade:
1 small apple, peeled, cored and grated
1 small hard pear, peeled, cored and grated
2 tablespoons chopped onion
4 tablespoons thinly sliced green shallots
4 tablespoons soy sauce
2 tablespoons sake*
½ cup water
1 tablespoon chopped garlic
2 tablespoons sesame seed oil*
2 teaspoons sesame seeds*
1 teaspoon freshly ground black pepper
2 tablespoons sugar
To serve:
carrot, boo* and parsley (optional)
Kim Chee (see page 119)

METHOD: Slice the beef very thinly into 5 cm (2 inch) squares. Place in a large bowl. Mix all the ingredients for the marinade together, then pour over the beef. Leave to marinate for at least 3 hours, preferably overnight.

Heat the pan until moderately hot. Add the beef and marinade and cook for 5 minutes or until the beef is tender, turning constantly.

Serve hot straight from the bulgogi pan, or transfer to a warmed serving dish if using a frying pan. Garnish, if liked, with flower shapes, cut from carrot and boo, and parsley. Serve with Kim Chee (see page 119).

SERVES 4

THAK JIM
CHICKEN IN SOY SAUCE WITH GINGER

3¾ cups water
1 chicken, weighing 1.25 kg (2½-2¾ lb), cut into serving portions
1 medium green pepper, cored, seeded and thinly sliced
1 medium red pepper, cored, seeded and thinly sliced
2 carrots, peeled and thinly sliced
8 mushrooms, sliced
Sauce:
¾ cup soy sauce
2 cups water
4 green shallots
2 teaspoons crushed garlic
1 tablespoon sugar
2 teaspoons freshly ground black pepper
1 tablespoons crushed fresh ginger*

METHOD: Bring the water to the boil in a large pan, add the chicken pieces and boil for 5 minutes.

Meanwhile, make the sauce: put all the ingredients in a pan, stir well, then bring to the boil.

Drain the chicken and add to the sauce with the peppers, carrots and mushrooms. Bring back to the boil, then lower the heat and simmer for 20 minutes or until the chicken is tender. Serve hot.
SERVES 4

THAK TUIGIM JANG
DEEP-FRIED CHICKEN WITH VEGETABLES IN SWEET SAUCE

500 g (1 lb) boned chicken, cut into 2.5 cm (1 inch) cubes
vegetable oil for deep-frying
2 medium carrots, peeled and sliced
2 medium potatoes, peeled and cut into 2.5 cm (1 inch) cubes
½ small red pepper, cored, seeded and thinly sliced
½ small green pepper, cored, seeded and thinly sliced
1 medium onion, peeled and chopped
Batter:
1 cup plain flour
2 eggs, well beaten
2 tablespoons water (approximately)
Sauce:
2 tablespoons soy sauce
2 tablespoons water
1 tablespoon sugar
2 teaspoons crushed fresh ginger*
2 teaspoons crushed garlic
2 tablespoons sake*
1 tablespoon sesame seed oil*
2 green shallots
½ teaspoon salt

METHOD: First, make the batter. Put the flour and eggs in a bowl and beat thoroughly until smooth. Add the water gradually, stirring until the batter is smooth.

Coat the chicken cubes in the batter. Heat the oil in a deep-fat fryer to 180°C/350°F, then add the chicken cubes and deep-fry until golden brown. Remove from the pan with a slotted spoon and drain on kitchen paper towels.

Blanch the carrots and potatoes in boiling water for 3 minutes, then drain and dry thoroughly. Deep-fry in the hot oil for 5 minutes, then remove from the pan with a slotted spoon and drain on paper towels.

To make the sauce, put all the ingredients in a pan and mix well. Bring to the boil, then remove from the heat.

Coat the base of a large heavy frying pan with oil. Heat gently, then add the chicken, carrots, potatoes, peppers and onion. Fry gently for about 1 minute, stirring constantly, then increase the heat and add the hot sauce. Cook for 1 minute, stirring and shaking the pan constantly over very high heat. Serve immediately.
SERVES 4

◁ *Marinated Beef in Sweet Sauce, served with Pickled Chinese Cabbage (see page 119)*

CHAP CHEE
SPICY VEGETABLES

4 cups water
200 g (7 oz) bean threads*
3 tablespoons vegetable oil
250 g (8 oz) Chinese cabbage, shredded
salt
1 large carrot, peeled and cut diagonally into matchstick strips
125 g (4 oz) fresh spinach leaves, cooked and roughly chopped
8 medium Chinese dried mushrooms, soaked in warm water for 30 minutes, then drained (optional)
Sauce:
1 tablespoon sesame seed oil*
1 tablespoon soy sauce
2 teaspoons sugar
2 teaspoons sesame seeds*
½ teaspoon salt

METHOD: Bring the water to the boil in a pan, add the bean threads and boil for 3 minutes. Drain and set aside.

Heat 2 tablespoons of the oil in a pan. When very hot, add the cabbage and salt to taste and fry for 2 minutes, tossing the leaves constantly. Remove from the pan and set aside.

Heat the remaining oil in the pan. Add the carrot and fry for 1 minute, stirring. Return the cabbage to the pan, add the spinach and the mushrooms, if using, and cook for a further 2 minutes, shaking the pan constantly.

To make the sauce: put all the ingredients in a pan and stir well. Bring to the boil, then add to the vegetable mixture with the bean threads. Mix well and heat through. Serve immediately.
SERVES 4

SHIKUMCHEE
SWEET SPINACH WITH GARLIC

For the best results, always use the youngest and freshest spinach available; large silverbeet leaves are not a good substitute.

750 g (1½ lb) fresh spinach leaves
3 tablespoons soy sauce
1 tablespoon sesame seeds*
1 tablespoon sesame seed oil*
1 tablespoon crushed garlic
2 tablespoons chopped green shallots
2 teaspoons sugar
salt
To garnish:
carrot, boo* and parsley (optional)

METHOD: Wash the spinach and discard the stalks. Bring a large pan of water to the boil, add the spinach and cook for exactly 3 minutes. Drain thoroughly.

Place the spinach on a serving plate and sprinkle the remaining ingredients on top. Garnish, if liked, with flower shapes, cut from carrot, boo and parsley. Serve hot.
SERVES 4

KAL BEE JIM
BEEF SPARERIBS IN TANGY SAUCE WITH CHESTNUTS

750 g (1½ lb) beef spareribs, trimmed of fat and cut into pieces 5 cm (2 inches) wide
Sauce:
3 tablespoons soy sauce
2 cups water
2 teaspoons sesame seed oil*
2 teaspoons sesame seeds*
1 tablespoon sugar
1 teaspoon freshly ground black pepper
1 teaspoon crushed garlic
8 dried chestnuts, soaked overnight
125 g (4 oz) bamboo shoot

METHOD: Parboil the beef for 20 minutes, then drain and set aside. Cook chestnuts in water until tender and chop finely.

To make the sauce: put all the ingredients in a pan and stir well. Bring to the boil, then add the beef and bring back to the boil. Lower the heat and simmer gently for 1 hour or until tender. Serve hot.
SERVES 4

YUK KWE
SPICED RAW BEEF

This is the Korean version of Steak Tartare. The egg yolk is broken at the table and mixed with the beef, pear and cucumber. Use either chopsticks or a fork for mixing and eating. If partially frozen beef is used, it will be easier to obtain very thin slices.

500 g (1 lb) beef, fillet or rump
2 teaspoons sugar
2 teaspoons sesame seeds*
1 tablespoon sesame seed oil*
1 tablespoon crushed garlic
salt
4 egg yolks (optional)
To garnish:
2 small hard pears, peeled, cored and sliced into matchstick strips
12 diagonal slices of cucumber, cut into matchstick strips
parsley sprigs
carrot (optional)

METHOD: Cut the meat into very thin slices no more than 3 mm (⅛ inch) thick, then cut the slices into matchstick strips. Place in a bowl with the remaining ingredients, except the egg yolks. Mix together, using the hands (their warmth will thaw the meat), then divide into 4 portions.

Divide the pear and cucumber strips equally between 4 individual serving plates, arranging them in separate piles. Place the meat mixture on top. If using egg yolks, mould the mixture into a neat shape and put an egg yolk in each hollow. Garnish with parsley sprigs and carrot 'flowers', if liked. Serve raw.
SERVES 4

▷ *Spicy Vegetables; Spiced Raw Beef*

Japanese cuisine is exquisite, aesthetic and sophisticated. Traditionally, visual feasting is part of a Japanese meal — you feed your eyes as well as your stomach. Despite the proximity to China and the use of many similar ingredients, the Japanese approach to cooking is entirely different with the emphasis on beautiful presentation and subtle flavours.

Japan is a country with a very small area, but because of its length it encompasses a wide range of climatic conditions and geographic differences. There is an endless assortment of foods, but this does not mean that the food is so plentiful that it is inexpensive!

For centuries, Japan was a closed port and was not subject to foreign influence until quite recently, which is most probably why this country developed such a unique, elegant style of cooking. Japanese food is made pleasing by the artistic way in which the food is arranged and garnished on beautiful ceramic plates or bowls. The Japanese have a strong sensitivity and awareness for natural colour, symmetry and general appearance of each prepared food. Hand-crafted serving dishes and bowls, often specially created by a potter, are carefully selected for each food. The Japanese have a talent of arranging the food and garnish to display contrast of colour, shapes and textures. Seasonal fresh flowers and leaves are a common garnish.

Preparation and cooking

Each food is prepared separately and thus, even when served together, the individual flavours and colourings are retained. Seasonings are delicate and fragrant.

Japan is probably one of the few countries in the world where people will pay any price to savour the very 'first' sweet strawberry, fragrant matsutake (pine mushroom) or juicy melon of the season. These are often packed individually in special boxes with elaborate cushioning, and sold as gifts.

Medium grain rice is served at all meals. So valued is this 'staff of life' grain, that the Japanese have an old saying, 'Tsukiyo ni kome no meshi'. Translated, this is 'Moonlight and boiled rice'. When you have become acquainted with the delights of Japanese cuisine you will appreciate the full meaning of this ancient proverb. Plain boiled rice does have a special satisfying flavour, and is delicious by itself.

Be sure to use shoyu* (Japanese light soy sauce) in these recipes; to use Chinese soy sauce instead would ruin the flavour of the dish. The same applies to miso (Japanese soy bean paste*), which is entirely different from Chinese soy bean paste*.

Certain holidays are celebrated in grand style: New Year is probably the most important. Food is prepared and placed in beautiful tiered, lacquered boxes. Friends, relatives and neighbours come to greet each other and food and drink are served. A rice patty made from glutinous (sweet) rice* is dropped into ozoni (a special New Year's soup). So sacred is this holiday that the 'o' is put before the word 'zoni' to specify the honorific form of the word. During this period, of almost one week's celebration, the shops are closed and virtually all of Japan is at a standstill.

Children's Day in May (formerly Boys' Day) is celebrated with fragrant cherry leaves wrapped around special rice cakes. The Japanese still observe these ancient traditions, despite the influence of the West.

The Japanese take extreme care and pride in growing the best fruit and vegetables; in fishing for only the freshest marine life; in hand-massaging their cattle and feeding them beer to produce the world's most expensive and beautifully marbled beef. The average housewife makes a daily trip to the market to buy the choicest fresh foods, even if she has a refrigerator. Menus are kept fairly simple with an entrée, a few side dishes, pickles, soup, rice and green tea.

Serving

The traditional Japanese meal is served on a low table with the diners sitting on cushions placed on the tatami (straw mat) floor. In the entrance of every home, shoes are removed and slippers put on, so dining at floor level is a very clean custom. In many homes, however, meals are now served at normal table height and chairs are used.

There are no matching place settings in Japan; after a traditional dinner there is a mountain of little dishes and plates to be cleared. Knives are not used for eating; the food is cut into small pieces during preparation and eaten with chopsticks, unless it is something like a whole fish which can be separated easily with chopsticks when cooked.

Japanese cooking is relatively simple. Most dishes are cooked in advance and served at room temperature, since sometimes there are only two burners on the gas stove. In the past, few Japanese kitchens had ovens, but, in recent years, portable ones have become available.

Sake* (rice wine) is the traditional accompaniment to Japanese food. It is served warm and enjoyed throughout the meal. Green tea is a national 'habit'; it is served frequently during the day and at meal times in fragile ceramic tea cups without handles. Green tea has a very delicate flavour, and is therefore most suited to Japanese cuisine.

This chapter provides a selection of the more popular Japanese recipes; essentially they are simple, light, delicious and beautifully presented — truly representative of an exquisite cuisine.

Pickles are an essential part of a Japanese meal as is hot Sake, a rice wine served throughout the meal.

△ *Bean Soup*

MISO SHIRU
BEAN SOUP

This is a traditional thick bean soup which can be served at any meal.

Years ago, it was the basic hot soup that was served for breakfast as a mainstay, but nowadays more and more people are turning to the Western-style breakfast and giving up the traditional Japanese-style meal.

Made with soya bean paste and bean curd, this soup is very nutritious, especially when it is served with rice. For a stronger flavour, substitute akamiso* for the shiromiso* and adjust the quantity used according to taste.

| 250 g (8 oz) shiromiso* |
| 5 cups Dashi (see right) |
| 300 g (11 oz) block tofu*, cut into bite-sized pieces |
| finely shredded green shallot, green part only, to garnish |

METHOD: Put the shiromiso and dashi in a pan and heat gently until dissolved, stirring constantly. Bring to the boil, add the tofu and heat through.

Pour into warmed soup bowls and garnish with the green shallot. Serve hot.
SERVES 4

DASHI
JAPANESE BASIC STOCK

Dashi is indispensable in Japanese cooking. Chicken stock or broth occasionally makes a suitable substitute, but to cook truly 'Japanese', one should always use dashi where stock or broth is called for in a recipe. Dashi is a light fish and seaweed stock. It is usually made as a 'first dashi' and generally used for the delicate flavouring of soups. The same basic ingredients are saved for making a 'second dashi', to

Soak the wakame in water to cover for 10 minutes. Drain, rinse under cold running water, then drain and cut into thin strips. Trim scallops and lightly simmer in water to cover for 3 to 4 minutes. Cut each into 4.

To make the sauce, put all the ingredients in a pan and stir well. Cook for 3 minutes until quite thick, stirring constantly.

Put the green shallots, wakame and prepared scallops in a bowl, pour over the sauce, then fold gently to mix. Transfer to individual serving dishes and serve at room temperature.

SERVES 4

HARUSAME SOUP
SPRING RAIN SOUP

This light soup has a wonderful aroma and chewy texture. It can be prepared at the table if wished, in which case each guest has a bowl of stock and adds ingredients to taste.

125 g (4 oz) dehydrated mung bean threads* or harusame*, soaked in boiling water for 30 minutes
2-3 shiitake*, soaked in boiling water for 20 minutes
4 cups Dashi (see opposite) or chicken stock
1 tablespoon sake*
salt
125 g (4 oz) peeled prawns
6-8 snow peas
1 gobo*, parboiled (optional)
4-6 green shallots
2 carrots
few cucumber strips
125 g (4 oz) napa*
few spinach leaves
To garnish:
1 teaspoon grated fresh ginger*
1 green shallot, finely shredded
2 teaspoons puréed daikon* (white radish)

METHOD: Drain the mung beans and cut into 5 cm (2 inch) lengths. Drain the mushrooms, reserving the liquid, and discard the stems.

Put the stock in a pan. Carefully pour in the reserved mushroom liquid, leaving any sandy sediment at the bottom – this should be discarded. Bring to the boil, then lower the heat and simmer for about 2 minutes. Add the sake and salt to taste.

Divide the stock between 4 warmed individual soup bowls. Arrange the other ingredients attractively on a serving dish, cutting the vegetables to make interesting shapes, if liked. Place the garnish ingredients on separate dishes. Serve at once.

SERVES 4

---

which katsuobushi* (dried bonito fish) and water are added. This second type of dashi is used for sauces and pan-fried dishes.

To save time, you may use one of the many excellent dashi powders which are available in foil packets.

10 cm (4 inch) square kombu*
5 cups water
½ cup flaked katsuobushi*
1½ teaspoons salt
1 teaspoon shoyu*

METHOD: Rinse the kombu and wipe with a damp cloth. Put the kombu and water in a pan and bring to the boil. Remove the kombu, add the katsuobushi to the pan and remove from the heat; leave to stand for 2 minutes. Strain, then add the remaining ingredients.

MAKES 5 CUPS

Note: The seaweed need not be wasted, cook it with a little shoyu* and sugar, then slice and serve as a 'nibble'.

NUTA NEGI
GREEN SHALLOTS WITH MISO

Green shallots make a delectable cooked vegetable – not pungent and piquant-flavoured as in their raw state.

2 bunches green shallots, cut into 5 cm (2 inch) lengths
3 strips of wakame* (optional)
15 fresh scallops
Sauce:
3 tablespoons shiromiso*
3 tablespoons Dashi (see left)
1 tablespoon su* (rice vinegar)
1 tablespoon water
1 teaspoon dry mustard

METHOD: Drop the green shallots into a pan of boiling water. Boil for 2½ minutes; drain and squeeze out excess moisture.

ASSORTED FRITTERS

Japanese deep-fried foods are noted for their delicacy, and extreme care is taken to use the lightest vegetable oils. The crisp batter is almost as thin as gauze, so the colour and texture of the ingredients show through faintly and look most attractive. Best results are obtained if all the ingredients for the batter are ice cold and the batter should be made just before using.

Fish fillets, strips of carrot, shiitake*, asparagus stalks, parsley and slices of yellow zucchini can be substituted for the prawns and vegetables suggested here. The dipping sauce reduces the oiliness of the Tempura and adds a delicate seasoning to the crispy coating.

500 g (1 lb) prawns
1 medium sweet potato, peeled and sliced into 5 mm (¼ inch) rounds
1 small eggplant, cut lengthwise into 5 mm (¼ inch) slices
8 snow peas
12 mushrooms, whole or sliced
1 onion, peeled and thinly sliced into rings
12 green beans, cut into 5 cm (2 inch) lengths
vegetable oil for deep-frying
Tentsuyu (Dipping Sauce):
2 cups Dashi (see page 130)
2 tablespoons shoyu*
3 tablespoons mirin*
pinch of salt
Batter:
½ cup plain flour
½ cup cornflour
1½ teaspoons baking powder
½ teaspoon salt
1 egg, lightly beaten
1 cup iced water
1 ice cube
To garnish:
4 tablespoons grated daikon* (white radish)
3 tablespoons grated fresh ginger*

METHOD: Peel and devein the prawns, leaving the last segment of the shell and tail intact. Pat the prawns and vegetables dry with kitchen paper towels. Arrange on a large serving dish, cover with plastic wrap and chill in the refrigerator until required.

To make the tentsuyu, put all the ingredients in a pan and stir well to combine. Heat through, then keep hot while making the batter.

To make the batter, put the dry ingredients in a chilled bowl and stir well. Mix together the beaten egg and water, then stir gently into the dry ingredients, taking care not to overmix. Add the ice cube.

Heat the oil in a deep fryer to 180°C/ 350°F. Dip the prawns and vegetables into the batter, a piece at a time, then fry a few pieces at a time in the hot oil until light golden. Drain on kitchen paper towels, then serve immediately in a folded napkin.

Pour the hot sauce into individual bowls and arrange the garnish on individual plates. Diners should then mix together the sauce and garnish according to taste, using it as a dip for the fritters. Serve hot.
SERVES 4

SLICED RAW FISH

Sashimi is a culinary miracle — raw fish without a fish smell or taste! Always use absolutely fresh fish; check for firm flesh, clear, bright eyes if the head is still attached, and no odour.

Octopus (parboiled), squid, abalone, bream and cuttlefish are some of the raw seafoods which can be prepared in this way; raw chicken breasts, sprinkled with lemon juice, can be substituted.

750 g (1½ lb) bream, tuna or other saltwater fish, filleted
2 cups daikon* (white radish), shredded
1 carrot, shredded
4-5 green shallots, shredded
few snow peas
few cooked, unshelled prawns
1 tablespoon wasabi*
few lemon wedges
1 tablespoon freshly grated ginger*
shoyu* to taste

METHOD: Remove any skin, blood and dark sections from the fish. Cut the flesh diagonally with a sharp knife into slices about 2.5 cm (1 inch) long and 5 mm (¼ inch) thick.

Arrange the shredded daikon, carrot and green shallots in mounds on a serving platter, together with the snow peas. Arrange the raw fish slices and cooked prawns on the platter.

Mix the wasabi to a thick paste with a little water. Place on the platter, with the lemon wedges and ginger.

To serve, pour shoyu into individual bowls, then allow each diner to add wasabi and ginger to his own bowl of shoyu according to taste. The fish and vegetables are then dipped into the sauce before eating. Serve with Japanese-style medium grain rice.
SERVES 4

CRAB AND CUCUMBER WITH VINEGAR SAUCE

This is an ideal dish for a buffet because it will keep well for several hours. If liked, prawns or abalone can be used instead of crab. Score the cucumber using a cannelling knife, or a fork, to give an attractive serrated edge.

1 small cucumber, 18-20 cm (7-8 inches) long
¼ teaspoon salt
125 g (4 oz) fresh crabmeat
Sauce:
5 tablespoons su* (rice vinegar)
4 tablespoons sugar
½ teaspoon salt
To garnish:
1 tablespoon sesame seeds*, toasted
few strips of lemon rind

METHOD: Score the cucumber lengthwise, slice into paper-thin rounds and sprinkle with the salt. Leave for 20 minutes.

Meanwhile, make the sauce: put all the ingredients in a bowl and stir well.

Squeeze the cucumber slices and discard the juice. Pour the sauce over the cucumber, add the crab and toss lightly.

Transfer to individual serving bowls and garnish with the sesame seeds and lemon rind. Serve cold.
SERVES 4

▷ *Sliced Raw Fish*

CHIRI NABE
FISH STEW

This dish can be prepared at the table like a fondue, if wished. Guests should eat from the pan, dipping the cooked morsels into the sauce.

15 cm/6 inch piece of kombu*
7 cups water
250 g (8 oz) filleted snapper, bream or other white fish, cut into serving pieces
1 bunch green shallots, sliced diagonally
4 fresh shiitake*, stems removed, or button mushrooms
300 g (11 oz) block tofu*, cut into 2.5 cm (1 inch) chunks
4 large napa* leaves, cut into 5 cm (2 inch) pieces
Dipping sauce:
½ cup shoyu*
¾ cup lemon juice
seasoning suggestions: minced green shallots, toasted sesame seeds*, freshly grated ginger*, grated daikon* (white radish), shichimi*

METHOD: Rinse the kombu, wipe with a damp cloth and place in a fondue pan or electric frying pan. Add the water, bring to the boil, then add the fish. Bring back to the boil and add the shallots, mushrooms, tofu and napa. Bring back to the boil, stirring constantly. The vegetables should then be crisp and tender and the fish cooked through.

To make the dipping sauce: mix together the shoyu and lemon juice, then add suggested seasonings according to taste. Divide between individual dishes.

Serve the fish stew hot, with the dipping sauce and steamed rice.

SERVES 4

SHAKE NO KASUZUKE
SALMON TROUT AND SAKE LEES

When fresh large trout is available, sometimes called salmon trout, this is an excellent way to preserve some for later use. This dish makes a quick entrée and will keep for several months in the refrigerator. The flavour of kasu* goes well with trout, but it is strongly flavoured and should therefore be eaten in small quantities – until you acquire a taste for it, that is!

4 fresh salmon trout steaks
1½ tablespoons salt
Marinade:
2 cups kasu*
1 cup sugar
To serve:
1 small lettuce, shredded
½ small daikon* (white radish), puréed

METHOD: Put the fish in a bowl and sprinkle both sides with the salt. Cover with plastic wrap or foil and leave in the refrigerator for 4 days to allow the flesh of the fish to become firm.

Drain the fish well, then pat dry with kitchen paper towels. Mix together the marinade ingredients and use to coat both sides of the fish. Place in a dish, cover and keep in the refrigerator for 7 days before serving.

Remove most of the marinade from the fish, then grill for about 7 minutes on one side only until the fish flakes easily when tested with a fork. Take care not to overcook as the marinade causes the fish to char easily. Serve hot with small mounds of shredded lettuce and puréed daikon.
SERVES 4

NIZAKANA
BRAISED FISH

This dish makes a quick, simple meal with plenty of flavour. Serve with rice and a green vegetable, with shichimi* and sansho* as condiments, if liked.

1 tablespoon vegetable oil
1 kg (2 lb) thick fish fillets, cut into serving pieces
1 medium onion, peeled, halved and cut into 1 cm (½ inch) thick slices
1 tablespoon sake*
2 tablespoons water
3 tablespoons shoyu*
2 tablespoons sugar
1 teaspoon freshly grated ginger*

METHOD: Place a frying pan over moderate heat, add the oil, then the fish and onion. Mix the remaining ingredients together, then pour into the pan. Cover and simmer for about 10 minutes until the fish flakes easily when tested with a fork. Serve the braised fish hot.
SERVES 4-6

SHIO YAKI
SALT GRILLED FISH

This method of preparing protein-rich fish is surprisingly simple – the fat in the skin of the fish oozes out during cooking and the salt creates moisture so that the flesh is deliciously moist. Hot steamed rice and green tea make good accompaniments.

1 mackerel or snapper, weighing 750 g (1½ lb)
salt
To serve:
few lemon wedges
shoyu* (optional)

METHOD: Remove the scales from the fish, leaving the skin intact. Clean the fish thoroughly and remove the head if wished, then sprinkle lightly inside and out with salt. Leave to stand for about 30 minutes.

Make 3 diagonal slashes on the surface of the fish. Grill under a preheated grill for about 5 minutes on each side, until the fish flakes easily when tested with a fork; do not overcook.

Serve hot with lemon wedges. Hand shoyu separately, if liked.
SERVES 4

◁ *Salt Grilled Fish (above); Salmon and Sake Lees*

CHAWANMUSHI
HOT CHICKEN AND EGG SOUP

Chawanmushi can be served as a soup course or light luncheon dish. Do not overcook the custard or steam over too high a heat, or the eggs will curdle and become tough.

Special ceramic chawanmushi cups with lids are available, but individual heatproof bowls or custard cups may be used instead.

½ boned chicken breast, cut into 8 slices
2 teaspoons shoyu*
2 cups Dashi (see page 130)
1½ teaspoons mirin*
½ teaspoon salt
3 eggs, lightly beaten
4 slices kamaboko*
4 mushrooms, sliced
¼ cup sliced bamboo shoot
4 snow peas or watercress sprigs to garnish

METHOD: Put the chicken slices in a bowl, sprinkle with half the shoyu and leave to marinate.

Meanwhile, put the dashi in a separate bowl. Add the mirin, remaining shoyu, salt and the eggs. Mix well.

Divide the chicken slices equally between 4 individual bowls. Divide the kamaboko, mushroom and bamboo shoot between the bowls. Pour the egg mixture carefully over the top and garnish with the snow peas or watercress.

Cover the bowls with lids or foil and place in a steamer or saucepan containing about 2.5 cm (1 inch) boiling water. Cover and steam over medium heat for 12 to 15 minutes until set. Serve immediately.

SERVES 4

TONKATSU
PORK CUTLETS

This dish was probably introduced to the Japanese by foreign traders some centuries ago. It is very popular and most suitable for anyone trying Japanese food for the first time, since it is similar to Western dishes. It is equally good served cold, or in sandwiches.

4-6 boned loin or butterfly pork chops, or fillet steaks
salt
freshly ground black pepper
flour for coating
2 eggs, beaten
panko* or breadcrumbs for coating
vegetable oil for deep-frying
To serve:
185 g (6 oz) cabbage, finely shredded
few parsley sprigs
tonkatsu sauce* (optional)

METHOD: Pound the pork with a mallet to flatten it slightly, then sprinkle lightly with salt and pepper. Coat with flour, dip in the egg, then coat with panko or breadcrumbs.

Heat the oil in a deep frying pan or deep-fat fryer to 180°C/350°F. Deep-fry the pork for 10 minutes, turning down the heat a little so that the pork cooks thoroughly; turn the pork once during frying to brown both sides.

Test the pork to make sure the meat is no longer pink, then remove from the pan with a slotted spoon and drain on kitchen paper towels. Cut each piece of pork into 3 or 4 slices, then reshape on a warmed serving dish.

Arrange the cabbage around the pork and garnish with parsley. Serve hot with tonkatsu sauce, if liked.
SERVES 4-6

BUTA TERIYAKI
PORK ON SKEWERS

Pork marinated in teriyaki sauce has an exquisite flavour, especially if cooked over a charcoal grill (hibachi). If this is not available, an ordinary grill may be used, although the flavour will not be quite so good.

If liked, green shallots, mushrooms and strips of green pepper can be added to the skewers, alternating with the pork. Use bamboo skewers if possible; these should be soaked in water for about 15 minutes before use.

As a variation, chicken, beef, prawns or fish may be used instead of pork.

1 kg (2 lb) pork fillet, thinly sliced
1 teaspoon grated fresh ginger*
1 medium onion, peeled and finely chopped
5 tablespoons shoyu*
4 tablespoons sugar
4 tablespoons sake*

METHOD: Put all the ingredients in a bowl, mix well, then leave to marinate for at least 1 hour.

Thread the pork on 4 skewers, reserving the marinade. Grill for 3 minutes on each side, basting frequently with the marinade. Serve immediately.
SERVES 4

OYAKO DOMBURI
CHICKEN AND EGGS WITH RICE

The literal translation of this recipe title is 'parent (chicken) and child (egg) in a bowl'. It makes a very filling meal for lunch. Try to keep the bowl covered until serving time to retain the heat.

1 cup Dashi (see page 130)
3 tablespoons shoyu*
2 tablespoons sake*
125 g (4 oz) chicken breast meat, thinly sliced
½ medium onion, peeled and sliced
125 g (4 oz) mushrooms, sliced
1½ cups medium grain rice, cooked and kept hot
5 eggs, lightly beaten
few green shallots, chopped, to garnish

METHOD: Put the Dashi in a pan and bring to the boil. Add the shoyu, sake, chicken, onion and mushrooms and cook for about 5 minutes.

Meanwhile, divide the hot rice between 4 warmed large serving bowls, cover and set aside.

Add the eggs to the pan and stir gently. Cook until the eggs are half set. Pour the mixture over the hot rice in the bowls, sprinkle with the green shallots and cover with lids. Serve immediately.
SERVES 4

MIZUTAKI
CHICKEN IN BROTH

Literally translated, mizutaki means 'water cooking'. This dish is traditionally cooked in a pan shaped like an upturned ring tin, with a chimney in the centre where hot charcoals are buried to provide the heat supply for the cooking. An electric frying pan or fondue pan can be used instead, so that guests can cook their own chicken and vegetables at the table.

Appearance plays a very important part in the art of Japanese cooking. Try to arrange the vegetables as artistically as possible on the serving dish – they should look like a beautiful picture.

8 dried shiitake*, soaked in warm water for 20 minutes
1 chicken, weighing 1.25 kg (2½-2¾ lb), boned and cut into 2.5 cm (1 inch) chunks
1 green pepper, cored, seeded and cut into long strips
½ cucumber, cut into strips
few carrots, trimmed
few snow peas
300 g (11 oz) block tofu*, cut into 2.5 cm (1 inch) cubes (optional)
1 medium napa*, sliced into 2.5 cm (1 inch) strips
few green shallots, cut into 5 cm (2 inch) lengths
4 cups Dashi (see page 130)
1 tablespoon sake*
1 small piece of kombu* (optional)
Gomatare (sesame sauce):
1 tablespoon shiromiso*
4 tablespoons sesame seeds*, toasted and crushed
3 tablespoons mirin*
1 tablespoon sugar
2 tablespoons shoyu*
½ cup Dashi (see page 130)
½ teaspoon salad oil

METHOD: Drain the mushrooms, squeeze dry, then discard the stems and slice the caps into thin strips.

Arrange the chicken and vegetables artistically on a large serving plate. Mix together all the sauce ingredients and divide between individual serving bowls.

Put the Dashi in a pan and stand in the centre of the table. Bring the Dashi to the boil, add the sake, kombu if using, and chicken and cook for 15 minutes. Let guests help themselves to chicken and vegetables, cooking the vegetables in the bubbling broth as required. Serve the sauce as a dip.
SERVES 4

△ *Pork on Skewers*

YAKITORI
GRILLED CHICKEN

This is one of the most popular of all Japanese grilled dishes. A charcoal grill (hibachi) imparts a flavour which is unsurpassed, but the dish can be cooked under an ordinary grill.

Use bamboo skewers if possible; these should be soaked in water for about 15 minutes before using.

1 kg (2-2¼ lb) boned chicken, cut into chunks
1 bunch green shallots, cut into 5 cm (2 inch) lengths
2 green peppers, cored, seeded and cut into 5 cm (2 inch) chunks

Marinade:
¾ cup shoyu*
¼ cup sugar
¾ cup sake*
To serve:
pinch of powdered sansho*

METHOD: Thread the chicken, green shallots and green peppers alternately on 4 skewers. Mix together the marinade ingredients and brush over the skewers. Leave to marinate for 30 minutes, basting occasionally.

Grill for 3 minutes, then dip the skewers in the marinade again, turn and grill for 2 minutes; do not overcook.

Serve hot with a pinch of sansho pepper.

SERVES 4

TEPPANYAKI
MIXED GRILL

Teppan means 'iron' and yaki means 'to fry'. Any combination of meat, seafood, or poultry can be used with vegetables in season for this dish. As illustrated, vegetables, such as radishes, chopped fresh spinach leaves, sliced green or red peppers, snow peas, green beans and green shallots are all suitable. Traditionally, a heavy iron griddle is used at the table, but an electric frying pan may be used instead.

At Japanese speciality restaurants, talented cooks bow before the diners and act out a 'show', waving sharp knives in the air while they prepare this scrumptious meal before your very eyes.

4 sirloin or fillet steaks, or 4 boned chicken breasts, cut into chunks
8 cooked, unshelled prawns
2 medium zucchini, sliced into julienne strips
2 medium onions, peeled and finely sliced
250 g (8 oz) fresh bean sprouts
250 g (8 oz) button mushrooms
1 tablespoon vegetable oil
Ponzu (tart sauce):
½ cup shoyu*
½ cup lime or lemon juice
½ cup mirin*
Karashi jyoyu (mustard sauce):
2 teaspoons dry mustard
2 teaspoons hot water
3 tablespoons shoyu*
2 tablespoons su* (rice vinegar)
1 teaspoon sesame seed oil*

METHOD: Arrange the beef or chicken, prawns and vegetables artistically on a large serving plate.

To make the ponzu sauce: mix together all the ingredients and pour into individual dishes. To make the karashi jyoyu sauce: mix the mustard and water to a paste, then add the remaining ingredients. Pour into individual dishes.

Heat a griddle or electric frying pan at the table. Add the oil, then some of the meat and prawns. As the meat becomes tender, add a few vegetables to the pan and cook until they are tender but still crisp.

Serve the meat, prawns and vegetables as they are ready, letting the guests dip them into their sauces while more teppanyaki is cooking.
SERVES 4

▷ *Mixed Grill*

KIMPIRA
CHILLI-FLAVOURED BURDOCK

Serve as an appetizer or accompaniment to any meal. Burdock is considered a nuisance weed in Australia, but in Japan gobo*, the root, is used as a vegetable.

3 long gobo*, skinned
1 small carrot, peeled
1 tablespoon vegetable oil
1 tablespoon shoyu*
1 tablespoon sugar
pinch of salt
pinch of dried chilli pepper flakes or chilli powder

METHOD: Cut the gobo and carrot into paper-thin 1 cm (½ inch) wide strips, using a vegetable peeler. Place in cold water until ready for use, then drain and pat dry.

Heat a frying pan. When hot, add the oil, then the vegetables and stir-fry for about 2 minutes until tender but still crisp. Add the remaining ingredients and stir-fry for 2 minutes. Serve hot or at room temperature.
SERVES 4

NIKO NO MISO YAKI
MEAT WITH MISO

Akamiso* is Japanese red soybean paste. It gives meat an entirely different flavour. Served with hot steamed rice and salad, this dish makes a quick family meal.

750 g (1½ lb) oyster blade steak, in one piece
Marinade:
4 tablespoons akamiso*
2 tablespoons shoyu*
1 tablespoon sugar
1 teaspoon grated fresh ginger*
1 green shallot, chopped
2 tablespoons vegetable oil
toasted sesame seeds* to garnish

METHOD: Cut the meat lengthwise through the middle, then cut into thin slices across the grain. Place the slices in a bowl with the akamiso, shoyu, sugar, ginger and green shallot. Mix well, then leave to marinate for 10 minutes.

Place a frying pan over high heat. Add the oil, then the meat and marinade. Stir-fry for about 2 minutes. Serve hot, sprinkled with toasted sesame seeds.
SERVES 4

SHIITAKE NO AMANIE
SWEET BLACK MUSHROOMS

Shiitake* is the legendary Black Forest mushroom so favoured by the Japanese and Chinese for its health-giving vitamins.

Shiitake is available in dehydrated form in speciality shops and markets. Although expensive it has an incomparable flavour. Chew the succulent pieces of these mushrooms slowly to appreciate their fabulous taste!

15 dried shiitake*, with large caps, soaked in warm water for 20 minutes
2 cups water
1½ teaspoons sugar
1-2 tablespoons mirin*
pinch of salt
2 teaspoons shoyu*
pinch of monosodium glutamate* (optional)
shredded green shallots and carrot slices to garnish

METHOD: Drain the mushrooms, reserving the soaking liquid, then discard the mushroom stems. Leave the caps whole or slice each one into 5 pieces.

Pour the mushroom liquid slowly into a pan, taking care to avoid including the sandy sediment at the bottom which should be discarded. Add the mushrooms and boil for 5 minutes. Add the remaining ingredients and cook for 5 minutes. If liked, sprinkle in a little more mirin.

Remove from the heat, then leave to stand for 10 minutes. Arrange the mushrooms in an attractive pattern on a serving plate. Garnish with the green shallots and carrot slices placed in the centre to resemble a flower head. Serve at room temperature, as an appetizer or side dish.
SERVES 4

HIJIKI TO ABURAGE
SEAWEED WITH FRIED BEAN CAKE

Japan is surrounded by water, so it is hardly surprising that seaweeds have become one of the major foodstuffs to the Japanese. These seaweeds are high in protein, starch, sugar, fat, Vitamins A, B_1, B_2, calcium, phosphorus, iron and trace elements.

5 tablespoons dry hijiki*
2 aburage*
1 teaspoon vegetable oil
⅔ cup Dashi (see page 130)
1 tablespoon mirin*
2½ teaspoons sugar
2 tablespoons shoyu*

METHOD: Pick out as much sediment as possible from the hijiki, then wash and soak in cold water for 1 hour. Drain, then rinse thoroughly under cold running water to remove the sand. Strain in a fine sieve.

Wash the aburage in boiling water to remove excess oil then cut lengthwise into 5 mm (¼ inch) slices.

Heat a frying pan, add the oil, then the hijiki. Fry for about 2 minutes, then add the aburage and Dashi. Simmer, uncovered, for 5 minutes.

Add the remaining ingredients, stir well and cook for 7 minutes or until all the liquid has evaporated. Serve hot in warmed individual serving dishes.
SERVES 4

GYOZA YAKI
FRIED DUMPLINGS

3 napa* leaves
250 g (½ lb) lean boned pork, finely minced
2 green shallots, chopped
1 garlic clove, peeled and crushed
½ teaspoon grated fresh ginger*
2 tablespoons shoyu*
½ teaspoon salt
1 tablespoon sesame seed oil*
½ packet round gyoza or wonton skins*
2 tablespoons vegetable oil
Dipping sauce:
2 tablespoons su* (rice vinegar)
2 tablespoons dry mustard
2 tablespoons shoyu*

METHOD: Blanch the napa quickly in boiling water, drain, then squeeze out excess moisture. Chop coarsely, then combine with the remaining ingredients, except the gyoza skins and vegetable oil.

Put 1 spoonful of the mixture on one half of a gyoza skin. Fold in half, enclosing the filling. Brush the inside edges with water and press together to seal. (For an authentic finish, pleat the top side as you seal the skin.) Repeat with the remaining filling mixture and skins.

Heat a frying pan, add the vegetable oil, then the gyoza, overlapping them slightly in a neat pattern, with the pleated sides on top. Cover and cook over moderate heat for about 5 minutes.

Add just enough hot water to cover the gyoza, then cover with a lid and cook until all the water has evaporated.

To make the dipping sauce: combine all the ingredients together and divide between individual dishes.

Serve the gyoza hot, with the sauce.
SERVES 4

SHIRA AE
VEGETABLES WITH TOFU SAUCE

This is a most interesting tangy white dressing for cooked vegetables.

6 aburage*
2 pieces konnyaku*, cut into 5 cm (2 inch) strips
3 small carrots, peeled and cut into 5 cm (2 inch) strips
1 cup Dashi (see page 130)
300 g (11 oz) block tofu*
4 tablespoons white sesame seeds*, toasted and crushed
2 tablespoons shiromiso*
2 tablespoons sugar
1 teaspoon salt
cucumber strips and carrot slice to garnish

METHOD: Wash the aburage in boiling water to remove the excess oil, then cut lengthwise into 5 mm (¼ inch) slices. Cook the konnyaku in boiling salted water for 2 minutes, then drain.

Cook the aburage, konnyaku and carrots in the dashi for about 5 minutes until the carrots are tender but still crisp and most of the dashi has evaporated. Leave to cool, then cut the vegetables into small pieces and place in a large serving bowl.

Wrap the tofu in a cloth and press down to squeeze out as much water as possible. Crush the tofu. Add the remaining ingredients, mix well, then pour the tofu dressing over the vegetables. Mix together, taking care not to crush the vegetables.

Garnish with cucumber strips and a carrot slice. Serve at room temperature.
SERVES 4

▽ *Meat with Vegetables*

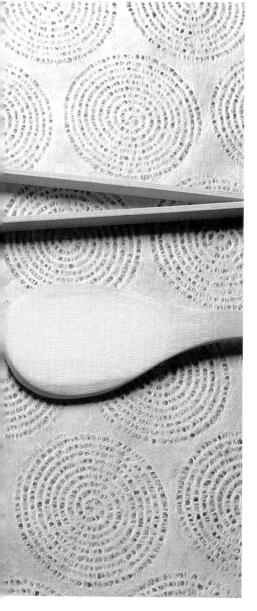

SUKIYAKI
MEAT WITH VEGETABLES

This extraordinary combination of ingredients with its tasty sauce is a delectable meal-in-one. It is especially good prepared at the table – the guests eat it little by little as it cooks, and more ingredients are added to the pan. Towards the end, as the juices blend together, the flavour is unsurpassed.

Be sure to serve sukiyaki with hot steamed rice. Vary the vegetables, according to season and taste.

125 g (4 oz) shiitake*, soaked in warm water for 20 minutes, or button mushrooms
95 g (3 oz) can shirataki*, or 125 g (4 oz) mung bean threads*, soaked in boiling water for 30 minutes
few pieces of beef suet
1 kg (2 lb) scotch fillet of fillet steak, thinly sliced
1 medium onion, peeled and sliced into rings
2 bunches green shallots, cut into 5 cm (2 inch) lengths
1 carrot, thinly sliced into squares
150 g (5 oz) water chestnuts* or bamboo shoot, sliced
few spinach and/or napa* leaves, cut into 4 cm (1½ inch) slices
300 g (11 oz) block tofu*, diced
Sauce:
½ cup shoyu*
¼ cup sugar
½ cup Dashi (see page 130)
½ cup mirin*
To serve:
4 eggs (optional)
shoyu*, to taste (optional)

METHOD: If using shiitake, drain, squeeze dry then discard stems and slice the caps. If using mung bean threads, drain, then cut into 5 cm (2 inch) lengths.

Heat an electric frying pan at the table. Add the suet and render some of the fat, then remove. Add half the meat and cook for a few minutes.

Mix together the sauce ingredients, then add a little sauce to the pan and mix with the meat. Push this mixture to one side of the pan, then arrange half the remaining ingredients in the other side of the pan. Pour over half the remaining sauce.

Cook over high heat for 3 to 4 minutes, turning the ingredients gently to cook both the top and bottom; do not overstir as the ingredients should still remain whole after cooking.

Push the cooked ingredients carefully to one side of the pan, then continue adding more ingredients and sauce to the pan while the guests are helping themselves to the cooked half.

If liked, provide each diner with an individual bowl into which he may crack an egg. The diner then mixes the egg with shoyu according to taste and dips morsels of hot food into this mixture; the heat of the food will cook the egg slightly.
SERVES 4-6

SHIMEJI
TREE OYSTER MUSHROOMS

The shimeji (tree oyster) mushroom has been cultivated in Japan for years as a fresh fungi 'vegetable'. It is now becoming more widely available because it can be grown easily under controlled conditions. This mushroom is occasionally referred to as the 'shellfish of the forest' because it has a slight shellfish flavour.*

250 g (8 oz) fresh shimeji* (oyster mushrooms)
1½ teaspoons butter
1 garlic clove, peeled and crushed
1 teaspoon sake*
3 tablespoons chicken stock
salt
freshly ground black pepper

METHOD: Tear the shimeji into bite-sized pieces. Melt the butter in a frying pan over low heat. Add the garlic and stir-fry for 30 seconds, then add the shimeji and sake. Stir-fry for 1 minute, then add the remaining ingredients and cook for 2 minutes. Serve immediately, as a side dish.
SERVES 4

NASU NO KARASHI
MUSTARD-PICKLED EGGPLANT

This spicy pickle will add spark to any dinner. It is an unusual way to blend ingredients.

1 medium eggplant
3 cups water
1 tablespoon salt
Dressing:
1 teaspoon dry mustard
3 tablespoons shoyu*
3 tablspoons mirin*
3 tablespoons sugar

METHOD: Cut the eggplant crossways into slices about 2.5 mm (⅛ inch) thick, then cut the slices into quarters. Soak in the water, with the salt added, for 1 hour.

Meanwhile, make the dressing. Put all the ingredients in a bowl and stir well.

Drain the eggplant and pat dry with kitchen paper towels. Arrange in a glass serving bowl and pour over the dressing.

Cover with plastic wrap and chill in the refrigerator for several hours or overnight before serving, to allow the flavours to develop.
SERVES 4

NIGIRI ZUSHI
RICE BALLS WITH TOPPING

This is the Japanese snack which is prepared at the popular sushi bars.

The tuna or bream topping given here can be replaced with prawns. These should be peeled, deveined and boiled briefly, with a toothpick inserted along the underside to prevent them curling. Cut them in half, keeping the back side intact, then place on top of the wasabi.*

Another variation is to serve the rice ovals topped with rectangular pieces of thin omelet. These make marvellous hors d'oeuvre.

1 tablespoon su* (rice vinegar)
1 quantity of Sushi (see page 144)
1 tablespoon (approximately) wasabi*, mixed to a paste with water
30 small slices (approximately) of raw fresh tuna or bream
To serve:
few parsley sprigs
few slices beni-shoga*
shoyu* to taste

METHOD: Moisten the hands with a little su. Scoop up 2 tablespoons rice in one hand then, with the other hand, squeeze the rice into an egg-shaped oval, about 5 cm (2 inches) long. Dab the top with wasabi paste, then cover with a slice of fish, pressing it down firmly. Repeat with the remaining rice, wasabi paste and fish, to make about 30 rice ovals.

Arrange the rice ovals on a tray and garnish with the parsley and beni-shoga. Hand shoya separately as a dip for the fish. Serve cold with plenty of green tea.
MAKES ABOUT 30

HORENSO TAMAGO MAKI
OMELET SPINACH ROLL

This dish presents spinach and egg together in an interesting way. The colourful green spinach encircled by the yellow of the omelet resembles a pretty flower.

375 g (12 oz) fresh spinach leaves, washed
¾ teaspoon shoyu*
2 eggs, lightly beaten
pinch of salt
1 teaspoon sugar
little vegetable oil
shoyu* to taste

METHOD: Drop the spinach into a pan of rapidly boiling water and boil for about 1½ minutes until the leaves are wilted and bright green. Drain and rinse twice in cold water.

Hold the spinach leaves, stems together, then squeeze out the water and trim off any hard stems. Sprinkle with the shoyu. Divide in half and shape into 2 long rolls.

Put the eggs, salt and sugar in a bowl and mix well (do not overbeat or the eggs will become frothy).

Heat a 20 cm (8 inch) frying pan. Coat the base of the pan with oil, then add half the egg mixture, twirling the pan so that the egg mixture coats the base. Cook over moderate heat, until the egg sets and the surface is dry to the touch.

Transfer to a sudare (bamboo mat) or clean cloth. Place one of the spinach rolls on the edge of the omelet. Roll up the omelet firmly, enclosing the spinach, using the mat or cloth as an outer support. Repeat with the remaining egg mixture and spinach.

Leave the rolls to rest for a few minutes, then carefully cut into 2.5 cm (1 inch) slices. Arrange on a serving plate. Serve cold, with a bowl of shoyu as a dip.
SERVES 4

GOHAN
PLAIN STEAMED RICE

The Japanese prefer medium or short grain rice because it cooks to a fluffy mass that clings together but is not sticky. This type of rice has an entirely different texture from long grain rice, which has a tendency to be drier with separate grains.

In Japan, a bowl of rice is usually eaten with every meal. It is generally served plain, with the entrée and side dishes. However, there are speciality dishes using rice with various combinations of meat, fish, poultry and vegetables.

The amount of water required to cook the rice will vary according to its origin and the length of time it has been stored since the harvest; the quantity given in this recipe is therefore only an approximate guide. If you are lucky enough to have an electric rice steamer, it will produce perfect rice every time you use it! No salt is added to plain rice in the cooking stage.

3 cups short or medium grain rice
3 cups water

METHOD: Wash the rice thoroughly under cold running water rubbing it well between the palms of the hands. Drain and repeat this process about 3 times until the rinsing water is clear. Leave to drain in a colander for about 20 minutes.

Put the rice in a heavy pan, add the water, then cover and bring quickly to the boil. Lower the heat and simmer for 20 minutes, by which time most of the water will have been absorbed; do not remove the lid at any stage. Increase the heat and cook for about 20 seconds, then remove the pan from the heat. Leave to stand for 10 minutes, without removing the lid.

Fluff up the rice with a wet rice paddle or a fork. Serve hot in individual rice bowls or on a large serving plate.
SERVES 4-6

▷ *Mustard-Pickled Eggplant (centre);*
Omelet Spinach Roll

NAPA NO TSUKEMONO
CABBAGE PICKLES

Pickles appear on every Japanese menu; they go especially well with the blandness of the rice and tea and they also help to clear the palate of lingering tastes such as fish.

Many methods are used to preserve vegetables. These include the use of brine, rice bran, soya bean paste and mustard. This recipe, using brine, is one of the simplest ways of preserving. If kept in the brine in the refrigerator, the napa* will keep for about 1 week.

1 large head of napa*, trimmed and quartered
3 tablespoons coarse salt
3 tablespoons seeded raisins or stoned prunes
1 cup water
3 dried chillis

METHOD: Put the napa in a large glass bowl, sprinkling the layers with the salt. Add the remaining ingredients and mix well until the salt has dissolved.

Place a saucer on top of the cabbage, put a heavy weight on top, then leave to marinate for 12 hours.

Discard the raisins or prunes and wash the cabbage quickly. Squeeze out the excess moisture, then slice the cabbage into bite-sized pieces. Serve cold.
SERVES 4-6

Note: For extra flavour, add a little shoyu* and freshly grated ginger*, mixed with a little sugar, before serving.

SUSHI
BASIC VINEGARED RICE

The basic recipe for making all kinds of sushi is to combine medium grain rice with a vinegared sauce, but the variations are endless. It can be made into Nigiri Zushi (see page 142), or Chirashi Zushi, a kind of rice salad in which the sushi is tossed with the salad ingredients. Another variation is Makizushi, a rice roll covered with nori* and filled with seasoned ingredients.

When making sushi, add a 15 cm (6 inch) piece of kombu* – if available – to the pan of rice. Cook for 3 minutes, then remove.

3 cups medium grain rice
3 cups water
Vinegar sauce:
5 tablespoons su* (rice vinegar)
4 tablespoons sugar
2 teaspoons salt
To garnish:
1-2 tablespoons toasted sesame seeds*
beni-shoga* or sansho* (optional)

METHOD: Wash the rice thoroughly under cold running water, rubbing it well between the palms of the hands. Drain and repeat this process about 3 times until the rinsing water is clear. Drain.

Put the rice in a heavy pan, add the water and leave to soak for 1 hour. Cover the pan and bring quickly to the boil, then reduce the heat to very low and simmer for 15 minutes; do not remove the lid at any stage.

Turn off the heat and leave the rice to steam in its own heat for 10 minutes, then remove from the heat and leave to stand for 10 minutes.

Meanwhile, make the vinegar sauce: put the sauce ingredients in a small pan (not aluminium) and heat until the sugar has dissolved, stirring constantly. Set aside until required.

Fluff up the rice with a wet rice paddle or large fork, then transfer to a large stainless steel or ceramic bowl. Pour the vinegar sauce over the hot rice. Toss thoroughly but lightly, lifting the rice from the bottom up with the wet rice paddle or fork to produce the desired lustre.

Serve hot, sprinkled with toasted sesame seeds and garnished with beni-shoga or sansho, if liked.
SERVES 4-6

SEKIHAN
STEAMED PINK RICE WITH BEANS

This pale pink rice is a celebration dish, prepared for special occasions such as birthdays. For the rice to acquire a pink colour, preparation must be started the day before the dish is required.

¾ cup azuki*
750 g (1½ lb) mochigome*
goma jio*, made with 1 teaspoons black sesame seeds* and 2 teaspoons salt

METHOD: Pick over and wash the azuki, then put them in a pan and cover with water. Bring to the boil, then drain, cover with fresh cold water and bring to the boil again. Lower the heat, cover with a lid and simmer gently for about 40 minutes, adding more water to keep the beans covered. Drain and reserve the cooking liquid.

Wash the mochigome thoroughly, drain and place in a bowl. Cover with the reserved azuki liquid and leave to stand overnight to allow the rice to acquire a pinkish colour.

Drain the rice and reserve the liquid. Mix the mochigome and azuki together, taking care not to crush the beans. Line a steamer plate, or other heatproof plate, with a piece of cheesecloth (muslin). Bring the water in the steamer to the boil, then spread the rice and bean mixture on the cloth, patting it smooth and making a few vent holes in it. Steam over high heat for about 50 minutes until the rice is cooked, basting every 12 minutes with the reserved azuki liquid.

Divide between warmed individual serving bowls and sprinkle with goma jio. Serve hot or at room temperature.
SERVES 8-10

▽ *Steamed Pink Rice with Beans; Chilled Noodles; Noodles with Broth*

TSUKIMI UDON
NOODLES WITH BROTH

Noodles are consumed in large quantities, and with great relish, in Japan. 'Slurping' is good etiquette and everyone eats noodles with their meals or as a snack. There are many varieties of noodle in Japan – thick and wide ones, coloured ones and ones made from buckwheat. This recipe uses the traditional thick, wide udon*, and the egg on top is like a full moon – the title of the dish literally translated means 'seeing the moon noodles'.

500 g (1 lb) udon*
4 cups Dashi (see page 130)
1 tablespoon sugar
1½ teaspoons salt
1 tablespoon shoyu*
4 eggs
To garnish:
2 green shallots, thinly sliced
13 cm (5 inch) square piece of nori*, toasted and finely shredded

METHOD: Add the noodles to a large pan of boiling water, stirring constantly. Bring back to the boil, then add 1 cup cold water. Bring back to the boil again, then cook the noodles for 6 to 8 minutes until *al dente*. Drain, then rinse thoroughly under cold running water and drain again.

Put the Dashi, sugar, salt and shoyu in a large pan and stir well. Bring to the boil over high heat, then add the noodles. Bring back to the boil, stirring constantly, then cook until the noodles are heated through.

Pour into warmed individual bowls, then break 1 egg over each bowl. Cover the bowls with lids and the heat from the noodles will cook the eggs. Garnish with green shallots and nori shreds. Serve hot.
SERVES 4

HIYASHI SOMEN
CHILLED NOODLES

This is a most unusual way to eat noodles; it is very refreshing in the summer and looks most attractive. Guests help themselves to the somen*, then use individual bowls of sauce as a dip. If liked, you can top the somen with boiled fresh prawns or seasoned shiitake*. Grated fresh ginger* or wasabi* can also be served as an accompaniment.

500 g (1 lb) somen* (thin vermicelli)
Sauce:
2 cups Dashi (see page 130)
½ cup shoyu*
4 tablespoons sake*
1 tablespoon sugar
To garnish:
few ice cubes
few small tomatoes, quartered
few green shallots, shredded

METHOD: Cook the somen in plenty of boiling water for about 5 minutes until *al dente*. Drain, rinse thoroughly under cold running water and drain again. Place in a large shallow glass serving bowl and chill in the refrigerator.

Put the sauce ingredients in a pan and stir well. Bring to the boil, then lower the heat and simmer for 2 minutes. Leave to cool, then pour into individual glass bowls and chill in the refrigerator.

Garnish the chilled sauce with ice cubes, tomatoes and green shallots. Serve the sauce separately.
SERVES 4

KASUTERA
SPONGE CAKE

This light cake is not normally baked in Japanese kitchens – it is usually purchased from one of the many pastry shops in Japan. It was originally introduced several centuries ago by the Dutch traders who came to the port of Nagasaki. In recent years, small electric ovens have become part of the Japanese kitchen, and these have made it possible for cakes such as this one to be baked at home.

5 eggs, beaten
⅔ cup sugar
¼ cup honey
¾ cup plain flour
¾ teaspoon baking powder
2 tablespoons icing sugar to decorate

METHOD: Put the eggs in a bowl, then gradually beat in the sugar and honey. Beat for about 10 minutes until thick and pale, using an electric beater if possible. Sift the flour and baking powder together, then fold gently into the egg mixture.

Pour the mixture into a greased and floured 23 cm (9 inch) square cake tin. Bake in a preheated moderate oven (180°C/350°F) for 30 minutes. Leave the cake in the tin for 10 minutes, then transfer to a wire rack and leave to cool completely.

Sprinkle with icing sugar. Cut into squares before serving.
MAKES ONE 23 CM (9 INCH) CAKE

MATCHA ICE CREAM
GREEN TEA ICE CREAM

This ice cream with its pale, minty colour, makes a beautiful ending to a Japanese meal.

600 ml (2½ cups) vanilla ice cream, softened
1 tablespoon matcha*
1 can sweetened azuki beans* (optional)

METHOD: Blend together the ice cream and matcha, then freeze until required. Scoop into individual serving dishes and top with sweetened azuki beans, if liked.
SERVES 4

MOMO NO KANTEN
PEACH 'GELATIN'

Serve with tea, either as a snack or a dessert. Canned unsweetened crushed pineapple may be substituted for the peach pulp, if liked.

1 long block kanten*
2 cups water
1½ cups sugar
½ cup fresh peach pulp
juice of ½ lemon
2 egg whites

METHOD: Wash the kanten under cold running water, then put in a pan, cover with the water and leave to soak for 20 to 30 minutes. Bring to the boil over moderate heat until completely melted, then add the sugar and stir until dissolved. Strain through a very fine sieve, then stir in the peach pulp and lemon juice and leave to cool.

Beat the egg whites until stiff, then gradually fold in the cooled liquid. Pour into a shallow tin and chill in the refrigerator until set. Cut into 2.5 cm (1 inch) squares or diamond shapes. Serve chilled.
MAKES ABOUT 24

ZENZAI OR SHIRUKO
RED BEAN SOUP WITH RICE DUMPLINGS

This soup is served as a sweet snack, rather than as a dessert. The rice used in these little dumplings is glutinous rice flour* — sticky and satisfying — for true rice eaters!

250 g (8 oz) azuki*
1¼ cups sugar
½ teaspoon salt
Dango (dumplings):
½ package mochiko*

METHOD: Pick over and wash the azuki, then put them in a pan with 6¼ cups water. Bring to the boil, then lower the heat and simmer for 2 hours until the beans are soft.

Add more water to the pan to make the liquid up to 5 cups (some of the water will have evaporated during cooking). Add the sugar and salt and cook for 15 minutes, stirring occasionally.

Meanwhile, make the dumplings: mix the mochiko with enough water to make a stiff dough. Knead well, then pinch off tiny portions to form small balls, about the size of marbles. Make a small indentation in the side of each dumpling.

Bring the azuki soup back to the boil, then drop the dumplings into the soup. Cook until the dumplings rise to the surface. Divide between warmed individual bowls. Serve hot.

SERVES 4

◁ *Green Tea Ice Cream; Peach 'Gelatin'*

Philippine cooking is a happy marriage of many fine foods from many different countries. Initially influenced by the Malays, Spanish, American, Chinese and Japanese, truc Philippine cuisine has developed into a rather unique one.

The Filipinos are a very hospitable people: they love to eat with friends and they love their fiestas and the related pageantry. Their fiestas date back to ancient Malay rites, probably as early as A.D. 1300 when the Malays came to the Philippine Islands. Since then the Spanish, Americans, Chinese and Japanese have all influenced the Filipino-Asian tropical diet, and Philippine cuisine has subsequently emerged as a rather unique, international one.

The use of certain vegetables, spices and cooking methods is reminiscent of the early strong Spanish influence, yet other foods definitely display the Chinese style of cooking. Being in the tropical zone, there is a great similarity to other South-East Asian countries in the abundance of tropical fruits, such as bananas, mangoes, coconuts, pomelos, guavas, papayas, custard apples and pineapples.

Traditions

The Filipinos are not such avid tea drinkers as the Japanese and the Chinese; they have their own favourite drinks. Tuba is a potent brew made from the fermented sap of the coconut palm, and basi, a sweeter but just as powerful drink made from fermented sugar-cane juice. They also enjoy coffee, rich hot chocolate and milk. The Spanish custom of *meriendas* is observed in the Philippines. During these morning or afternoon coffee breaks, cakes, tarts and sweet fritters are served. Glutinous (sweet) rice* is the basis of many of the sweet delicacies.

Banquets are prepared for most festive occasions, a roast suckling pig is cooked over hot coals and the table is laden with accompanying dishes and elaborate arrangements of fresh fruit. Everyday food is fairly simple. Full use is made of the wealth of seafood found in the waters surrounding the islands. Rice, fish and vegetables, fried or combined with meat, is the standard diet. Coconut is used extensively.

Ingredients

The Philippine Islanders enjoy the taste of their famous fish paste bagoong*, pronounced ba-go-ong, as well as patis*, the clear fish liquid sauce. Bagoong tastes a little like anchovies, although there are dozens of varieties. It is made by putting salt and fresh fish or shrimp in a ceramic pot and letting the mixture ferment for days or weeks. Bagoong comes as a thick paste, sometimes with bits of the fish still visible. Patis, on the other hand, is a clear amber liquid that has been strained, boiled and refined. In general, patis blends easily into soups and broths while bagoong, like a relish, is eaten with dry fish or chunky stews. Bagoong and patis appear at every Filipino meal – rather like the salt and pepper which we use.

The Filipinos are also famed for their adopo style of cooking. Pork, chicken or beef is marinated in vinegar with lots of garlic then simmered gently until the meat is tender. The cool tangy flavour of the vinegar results in a dish that has a distinct flavour. In its variations, adopo turns up everywhere. It can be cooked with coconut, bagoong and seafood enthusiasts like a version using small squid with the purplish 'ink' of the squid. The flavour of adopo stews seem to develop after cooking so if possible make them a day or two in advance.

Filipinos have a sweet tooth and pudding is usually served with a meal. They are famous for their wide range of creamy ice creams which are made from local fruit and other more unusual flavourings like yam.

Cooking utensils

A clay Lalayok is the old, traditional utensil used for cooking many Filipino soups, stews, casserole type dishes. Rice is also cooked in a lalayok which may be first lined with banana leaves to stop the rice burning to the bottom of the pot.

Today most modern city dwellers use western style saucepans, frying pans and casseroles. The traditional carajay – pronounced 'cara-hai' – is rounded like the Chinese wok and is useful for stir-fried noodle dishes.

Flat dinner plates are used along with knives, forks and spoons, and bowls are used for soup, so it is easy to cook and serve Filipino dishes in a western kitchen.

Filipino recipes do not yet have the universal appeal or variety of Chinese or Japanese foods, but the recipes in this chapter provide an introduction to this unusual cuisine.

Rice Fritters, a traditional Philippine snack, and the pudding, Leche Flan are evidence of the cosmopolitan influence on the cuisine of these beautiful islands.

HIPON REBOSADO
FRIED PRAWNS IN SWEET-SOUR SAUCE

Although there is a Chinese influence, sweet and sour sauce is seldom served in the Philippines – this is an exception. Serve as an appetizer.

24 raw prawns
½ teaspoon salt
freshly ground black pepper
vegetable oil for frying
Sauce:
2 tablespoons cornflour
1 cup cold water
½ cup cider vinegar
¼ cup dark brown sugar
1½ teaspoons salt
Batter:
1 cup flour
1 cup water
1 tablespoon vegetable oil
1 egg white

METHOD: Remove heads from prawns, then remove the shell down to the last segment leaving this and the tail intact. Make a deep incision down the back of each prawn and remove the intestine with the point of a knife. Wash under cold water, pat dry with kitchen paper towels and season with salt and pepper.

To make the sauce, in a small saucepan combine the cornflour with a little of the water and stir until it forms a smooth paste, then add the remaining water, vinegar, sugar and salt. Bring slowly to the boil, stirring, then set aside and keep warm.

To make the batter, place the flour in a deep bowl, make a well in the centre, and add the water and vegetable oil. Gradually stir in the flour with a fork to form a smooth creamy batter. Beat the egg white to a stiff froth and fold in.

Pour the oil for frying into a wok or deep frying pan to a depth of 5 cm (2 inches) and heat until a light haze forms above it. Holding the prawns by the tail dip into the batter and drop immediately into the hot oil. Fry 4 at a time, turning them once, until golden and crisp. Transfer them to a dish lined with crumpled paper and keep warm.

To serve, arrange on a heated platter and serve with the hot sweet-sour sauce.
SERVES 4

ESCABECHE
HOT PICKLED FISH

As fish is plentiful in the seas surrounding the Philippine Islands, it features a great deal in Philippine cooking.

This method of preparing fish is the most common in Philippine cuisine, and it is the result of the many different foreign influences.

1 kg (2-2¼ lb) cleaned snapper, sea bream or other white fish
salt
flour for coating
3 tablespoons vegetable oil
3 garlic cloves, peeled and crushed
1 teaspoon grated fresh ginger*
1 large onion, peeled and thinly sliced into rings
1 large green pepper, cored, seeded and sliced into 5 mm (¼ inch) strips
1 tablespoon cornflour
1½ cups water
3 tablespoons cider vinegar
1 tablespoon brown sugar

METHOD: Wash the fish, pat dry with kitchen paper towels. Leave the fish whole or slice into steaks, then sprinkle lightly with salt and flour.

Heat a frying pan over moderate heat. Add 2 tablespoons oil, then add the fish. Fry until the fish is crisp and brown on all sides, then remove from the pan and set aside.

Add the remaining oil to the pan with the garlic and ginger. Fry until brown, then add the onion and green pepper. Stir-fry for 1 minute, then remove from the pan and set aside.

Mix the cornflour to a paste with a little of the water, then add to the pan with the remaining water, the vinegar, sugar and ½ teaspoon salt. Bring to the boil, then lower the heat and simmer until thickened, stirring constantly. Add the fish, bring the sauce back to the boil, then cover and cook for about 5 minutes.

Add the fried vegetables to the fish in the pan and stir-fry the mixture for 1 minute to heat through.

Carefully transfer the fish to a warmed serving dish. Arrange the vegetables around the fish. Taste and adjust the seasoning of the sauce, then pour over the fish and vegetables. Serve the hot pickled fish immediately.
SERVES 4-6

GUINATAAN HIPON
PRAWNS IN COCONUT

Serve this dish hot with a steaming bowl of boiled rice.

750 g (1½ lb) raw prawns
2 cups thick coconut milk*
4 cloves garlic, chopped
2 teaspoons grated fresh ginger*
1 teaspoon salt
freshly ground black pepper

METHOD: Wash prawns but do not shell them. Put into a saucepan with remaining ingredients and bring to the boil, stirring. Reduce heat and simmer uncovered for 15 minutes, stirring frequently.
SERVES 6

TINOLA
CHICKEN GINGER SOUP

2 half breasts chicken
3 chicken marylands
4 tablespoons vegetable oil
1½ teaspoons grated fresh ginger*
1 onion, thinly sliced
1 teaspoon salt
6 cups water
4-5 young spinach leaves, or 2 silverbeet leaves, cut into 5 cm (2 inch) pieces

METHOD: Cut each chicken breast into 3, sever drumsticks and cut each drumstick and thigh into 2.

Heat 2 tablespoons of the oil in a medium saucepan, add the ginger and onion and cook, stirring, for about 5 minutes; do not allow to brown. Transfer to a small plate and set aside.

Add the remaining oil to the pan and brown chicken on all sides – this is best done in several lots; do not overcrowd the pan. Return all the chicken, ginger and onion to the pan, add the salt and water and bring to the boil. Reduce heat and partially cover the pan, then simmer for 30 to 40 minutes. Remove from heat, add spinach leaves and serve.
SERVES 6

◁ *Deep-Fried Prawn Cakes*

UKOY
DEEP-FRIED PRAWN CAKES

In the Philippines, traditional cooks like to leave the prawns in their shells for this dish.

½ cup boiling water
10 medium raw prawns, shelled and deveined
1 teaspoon ground paprika
1 teaspoon salt
½ cup rice flour*
½ cup cornflour
1 sweet potato (about 250 g/8 oz), peeled and coarsely grated
1 medium butternut squash (about 375 g/12 oz), peeled, seeded and coarsely grated
2 cups vegetable oil
¼ cup finely chopped green shallot
Garlic Sauce (page 152)

METHOD: Combine the water, prawns, paprika and salt in a heavy saucepan and bring to the boil over high heat. Reduce the heat to low and simmer for about 3 minutes or until the prawns are firm and pink. Transfer the prawns to the kitchen paper towels and strain the cooking liquid through a fine sieve into a bowl. Measure the liquid, add enough fresh water to make 1 cup and set aside.

In a deep bowl, combine the rice flour and cornflour. Pour in the prawn cooking liquid and beat until the liquid is absorbed. Then add the grated sweet potato and squash and beat vigorously with a wooden spoon until the mixture is well combined.

Pour the oil into a heavy frying pan. The oil should be about 1 cm (½ inch) deep; if necessary add more. Heat the oil until it is very hot but not smoking.

To make each cake, spoon about ⅓ cup of the vegetable mixture onto a saucer, sprinkle a teaspoon or two of the green shallots on top and lightly press a prawn into the centre. Then holding the saucer close to the surface of the oil, slide the ukoy into it with the aid of a spoon. Fry the cakes, 3 or 4 at a time, for about 3 minutes, spooning the oil over each cake; then turn them carefully and fry for another 3 minutes, regulating the heat so they colour richly and evenly without burning. As each ukoy browns transfer it to kitchen paper towels to drain.

While they are still hot, arrange the ukoy, prawn side up, on a heated platter and moisten each cake with a little of the garlic sauce. Pour the remaining sauce into a bowl or sauceboat. Serve at once garnished with cooked, shelled prawns and lemon slices.
MAKES 10

LUMPIA
FILLED EGG ROLLS

Lumpia may be eaten 'fresh' or deep-fried, and the variety of fillings is endless, depending on the cook's culinary imagination and what happens to be available. They are always served with a distinctive brown dipping sauce and sometimes a vinegary garlic sauce (see Garlic Sauce, right).

Ready-made wrappers are sold in specialist stores, but they can easily be made at home, following this recipe for 'fresh' lumpia.

Filling:
3 tablespoons vegetable oil
1 large onion, peeled and sliced
2 garlic cloves, peeled and crushed
250 g (8 oz) boned pork, diced
60 g (2 oz) cooked ham, chopped
125 g (4 oz) prawns, peeled and chopped
½ cup cooked garbanzo beans*
1 medium carrot, peeled and cut into julienne strips
250 g (8 oz) green beans, topped, tailed and cut into julienne strips
1 cup diced, parboiled potatoes
2 cups shredded cabbage
1 teaspoon salt, or to taste
Wrappers:
2 eggs, separated
½ cup cornflour
1 cup water
vegetable oil for frying
18-20 small lettuce leaves
Brown dipping sauce:
1 cup chicken stock
2 tablespoons light soy sauce
5 tablespoons brown sugar
1 teaspoon salt
2 tablespoons cornflour
1 garlic clove, peeled and crushed
To garnish:
parsley sprigs

METHOD: To make the filling, heat a wok or deep frying pan over low heat. Add the oil, then the onion and garlic. Fry gently for a few minutes, then add the pork, ham, prawns and beans. Cook gently for about 2 minutes. Add the vegetables, except the cabbage, cover and simmer for about 5 minutes, then add the cabbage and salt. Cover again and cook until the vegetables are tender but still crisp. Drain off any excess liquid, then leave to cool. To make the wrappers: beat the egg whites until stiff. Beat the egg yolks lightly, then add to the whites. Blend the cornflour and water together, then add to the egg mixture and mix well.

Heat a 20 cm (8 inch) frying pan over moderate heat and brush with oil. Pour about 2 tablespoons of the batter into the pan, tilting the pan so that the mixture spreads to cover the base thinly. Cook until set and firm, like a thin pancake, then remove from the pan and set aside while cooking the remainder.

Put 1 lettuce leaf on each wrapper, then put a spoonful of the prepared cooled filling in the centre. Fold the bottom end over the fillings, then roll up to enclose the filling completely. Arrange the lumpia on a serving dish.

To make the sauce: put all the ingredients except the garlic in a pan. Mix well and cook gently until the mixture thickens, stirring constantly. Float the garlic on top of the sauce. Arrange 2 lumpias on each serving plate, spoon a little sauce over the top and garnish with parsley. Serve at room temperature.

MAKES 18-20

GARLIC SAUCE

This pungent sauce is served as an accompaniment to fried Lumpia (see left) and Ukoy (see page 151).

8 garlic cloves
1½ teaspoons salt
1 cup malt or cider vinegar

METHOD: With the flat of a broad kitchen knife smash each clove of garlic. Remove outside skins. Sprinkle salt over the garlic and, using the broad of the knife or the back of a wooden spoon, crush the garlic and salt to a smooth paste. Put into a small bowl and stir in the vinegar vigorously with a spoon to mix the ingredients thoroughly, or blend in an electric blender.

MAKES 1 CUP

ADOBONG MANOK
CHICKEN ADOBO WITH COCONUT

The tang of vinegar is characteristic of adobo-style cooking and gives a distinctive flavour to many Philippine dishes. It is said this dish is best 1 or even 2 days after cooking.

4 half breasts chicken
3 chicken marylands
4 garlic cloves, chopped
½ cup cider vinegar
1 teaspoon salt
½ teaspoon whole peppercorns
2 tablespoons light soy sauce
1½ cups water
3 tablespoons lard or oil
2 tablespoons thick coconut milk*

METHOD: Cut chicken breasts in two. Sever drumsticks from thighs and cut off knuckle ends. Put into a bowl with the garlic, vinegar, salt, peppercorns and soy sauce. Marinate for 30 minutes.

Place the chicken mixture in a saucepan with the water, bring to the boil, reduce heat and simmer covered for 20 minutes. Remove the chicken then, over medium heat, boil the liquor until reduced to ¾ cup.

Heat the lard or oil in a frying pan, add the chicken and brown on both sides – do not overcrowd the pan; this is best done in two lots. Remove chicken pieces to a hot platter as they are done and keep warm. Heat the sauce, add the coconut milk and cook for 1 minute. Spoon the sauce over the chicken and serve.
SERVES 6

CHICKEN AND PORK EN ADOBO
CHICKEN AND PORK STEW

Adobo is a cooking style rather than a recipe, and there are as many variations as there are cooks who make it. This version is a spicy combination of pork and chicken, but it can be made with only one meat if preferred. It tastes better 2 to 3 days after it has been cooked, but it is so good that there is rarely any left to be kept for later!

1 kg (2 lb) boned lean pork, cut into chunks
500 g (1 lb) chicken breast meat, cut into chunks
1 garlic clove, peeled and crushed
2 bay leaves
2 medium onions, peeled and quartered
½ cup cider vinegar
1 tablespoon soy sauce
salt
freshly ground black pepper
1½ cups water
1 tablespoon lard or oil

METHOD: Put the pork and chicken in a pan, then add the garlic, bay leaves, onions, vinegar, soy sauce and salt and pepper to taste. Stir well, then leave to marinate for 30 minutes.

Add the water to the pan and bring to the boil. Lower the heat and simmer for 45 minutes to 1 hour, until the meat is tender and the cooking liquid has reduced to about ½ cup. Remove meat from pan, strain the cooking liquid and reserve.

Melt the lard in the cleaned pan. Add the pork and chicken and fry over brisk heat until browned. Add the reserved cooking liquid and simmer for about 5 minutes.

Serve hot with rice.
SERVES 6-8

△ *Chicken and Pork Stew; Filled Egg Rolls*

PANCIT GUISADO
NOODLES WITH MEAT AND VEGETABLES

There are many variations of pancit; it can be prepared with any kind of meat that is available. It is similar to Chinese chow mein, and no doubt the Chinese have influenced the dish.

250 g (8 oz) miti*
3 tablespoons vegetable oil
1 garlic clove, peeled and crushed
250 g (8 oz) boned lean pork, thinly sliced
250 g (8 oz) chicken breast meat, thinly sliced
250 g (8 oz) fresh prawns, peeled, deveined and diced
1 medium onion, peeled and thinly sliced
1 cup shredded cabbage
2 tablespoons patis*
¾ cup chicken stock
pinch of paprika
½ teaspoon salt
freshly ground black pepper
To garnish:
2 hard-boiled eggs, quartered
2 green shallots, chopped
few lemon wedges

METHOD: Cook the noodles in boiling water for about 2 minutes until slightly undercooked. Drain, rinse under cold running water, then drain again. Place in a bowl with 1 tablespoon of the oil and mix.

Heat a wok or deep frying pan over moderate heat. Add 1 tablespoon of the oil, then add the noodles. Fry until golden brown on all sides, then remove the noodles from the pan and set aside.

Wipe the pan clean with kitchen paper towels, then add 1 tablespoon of the oil and the garlic. Fry until the garlic is brown, then add the pork and fry for 5 minutes. Add the chicken and prawns, stir-fry for 2 minutes over high heat, then remove all the ingredients from the pan; set aside.

Wipe the pan clean again with kitchen paper towels and place over high heat. When it is very hot, add the remaining oil, then the onion and cabbage. Stir-fry for about 4 minutes until the onion is translucent but the cabbage is still undercooked and crunchy.

Add the remaining ingredients, stir well, then add the cooked meat and fish mixture. Heat through for 2 minutes until most of the juices have evaporated, stirring constantly.

Add the noodles to the pan, toss well and cook until heated through.

Pile on to a warmed serving dish. Garnish with the eggs, green shallots and lemon wedges. Serve hot.
SERVES 4-6

CHICKEN WITH SOTANGHON
CHICKEN AND NOODLES

Sotanghon is the Philippines name for cellophane noodles. Annatto seeds are small red seeds which are used for colouring Filipino food; as these are, as yet, unobtainable in Australia, a good substitute is a mixture of paprika and turmeric.*

2 chicken breasts
2 chicken marylands
6 cups water
salt
2 onions, sliced
2 tablespoons vegetable oil
2 garlic cloves, crushed
1 teaspoon paprika
1 teaspoon turmeric
freshly ground black pepper
185 g (6 oz) cellophane noodles*, soaked and cut into 2.5 cm (1 inch) lengths
8 Chinese dried mushrooms, soaked for 30 minutes in warm water, then stems discarded and caps chopped
8 green shallots, shredded diagonally

△ *Chicken and Noodles; Noodles with Meat and Vegetables*

METHOD: Put chicken pieces in a saucepan, add the water, 1 teaspoon salt and 1 sliced onion, and bring to the boil. Cover, reduce the heat and simmer for 20 to 25 minutes. Remove chicken, strain stock and reserve. Remove chicken bones and, if liked, the skin from the flesh. Reserve chicken flesh.

Heat the oil in a saucepan and gently fry the remaining onion and garlic until soft and golden. Add the paprika, turmeric and reserved chicken stock, salt and freshly ground pepper to taste, and bring to the boil. Add the drained noodles and mushrooms and simmer, half-covered, for 15 minutes. Add the shredded shallots and serve.
SERVES 6

CAMOTO FRITO
SWEET POTATO CHIPS

These delicious crisps can be served hot, sprinkled with icing sugar in the Filipino manner or with salt in the Western style.

1 kg (2 lb) sweet potatoes
vegetable oil for deep-frying
icing sugar or salt

METHOD: Peel the sweet potatoes and cut them into paper-thin slices. Drop the slices into a bowl of water with a few ice cubes and stand for 15 minutes.

Pour oil into a wok or deep-fat fryer to a depth of 6 cm (2½ inches) and heat. Drain the sweet potatoes and dry thoroughly on kitchen paper towels. When oil is heated and a light haze forms, place the chips (in several batches) in a frying basket or scoop and lower into the hot oil. Let them fry for 3 to 4 minutes or until they are a light golden colour. As they brown, transfer to kitchen paper towels to drain. Serve warm.
SERVES 4-6

PAELLA
RICE WITH PORK, CHICKEN AND SEAFOOD

This is not unlike the famous Spanish dish of rice and things from land and sea – the Spanish made a lasting impact on the food of the Philippines.

1.5 kg (3 lb) chicken joints (breasts, thighs)
500 g (1 lb) pork spareribs
2 chorizos (spicy Spanish sausage) (optional)
500 g (1 lb) raw prawns, shelled and deveined
4 tablespoons olive oil
2 onions, sliced
½ teaspoon saffron threads, soaked in 1 tablespoon boiling water for 30 minutes
4 garlic cloves
2 cups long grain rice, washed
3 tomatoes, peeled, seeded and quartered
4 cups boiling chicken stock
1 cup green peas
2 canned pimientos

METHOD: Cut chicken breast and thighs in two. Cut spareribs into 2.5 cm (1 inch) slices. Poach the chorizos in water to cover for about 5 minutes, then drain. Wash the prawns.

In a large frying pan heat 2 tablespoons of the oil and quickly fry the chicken, then the pork, then the sausages on all sides for just long enough to brown them. Cut sausages in 3 or 4 lengths. Set aside.

Add remaining oil to pan and fry the onions until soft and golden, then add the garlic and cook for 30 seconds. Add the rice and fry, stirring, until each grain is coated with oil. Add tomatoes, boiling stock, and the saffron with its liquid, and cook, stirring, until stock comes to the boil.

Add the browned chicken, pork and chorizos, arranging them in a pattern on top of the rice. Scatter over the peas, cover (if you have no lid, use a large sheet of aluminium foil) and cook over a low heat for 15 minutes. Add the prawns, pushing them into the rice, cover and cook for a further 15 minutes. Add more stock if the surface appears to dry out. Decorate with strips of pimiento.
SERVES 6-8

COCONUT ICE CREAM

There are many delicious ice creams made in the Philippines; fruit flavours are popular and one of the best is this rich coconut ice.

1½ cups milk
1 cup desiccated coconut
1½ cups cream
2 eggs
2 egg yolks
½ cup sugar
¼ teaspoon salt

METHOD: Scald the milk, desiccated coconut and cream in a heavy saucepan over a low heat. This should be done very slowly, taking about 15 to 20 minutes. Push the mixture through a fine sieve, squeezing out as much of the coconut as possible. Discard the coconut.

Using electric beaters, beat the eggs and egg yolks in a heatproof bowl until thick and mousse-like. Place the bowl over a saucepan of boiling water, stir in some of the rich scalded coconut milk, then add the remaining coconut milk and cook, stirring, until thick (the mixture should coat the back of a metal spoon). Remove from heat and cool quickly over cold water, stirring occasionally. Pour mixture into metal ice cream trays. Cover with foil or waxed paper.

Place in freezing compartment pre-set to maximum or coldest setting. Allow mixture to semi-freeze. Transfer to a chilled mixing bowl, break up and beat thoroughly. Replace mixture in ice cream trays, cover and freeze until frozen hard, about 2 to 3 hours. Store in freezing compartment at normal setting.
MAKES ABOUT 3½ CUPS

Note: If you have an electric sorbetier or ice cream maker follow manufacturer's instructions. As a general guide: make the ice cream mixture, pour it into the sorbetier and put in the freezer. Switch machine on and process until firm. Remove paddle, store as above.

As a general rule homemade ice creams tend to freeze harder than bought ones. They reach their peak of flavour and texture after ripening for 2 to 6 hours and are best eaten within 48 hours of being made.

LECHE FLAN
CARAMEL CUSTARD

Inherited from the Spanish, this version of the French Crème Renversée au Caramel is made with evaporated milk which is used in many desserts in the Pacific and gives a distinctive flavour. Lime is also a popular flavour for the flan.

½ cup sugar
½ cup water
1½ cups canned evaporated milk
1 cup milk
3 whole eggs
2 egg yolks
½ cup caster sugar
2 teaspoons vanilla essence or 4 teaspoons grated lime rind

METHOD: Put sugar and water into a small saucepan and heat without stirring until a caramel colour. Pour into a 6-cup oven-proof dish – a soufflé dish is ideal.

Gently heat the evaporated milk and fresh milk. In a large bowl beat the eggs and egg yolks with the caster sugar. Gradually beat in the hot milk then add the vanilla or grated lime rind. Strain the custard and pour into the caramel mould.

Set mould in a baking dish and pour in boiling water to come halfway up the side of the mould. Bake in a moderately slow oven (160°C/325°F) for 35 to 40 minutes. Remove from oven and cool. When cold, cover and chill in refrigerator overnight.

To serve, run a knife around the edge, invert a chilled serving plate over the mould then, grasping them firmly, turn them over so the flan slips out onto the serving plate. Serve chilled.
SERVES 6-8

BOMBONES DE ARROZ
RICE FRITTERS

As is the case in many Asian countries, rice is often used as an ingredient for desserts. These are not eaten after a meal in the Western manner, but as snacks between meals.

1 cup cooked medium grain rice
2 eggs, beaten
3 tablespoons sugar
½ teaspoon vanilla essence
½ cup plain flour
1 tablespoon baking powder
pinch of salt
¼ cup desiccated coconut
vegetable oil for deep-frying
sifted icing sugar for sprinkling

METHOD: Put the rice, eggs, sugar and vanilla in a bowl and mix well. Sift together the flour, baking powder and salt, then stir into the rice mixture. Stir in the desiccated coconut.

Heat the oil in a deep-fat fryer to 180°C/350°F. Drop tablespoonfuls of the mixture into the hot oil, one at a time, and deep-fry until golden brown on all sides. Drain on kitchen paper towels. Transfer the rice fritters to a serving dish, then sprinkle with a generous amount of icing sugar. Serve hot.
MAKES ABOUT 20

▽ *Coconut Ice Cream; Rice Fritters*

This area comprises of such a variety of races, landscapes and cultures that shared cooking and eating traditions would seem unlikely. Surprisingly, there is a certain similarity among the recipes in the region due to the exchange of foodstuffs, goods, spices and culinary ideas across the South China Sea.

Many dishes of Malaysia, Singapore and Indonesia show how this South-East Asian cuisine has been affected by travellers and immigrants: there is evidence of Indian, Chinese, Dutch and even British influence but all dishes are essentially local in origin and flavour; in the Indonesian word – asli.

There are other common factors. The Malay Peninsula and the islands share a tropical monsoon climate and large areas are extremely fertile. The South China Sea contains plenty of fish and seafood. The staple food is rice, which is harvested with appropriate ceremony from the flooded fields or sawah which make a mosaic of the contours of every hillside. Spices are important, especially cumin, galingale*, lemon grass*, ginger, cloves, tamarind*, cinnamon and turmeric.

Cooking Techniques and Utensils

People tend to cook in the same way throughout the area. Charcoal stoves are used to provide the intense heat needed for rapid frying or grilling.

Meat and vegetables are usually cut into small pieces before cooking, either to enable them to be cooked very quickly, or to increase the absorption of spice and sauce flavourings during slow simmering.

Almost all the essential utensils needed for Indonesian and Malaysian cooking can be found in any kitchen anywhere in the world. There are three special items, however, that are worth buying if Indonesian and Malaysian dishes are to be cooked often. The first is a wajan, a round-bottomed frying pan which is more generally known by its Chinese name of wok. It sits comfortably on a charcoal stove or gas ring and is ideally shaped to spread heat evenly while stir-frying. A wajan is, however, unsuitable for cooking on an electric hotplate (although it can be used with the aid of a ring that fits around the wok). A wide, flat-bottomed, heavy pan can be used instead.

The second item is a rice steamer which is a very useful piece of equipment for all Oriental cooking where rice is to be cooked often, because it practically guarantees perfectly cooked rice every time.

The third item, which is perhaps the most important, is an ulek-ulek (pestle) and a cobek (mortar) made of wood or stone. Many of the recipes in this chapter require garlic, chillis and other ingredients to be pounded to a paste and although this can be achieved in an electric blender, care must be taken not to let the paste get too watery.

Ingredients

Apart from rice and spices, many other specialist ingredients are widely used throughout the Indonesian-Malaysian world. Coconut palms grow every-

where and the coconut flesh and oil are added to many meat dishes and sweets. Santen* (coconut milk) is made by pressing the natural oils out of the flesh of the coconut and mixing them with water. It is used constantly, and imparts a distinctive but delicate flavour to dishes.

Another ingredient widely used is the pungent, dark-coloured shrimp paste which the Indonesians call terasi*; use in tiny quantities.

Three different chillis give Indonesian food its hot reputation: lombok hijau* (green), lombok merah* (red) and lombok rawit*. It is true that Indonesians are accustomed to eating hot peppers and find it hard to go without them, but this does not mean that all Indonesian food has to be hot; any of the recipes given here can equally well be made with little or no chilli. Boiled rice or a few slices of raw cucumber will cool the mouth quickly if too much chilli has been eaten.

Serving

Although an everyday family meal may simply consist of rice, served with one or two dishes of vegetables and possibly a little meat or fish, even the most minor social occasion in Malaysia, Indonesia or Singapore calls for plenty of good food. Any celebration is likely to be accompanied by an elaborate array of side dishes, relishes, sauces, Serundeng (see page 163), Krupuk (see page 163) and huge amounts of rice. The Dutch in the islands adapted the custom for their own use and called it rijsttafel*, or rice table. There are no separate courses at a meal of this kind, but the sweet usually appears some time towards the end of the meal.

Almost all the dishes in this chapter can be eaten with a fork. A spoon is useful when eating dishes which have a sauce, or large quantities of rice. Chopsticks are not used for Indonesian or Malaysian food.

China tea is a good drink to take with food of this kind.

Origins

The country or origin of a recipe is given in many recipes. If no origin is given, the dish belongs about equally to Singapore, Malaysia and Indonesia.

Lamb Sate, one of the most popular of Indonesian dishes, served with the accompaniments of Peanut and Chilli Sauces.

SOTO MADURA
SPICY BEEF SOUP
INDONESIA

This is a rich meaty soup which can be served as a first course, or with other dishes as part of a main course.

7 cups water
500 g (1 lb) boned brisket or beef, trimmed
salt
freshly ground black pepper
90 g (3 oz) peeled green prawns
4 macadamias or kemiri*
6 brown shallots or 1 onion, peeled and sliced
3 garlic cloves, peeled
2 teaspoons grated fresh ginger*
2 tablespoons corn oil
1 teaspoon ground turmeric
½ teaspoon ground chilli (optional)
To garnish:
1 tablespoon chopped coriander leaves*
1 tablespoon chopped onion, fried
4 lemon slices

METHOD: Bring the water to the boil in a large pan. Add the beef with a little salt and pepper, then cover and simmer for 40 minutes.

Strain and reserve the cooking liquid. Cut the beef into small cubes, discarding any fat and gristle.

Mince or finely chop in a blender the prawns, kemiri, 3 shallots, garlic and ginger. Heat 1 tablespoon of the oil in a pan, add the minced mixture and fry for 1 minute. Stir in the turmeric and half the reserved cooking liquid. Cover and simmer for 15 minutes.

Meanwhile, finely chop the remaining shallots. Heat the remaining oil in a large pan, add the shallots and fry until golden brown. Add the beef, 2 tablespoons of the reserved cooking liquid, a little salt and the chilli powder, if using. Cover and simmer for 2 minutes.

Strain the prawn and macadamia liquid into the beef mixture, then add the remaining reserved cooking liquid. Bring to the boil, then lower the heat, cover and simmer for 40 to 50 minutes.

Taste and adjust the seasoning, then pour into a warmed soup tureen. Garnish with the coriander, onion and lemon slices.
SERVES 6

SOTO AYAM
SPICED CHICKEN SOUP

6 cups water
1.2 kg (2½ lb) chicken, quartered
4 green King prawns, halved and deveined
salt
freshly ground black pepper
2 macadamias or kemiri*, chopped
4 brown shallots or 1 onion, peeled and chopped
2 garlic cloves, peeled and chopped
2 teaspoons grated fresh ginger*
pinch of ground turmeric
pinch of chilli powder
vegetable oil for shallow frying
1 tablespoon light soy sauce
1 cup bean sprouts, washed
1 potato, peeled and sliced into very thin rounds
To garnish:
few lemon slices
coriander leaves*

METHOD: Bring the water to the boil in a large pan. Add the chicken, prawns and salt and pepper to taste, then cover and simmer for 40 minutes.

Strain and reserve 5 cups of the cooking liquid. Shred the meat from the chicken. Shell the prawns and discard the heads, then cut each into 4 or 5 pieces.

Put the macadamias, brown shallots, garlic and ginger in a *cobek* or electric blender and grind to a very smooth paste. Add the ground turmeric and chilli powder and mix well.

Heat 2 tablespoons oil in a wok or deep frying pan, add the spice paste and fry for a few seconds. Stir in 1¼ cups of the reserved cooking liquid, the soy sauce, chicken and prawns. Simmer for 10 minutes, then add the remaining cooking liquid and simmer for a further 10 minutes. Add the washed bean sprouts, taste and adjust the seasoning if necessary, then continue cooking for 3 minutes.

Meanwhile, heat a little oil in a frying pan, add the potato slices and fry until crisp on both sides.

Divide the potato slices equally between 4 to 6 warmed soup bowls. Ladle the soup into bowls, then garnish with the lemon slices and coriander. Serve hot.
SERVES 4-6

SAYUR LODEH JAKARTA
CREAMY VEGETABLE SOUP
INDONESIA

This soup becomes a rich vegetable stew if more vegetables are added and the quantity of water decreased. It can then be served as one of the side dishes at a rijsttafel*.

1 medium eggplant, sliced
salt
4 macadamias or kemeri*, chopped
4 brown shallots or 1 small onion, peeled and finely sliced
1 teaspoon terasi* (dried shrimp paste)
2 garlic cloves, peeled and chopped
1 red or green chilli, chopped (optional)
30 g (1 oz) ebi* (dried shrimps)
5 cups water
2 teaspoons ground coriander
pinch ground sereh*
2 daun jerek purut*
½ teaspoon brown sugar
60 g (2 oz) green beans, topped, tailed and cut into 2.5 cm (1 inch) lengths
60 g (2 oz) white cabbage, shredded, or cauliflower florets, chopped
60 g (2 oz) bamboo shoots, finely sliced
60 g (2 oz) watercress, stalks removed (optional)
60 g (2 oz) creamed coconut*

METHOD: Sprinkle the eggplant slices with salt, leave to stand for 30 minutes, then rinse under cold running water.

Meanwhile, put the macadamias in a *cobek* or blender with the shallots, shrimp paste, garlic and chilli and work to a very smooth paste. Transfer to a small pan. Add the dried shrimps and ½ cup water and boil for 2 to 3 minutes.

Strain the liquid into a clean pan. Add the remaining water, coriander, sereh, daun jeruk purut and sugar. Bring to the boil, then add the vegetables except the watercress. Simmer for 5 minutes.

Add the watercress, if using, and the creamed coconut and simmer until the coconut has dissolved, stirring constantly. Taste and adjust the seasoning, then pour into a warmed soup tureen. Serve hot.
SERVES 4

◁ *Spiced Grilled Soup; Prawn and Vermicelli Soup*

MIE BAKSO
NOODLE SOUP WITH MEATBALLS
INDONESIA

Bakso or baso, is a cake or ball made of meat, fish, prawns or bean curd, or a combination of these. In this recipe, the bakso is made with beef. The meatballs may be made in advance to avoid preparing and cooking just before serving.

Soup:
125 g (4 oz) egg noodles
salt
2 tablespoons vegetable oil
3 brown shallots, peeled and finely sliced
2 garlic cloves, peeled and finely sliced
1 teaspoon grated fresh ginger*
1 tablespoon light soy sauce
6 cups beef stock
4 green shallots, cut into thin rounds
2 carrots, peeled and cut into thin rounds
60 g (2 oz) snow peas, topped and tailed
3 Chinese cabbage leaves, finely sliced
freshly ground black pepper
Meatballs:
250 g (8 oz) lean beef
3 tablespoons cornflour
1 egg white
2 teaspoons coarse sea salt

METHOD: Bring a large pan of water to the boil. Add the noodles and ½ teaspoon salt and boil for 5 minutes. Drain, rinse under cold running water, then drain and set aside.

To make the meatballs, work the beef through the fine blade of a mincer several times, or chop finely in a food processor, until it is almost a paste. Transfer to a bowl, add the cornflour, egg white and salt and pepper to taste. Mix well, then shape into small balls, about the size of marbles. Drop them one by one into a bowl containing 3 cups water and the coarse sea salt.

Bring 2½ cups water to the boil in a large pan. Add a pinch of salt, then remove the meatballs from the salted water with a slotted spoon and drop them one at a time into the boiling water. Boil for 5 to 8 minutes, then drain and set aside.

Just before serving, heat the oil in a large pan. Add the shallots and garlic and fry for 1 minute, stirring continuously. Add the ginger, soy sauce, stock, green shallots and carrots. Simmer for 5 minutes, then add the snow peas and cabbage leaves. Taste and adjust the seasoning, then simmer for a further 3 to 4 minutes.

Add the noodles and meatballs, increase the heat and cook for a further 1 minute. Serve immediately.
SERVES 6-8

LAKSA LEMAK
PRAWN AND VERMICELLI SOUP
SINGAPORE

This soup is traditionally garnished with Sambal Bajak (see page 180), but since this is hot and spicy, you may prefer to serve it in a separate bowl so that guests can help themselves according to taste.

2½ cups water
125 g (4 oz) pork fillet or chicken breast meat
salt
freshly ground black pepper
185 g (6 oz) laksa* (rice vermicelli)
1½ tablespoons vegetable oil
5 brown shallots or 1 small onion, peeled and finely sliced
4 green shallots, cut into 1 cm (½ inch) lengths
2 garlic cloves, peeled and crushed
1 teaspoon ground ginger
1 teaspoon ground coriander
½ teaspoon ground turmeric
185 g (6 oz) peeled green prawns
1¼ cups thick santen* (coconut milk)
600 g (2 × 11 oz blocks) tahu* (bean curd), cut into thick strips
2 cups bean sprouts, washed
1-2 teaspoons Sambal Bajak (see page 180) to garnish (optional)

METHOD: Bring the water to the boil in a large pan. Add the pork or chicken and salt and pepper to taste. Cover and simmer for 40 minutes.

Strain and reserve the cooking liquid. Cut the meat into small cubes. Put the rice vermicelli in a pan and cover with boiling water. Cover and leave to stand for 5 minutes. Drain thoroughly.

Heat the oil in a wok or deep frying pan, add the brown shallots and fry for 1 minute, then add the green shallots, garlic and spices. Fry for 30 seconds, stirring constantly, then add the meat and prawns. Stir-fry for 1 minute, then add the reserved cooking liquid and simmer for 25 minutes.

Add the rice vermicelli and coconut milk and bring very slowly to the boil, stirring gently to prevent the coconut milk from curdling. Add the bean curd and bean sprouts and simmer for 5 to 8 minutes, stirring occasionally.

Pour into a warmed soup tureen, then garnish with the Sambal Bajak, if using. Serve hot.
SERVES 4-6

MARTABAK
STUFFED SAVOURY PANCAKES
INDONESIA/SINGAPORE

Strictly speaking, Martabak are not pancakes at all, but quick-fried envelopes of very thin dough, stuffed with minced meat and spices. They are very popular as snacks to be eaten in the open air; you can buy them at Indonesian market stalls or from street vendors who will make them especially for you, absolutely fresh and with ingredients to suit your taste.

If you are making them at home, they can accompany a meal, or be served with drinks beforehand, or they can be eaten as a snack at any time of day. Cold Martabak are excellent as part of a packed lunch.

This recipe gives instructions for making your own dough, but if preferred you can buy packets of wun tun* (wonton) skins from Chinese supermarkets and use them for the casing instead – a quarter of a 100 g (3¾ oz) package is the right quantity for this amount of filling.

Dough:
2½ cups plain flour
salt
2 eggs
water to mix
Filling:
1 tablespoon oil
1-2 large onions, peeled and finely sliced
2 garlic cloves, peeled and crushed
1 teaspoon ground coriander
½ teaspoon ground cumin
½ teaspoon ground ginger
½ teaspoon chilli powder
½ teaspoon ground turmeric
1 teaspoon sereh powder*
salt
500 g (1 lb) cooked lamb or beef, minced
To finish:
2-3 eggs, according to taste
5 green shallots, chopped
¼ cup coriander leaves*, chopped
vegetable oil for shallow-frying

METHOD: To make the dough, sift the flour and salt into a bowl, break in the eggs and mix well. Knead thoroughly, adding enough water to make a smooth, firm dough.

Roll the dough into a ball on a board lightly sprinkled with cornflour. Flatten the ball with a rolling pin and very carefully pull it into the thinnest possible sheet. Cut the dough into 7.5 cm (3 inch) squares, then chill in the refrigerator until required.

To make the filling, heat the oil in a wok or deep frying pan, add the onions and garlic and fry gently until soft. Add the spices and salt and fry for 30 seconds, stirring constantly. Add the meat, stir well and fry for 1 to 2 minutes, stirring constantly. Leave to cool for 30 minutes to 1 hour.

To finish, break the eggs into the filling. Add the green shallots and coriander and stir well. Place a few squares of dough on a board, lightly sprinkled with cornflour. Place a tablespoon of filling on each square and put another square on top, then press the edges of the dough together firmly to seal.

Heat 5 tablespoons of oil in a frying pan. When the oil is very hot, add the martabak and press down with a fish slice for a few seconds. Fry for about 1 minute on each side, turning them once only. Remove from the pan with a slotted spoon and drain on kitchen paper towels. Repeat with the remaining ingredients, adding more oil to the pan as required. Serve hot or cold, cut into triangles if preferred.
SERVES 6-8

Note: When cooked, the martabak should be flat and evenly filled with meat; the casing should be quite crisp around the edges, but soft in the centre.

REMPEYEK KACANG
SAVOURY PEANUT BRITTLE

These little peanut snacks are delicious at any time of day, but they go particularly well with pre-dinner drinks. It is advisable to use very fine rice powder* to make them – ordinary rice flour does not give the best results. If stored in an airtight container, Rempeyek will keep for at least 2 weeks.

2 macadamias or kemiri*, chopped
1 garlic clove, peeled and chopped
2 teaspoons ground coriander
1 teaspoon salt
1 cup rice powder*
1 cup water
1 cup whole shelled peanuts, halved if large
1¼ cups vegetable oil

METHOD: Put the macadamias and garlic in a *cobek* or food processor and work to a very smooth paste. Add the coriander and salt and stir well, then mix in the rice powder and water to make a smooth, liquid batter. Stir in the peanuts.

Heat 5 tablespoons of the oil in a non-stick frying pan. Place spoonfuls of the batter in the pan. Fry each one for 1 minute, then remove from the pan with a slotted spoon and drain on kitchen paper towels. Repeat until all the batter is used up, adding more oil to the pan as necessary.

Stir the uncooked batter from time to time, adding a little water if it becomes dry while standing.

Pour the remaining oil into a wok or deep-fat fryer. Add any remaining oil from the pan and heat to 180°C/350°F. Add about 8 rempeyek to the pan and fry for about 1 minute until golden brown, turning them several times during frying. Drain and repeat with the remaining rempeyek. Leave until cold before serving.
MAKES 50-55

PERGEDEL JAGUNG
CORN FRITTERS

These can be served as a snack on their own, or as part of a meal with other vegetables.

6 corn on the cob, or 300 g (11 oz) can sweetcorn, drained
90 g (3 oz) peeled prawns (optional)
4 brown shallots, peeled
2 garlic cloves, peeled
1 red chilli or ½ teaspoon chilli powder (optional)
1 teaspoon ground coriander
salt
1 large egg, beaten
vegetable oil for shallow-frying

METHOD: If you are using corn on the cob, grate the kernels off the cobs. Mince or finely chop in a food processor the prawns, if using, shallots, garlic, and chilli, if using. Mix with the corn, then add the coriander and salt to taste. Add the egg and beat thoroughly.

Heat 5 tablespoons oil in a frying pan, then drop a heaped tablespoonful of the mixture into the pan. Flatten with a fork, then repeat this process until there are 5 or 6 fritters in the pan. Fry for about 2½ minutes, then turn over and cook the other side. Remove from the pan with a slotted spoon and drain on kitchen paper towels. Repeat until all the mixture is used, adding more oil to the pan as necessary. Serve hot or cold.
SERVES 4

▷ *Savoury Peanut Brittle*

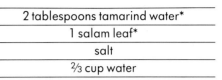

SERUNDENG
ROAST GRATED COCONUT WITH PEANUTS
INDONESIA

Serundeng is an Indonesian side dish which has both a delicious taste and texture. Serve guests with a very small quantity as a little goes a long way.

If stored in an airtight container, Serundeng will keep for several weeks.

7 tablespoons vegetable oil
½ cup whole shelled peanuts
3 macadamias or kemiri*, chopped
1 onion, peeled and chopped
2 garlic cloves, peeled and chopped
½ teaspoon terasi* (dried shrimp paste)
2 teaspoons ground coriander
pinch of ground cumin
pinch of ground laos*
1 cup desiccated coconut
1 teaspoon brown sugar
2 tablespoons tamarind water*
1 salam leaf*
salt
⅔ cup water

METHOD: Heat 5 tablespoons of the oil in a small frying pan, add the peanuts and fry for about 5 minutes until just brown, shaking the pan constantly. Remove from the pan and leave to cool. Put the macadamias, onions, garlic and dried shrimp paste in a *cobek* or food processor and work to a smooth paste. Stir in the coriander, cumin and laos.

Heat the remaining oil in a wok or deep frying pan. Add the spice paste and fry for 1 minute, stirring constantly. Stir in the coconut, then the sugar, tamarind water, salam leaf and salt to taste. Stir-fry for a few minutes, then add the water and simmer until the water is completely absorbed. Cover and cook gently for 50 minutes to 1 hour until golden brown, stirring frequently.

Add the peanuts, then remove from the heat and cool before serving.
SERVES 4

KRUPUK
SHRIMP CRACKERS (CRISPS)

Krupuk, or Krupuk Udang, are sold in Chinese shops, supermarkets, and sometimes in delicatessens. When they are uncooked they look like thin, flat pink discs, about 10 cm (4 inches) long. When cooked, they are light and crisp and similar to the shrimp slices served in Chinese restaurants, although they are larger, brighter pink and, in most people's opinion, have more flavour. The Chinese name for them is kapeng.

To cook shrimp crackers, heat about 1¼ cups vegetable oil in a wok or deep frying pan. Drop the crackers into the pan, one at a time; they will immediately swell to several times their original size. Try to press the crackers reasonably flat with a fish slice during the first 1 to 2 seconds of frying, while they are still soft, otherwise they will buckle and twist and not cook properly. Fry for a few seconds further, then remove from the pan and drain off the excess oil. Leave to cool, then serve immediately, or store in an airtight container and eat with 24 hours. Serve with drinks or as part of a meal.

GERINTING UDANG
SPICED FRIED PRAWNS
SINGAPORE

This dish should really be made with freshly boiled prawns, but it is still delicious with precooked prawns from the fishmonger. Serve as a side dish with rice, or as a snack.

500 g (1 lb) peeled prawns, deveined
2 tablespoons tamarind water*
pinch of ground turmeric
1 teaspoon grated fresh ginger*
2 brown shallots or ½ onion, peeled and sliced
2 garlic cloves, peeled and crushed
1 tablespoon light soy sauce
⅔ cup vegetable oil
Batter:
⅔ cup rice powder* or plain flour
⅓ cup water
salt
freshly ground black pepper
1 small egg, beaten

METHOD: Discard the heads from the prawns, but leave on the tails. Place in a bowl with the tamarind water, turmeric, ginger, shallots, garlic and soy sauce. Stir well, then marinate for at least 30 minutes.

Meanwhile make the batter. Put the rice powder or flour in a bowl, then gradually stir in the water. Add salt and pepper to taste, then beat in the egg.

Drain the marinade from the prawns and shallots. Dip the prawns and shallots into the batter.

Heat the oil in a frying pan then add the prawns and shallots, one at a time until the bottom of the pan is covered. Fry until golden brown and crisp, then turn over and fry the underside. Serve hot or cold.
SERVES 4

SAMBAL GORENG UDANG DAN TELUR
PRAWNS AND EGGS IN SPICY COCONUT SAUCE

625 g (1¼ lb) King prawns, peeled
5 macadamias or kemiri*, chopped
3 red chillis, seeded and chopped, or 2 teaspoons sambal ulek*
1 small onion, peeled and chopped
2 garlic cloves, peeled and chopped
½ teaspoon terasi* (dried shrimp paste)
2 teaspoons ground coriander
1 teaspoon grated fresh ginger*
½ teaspoon sereh powder*
pinch of ground laos*
2 tablespoons vegetable oil
3 ripe tomatoes, skinned, seeded and chopped
salt
1 salam leaf*
2 daun jeruk purut* (optional)
⅔ cup water
⅔ cup thick santen* (coconut milk)
4 hard-boiled eggs, halved
90 g (3 oz) snow peas, topped and tailed
To garnish:
1 cooked, unpeeled King prawn
lemon twist

METHOD: Discard the heads from the prawns then cut each one in half and devein.

Put the macadamias, chillis or sambal ulek, onion, garlic, dried shrimp paste and ginger in a *cobek* or food processor and work to a very smooth paste. Add the spices and mix well.

Heat the oil in a pan, add the spice paste and fry for 1 minute, stirring constantly. Add the prawns, tomatoes and salt to taste, then cover and simmer gently for 2 minutes.

Stir in the salam leaf, daun jeruk purut, if using, and water, then increase the heat and boil uncovered, for 5 minutes.

Lower the heat, add the coconut milk and eggs and simmer for 8 minutes. Add the snow peas and simmer for 3 minutes or until they are quite tender and the sauce is thick. Taste and adjust the seasoning, then transfer to a serving dish and garnish with the prawn and lemon twist. Serve hot, with Serundeng (see page 163).
SERVES 4

freshly ground black pepper

vegetable oil for deep-frying

lemon slices to garnish

METHOD: Put all the ingredients except the oil in a bowl and mix well. Form the mixture into small balls about the size of walnuts, or flatten them into burger shapes.

Heat the oil in a wok or deep-fat fryer and fry the rempah-rempah for 1½ to 2 minutes until golden brown. Remove from the pan with a slotted spoon and drain on kitchen paper towels. Transfer to a serving dish and garnish with lemon slices. Serve hot or cold.
SERVES 6-8 AS A SIDE DISH

IKAN LEMAK
FISH IN COCONUT MILK
MALAYSIA

A mild, easy to make dish, known in Singapore as ikan moolie.

500 g (1 lb) fish steaks or fillets
4 brown shallots, or 1 onion, peeled and chopped
3 fresh red chillis, seeded and chopped, or 1 tablespoon sambal ulek*
1 tablespoon vegetable oil
1 cup thin santen* (coconut milk)
1 teaspoon ground turmeric
1 stalk lemon grass*
1 tablespoon tamarind water*
½ teaspoon salt
½ cup thick santen* (coconut milk)

METHOD: Large fish steaks can be cut in two, fillets into 4 serving portions. Rinse fish and pat dry. Pound the shallots and chillis in a *cobek*, mortar and pestle or in an electric blender. Heat the oil in a frying pan or saucepan and gently fry chilli mixture for 3 to 4 minutes.

Add the thin coconut milk, turmeric, lemon grass, tamarind water and bring slowly to the boil, stirring constantly. Simmer for 2 to 3 minutes, add the fish and salt and cook gently for 10 minutes. Add the thick coconut milk and stir carefully over low heat until gravy thickens.
SERVES 4

IKAN ASAM PEDAS
HOT SOUR FISH CURRY
MALAYSIA

Use Spanish mackerel, snapper, jewfish or other similar fish for this – gemfish steaks, cut into portions could also be used.

500 g (1 lb) fish steaks
salt
1 teaspoon ground turmeric
4 fresh red chillies, seeded and quartered, or 1 tablespoon sambal ulek*
3 garlic cloves, peeled
3 slices fresh ginger*, peeled
2 onions, peeled
½ teaspoon terasi* (dried shrimp paste)
½ cup vegetable oil
¼ cup tamarind water*
pinch of sugar

METHOD: Dry the fish steaks and rub with ½ teaspoon salt and the turmeric. Put the chillis, garlic, ginger, 1 onion, quartered, the shrimp paste and 1 tablespoon water in a *cobek* or electric blender and work to a fine paste.

Heat the oil in a pan and fry fish for a minute or two on each side until golden. Drain and set aside.

Pour all but a tablespoon of the oil off and gently fry the remaining onion, sliced, until golden. Add the ground ingredients and cook gently, stirring, for 2 to 3 minutes. Add tamarind water, ½ cup water, salt and

sugar to taste, then the fried fish, cooking for 2 to 3 more minutes to complete the cooking of the fish.
SERVES 4

REMPAH-REMPAH
PRAWN AND BEAN SPROUT FRITTERS
MALAYSIA

These are normally made without prawns, but their addition certainly makes the fritters tastier. Serve as a side dish with a rice meal, or as a snack with drinks.

125 g (4 oz) peeled prawns, minced
250 g (8 oz) bean sprouts
4 green shallots, thinly sliced
2 brown shallots or ½ small onion, peeled and finely sliced
2 garlic cloves, peeled and crushed
2 tablespoons chopped coriander leaves* (optional)
2 teaspoons grated fresh ginger*
2 tablespoons grated coconut flesh (optional)
½ cup rice flour or self-raising flour
1 teaspoon baking powder
1 teaspoon ground coriander
½ teaspoon chilli powder
3 tablespoons water
1 egg, beaten
salt

△ *Spiced Fried Prawns; Prawns and Egg in Spicy Coconut Sauce; Prawn and Bean Sprout Fritters*

▷ *Spiced Poached Trout; Aromatic Baked Fish*

PAIS IKAN
AROMATIC BAKED FISH
INDONESIA

There are variations of this dish all over Indonesia, and it has many different names. This version is from Sunda, in West Java. If preferred, the coconut milk can be omitted, in which case the spice mixture (bumbu*) should be scraped off the fish after baking, and the fish grilled simply with oil or butter.

1.5 kg (3 lb) large fish, whole or in a piece
salt
10 brown shallots or 1 medium onion, peeled and finely sliced
1 cm (½ inch) piece of fresh ginger*, peeled and cut into thin strips
4 stalks lemon grass*, cut into thin rounds, or 1½ teaspoons sereh powder*
3 green chillis, seeded and cut into thin rounds, or 1 teaspoon chilli powder
1½ teaspoons ground turmeric
3 daun jeruk purut*
3 tablespoons chopped mint
3 whole cloves
pinch of grated nutmeg
pinch of ground cumin
pinch of ground laos*
2 teaspoons brown sugar
1 tablespoon dark soy sauce
juice of 1 small lime or ½ lemon
1¼ cups thick santen* (coconut milk)
1 tablespoon vegetable oil or melted butter

METHOD: Make several shallow cuts on each side of the fish, spacing them fairly wide apart. Discard the head, score the skin and rub with a little salt.

Put the remaining ingredients, except the coconut milk and oil or butter, in a bowl. Mix well, then rub all over the fish. Wrap in foil and cook in a preheated moderate oven (180°C/350°F) for 35 to 45 minutes.

Remove the foil from the fish, then scrape the spice mixture into a small pan. Add the coconut milk, bring to the boil, then lower the heat and simmer until the mixture is quite thick.

Put the fish in a shallow flameproof dish. Strain the spice and coconut milk mixture over the top, then add the oil or butter. Grill under a preheated hot grill turning the fish once, until golden brown on both sides. Serve hot or cold.
SERVES 4-6

SAMBAL SOTONG
SQUID IN RED CHILLI SAUCE
SINGAPORE

Despite its name, this is a main dish, not a relish. The chillis give the dish a good red colour, but if you find they make it too hot, use paprika or sweet red peppers instead.

1 kg (2 lb) squid
1 tablespoon white vinegar
3 cups water
5 macadamias or kemiri*, chopped
6 large red chillis, seeded and chopped
6 brown shallots or 1 onion, peeled and chopped
½ teaspoon terasi* (dried shrimp paste) (optional)
2 teaspoons grated fresh ginger*
pinch of ground cumin
pinch of ground turmeric
pinch of sereh powder*
2 tablespoons vegetable oil
3 tablespoons tamarind water*
1 teaspoon brown sugar
salt

METHOD: Clean the squid, discarding the ink sac and head. Chop the tentacles into 1 cm (½ inch) lengths, then cut the squid into small squares. Mix the vinegar with 2½ cups of the water, then use to rinse the squid. Drain immediately.

Put the macadamias, chillis, shallots and shrimp paste in a *cobek* or blender and work to a very smooth paste. Add the spices and mix well.

Heat the oil in a pan, add the spice paste and fry for 1 minute, stirring constantly. Add the squid and tamarind water and fry for a further 3 minutes. Stir in the sugar, salt and remaining water and simmer for 5 to 6 minutes, stirring frequently. Serve hot.
SERVES 4-6

PANGEK IKAN
SPICED POACHED TROUT
INDONESIA

This way of cooking river fish is well known in West Sumatra. Paku* or pakis – young fern shoots – are used to add an alluring, quite indefinable flavour to the dish. In Indonesia, large quantities of fish are cooked at the same time in a deep earthenware pot and the fish are removed from the pot as and when required. It is possible to keep the dish in the refrigerator for as long as 1 week, but the whole dish must be reheated before serving.

8 small river trout, cleaned
salt
8 kemiri*, chopped
4 red chillis, chopped, or 1 tablespoon sambal ulek*
8 green shallots, peeled and chopped
4 garlic cloves, peeled and chopped
2 teaspoons ground ginger
1 teaspoon turmeric powder
½ teaspoon laos powder*
3 cups very thick santen*
7 tablespoons tamarind water*
625 g (1¼ lb) paku*
2 salam leaves*
40 g (1½ oz) mint sprigs

METHOD: Rub the fish with salt. Put the kemiri, chillis, if using, shallots and garlic in a *cobek* or mortar and pound to a very smooth paste. Add the spices, santen, tamarind water, and 1 teaspoon salt and mix well. Line a flameproof casserole with a layer of paku. Arrange a single layer of trout on top, then cover with more paku. Repeat these layers until all the trout and paku have been used, finishing with paku.

Arrange the salam leaves and mint on top, then pour over the spice mixture. Cover with a tight-fitting lid and simmer gently for 1 hour. Serve hot.
SERVES 4

GORENG SOTONG
FRIED SQUID
SINGAPORE

The secret of this dish is the marinade, which needs at least 2 hours to be effective – preferably longer. Serve Goreng Sotong as a side dish with rice, or by itself as a first course.

750 g (1½ lb) squid
4 tablespoons tamarind water*

½ teaspoon ground turmeric
2 teaspoons grated fresh ginger*
pinch of chilli powder
4 brown shallots, peeled and sliced
3 garlic cloves, peeled and crushed
½ teaspoon salt
1 teaspoon dark soy sauce (optional)
4 tablespoons vegetable oil

METHOD: Clean the squid, discarding the ink sac and head. Chop the tentacles into 2.5 cm (1 inch) lengths, then slice the squid into thin rings.

Put the squid in a bowl with all the remaining ingredients except the oil. Leave to marinate for at least 2 hours.

Drain the squid and discard the marinade. Heat the oil in a wok or frying pan and stir-fry the squid for 3 to 4 minutes. Remove from the pan with a slotted spoon and drain on kitchen paper towels. Serve hot.
SERVES 4

KEPITING PEDAS
CRAB WITH CHILLI
SINGAPORE

One of the best-loved dishes, our mud-crabs are excellent cooked this way. Live or raw crabs are best for this dish. (See note for killing instructions.) In Singapore, the crab is eaten with the fingers, but a fork can be used to help extract the crabmeat from its shell.

2 medium or 1 large crab, or 6 blue swimmers
3 tablespoons vegetable oil
1 tablespoon lemon juice
salt
Sauce:
5 red chillis, seeded and chopped
1 onion, peeled and chopped
2 garlic cloves, peeled and chopped
2 teaspoons grated fresh ginger*
2 tablespoons vegetable oil
2 ripe tomatoes, skinned, seeded and chopped, or 2 teaspoons tomato paste
1 teaspoon sugar
1 tablespoon light soy sauce
3 tablespoons water

METHOD: Clean the crabs thoroughly, then cut each body into 2 or 4 pieces. Chop the claws into 2 or 3 pieces if they are very large.

Heat the oil in a frying pan, add the crab pieces and fry for 5 minutes, stirring constantly. Add the lemon juice and salt to taste, remove from the heat and keep hot.

To make the sauce, put the chillis, onion and garlic with ginger in a *cobek* or blender and work to a very smooth paste.

Heat the oil in a wok or a deep frying pan. Add the spice paste and fry for 1 minute, stirring constantly. Add the tomatoes, sugar and soy sauce and stir-fry for 2 minutes, then stir in the water. Add salt if necessary and simmer for a further 1 minute.

Add the crab and stir to coat each piece in the sauce. Serve hot.
SERVES 4

Note: If using live crabs the best way to handle them is to wrap in paper and put in freezer long enough to numb them, or drown them in fresh water.

IKAN BAKAR
GRILLED FISH
INDONESIA

Both freshwater and sea fish can be cooked in this way – the secret is simply that the fish must be absolutely fresh. For optimum flavour, cook the fish over a charcoal barbecue.

4 fresh trout or bream, cleaned
juice of 1 lime or 1 tablespoon white vinegar
2 garlic cloves, peeled and crushed
salt
Sauce:
2 tomatoes, skinned
2 red chillis
1 teaspoon terasi* (dried shrimp paste)
2 brown shallots or ½ small onion, peeled
1 teaspoon dark soy sauce (optional)

METHOD: Make several shallow cuts on both sides of the fish, then rub with the lime juice or vinegar, the garlic and salt. Leave to stand for 30 minutes.

Grill the fish under a preheated hot grill for 10 to 15 minutes until cooked through; turning them over once during cooking. Transfer to a baking tray lined with foil, arranging them side by side in a single layer.

To make the sauce, put the tomatoes, chillis, dried shrimp paste and shallots under the grill for 2 minutes. Transfer the chillis, dried shrimp paste and shallots to a *cobek* or blender and work until the mixture forms a paste.

Put the paste in a pan with the tomatoes and soy sauce, if using. Heat gently for 1 minute, breaking the tomatoes down with a wooden spoon.

Pour the sauce over the fish, then return to the hot grill and cook for 1 minute. Serve immediately.
SERVES 4

SATE AYAM
CHICKEN SATE

This is one of the easiest and most versatile kinds of sate* to prepare, as well as being one of the most popular. It is equally good served with rice, eaten as a snack with drinks, or served with cucumber salad and Longtong (see page 178). Use bamboo skewers if available.

If you have a charcoal barbecue, use this for cooking sate, otherwise the grill or an ordinary gas or electric stove will give satisfactory results.

Sate Ayam can be served either on its own or with the sauces for Sate Kambing (see page 175). If serving without sauce, double the marinade quantities and brush over the meat during grilling.

1 kg (2 lb) boned chicken, skinned (preferably from breast and thigh)
1 tablespoon dark soy sauce
½ onion, peeled and finely sliced
1 garlic clove, peeled and crushed
pinch of chilli powder (optional)
1 tablespoon lemon juice (optional)

METHOD: Cut the chicken into 2.5 cm (1 inch) cubes. Mix together the remaining ingredients in a bowl. Add the chicken and stir to coat thoroughly, then cover and leave to marinate for at least 1 hour.

Divide the chicken pieces equally between 8 skewers and grill for 5 to 8 minutes, turning frequently. Serve hot.
SERVES 4

BOLA-BOLA TAHU
FRIED PRAWNS AND BEAN CURD BALLS
MALAYSIA

600 g (2 × 11 oz blocks) tahu* (bean curd)
250 g (8 oz) peeled prawns
2 garlic cloves, peeled and crushed (optional)
1 tablespoon cornflour
1 egg, beaten
salt
freshly ground black pepper
vegetable oil for deep-frying
Sauce:
3 tomatoes, peeled and chopped
2 green shallots, sliced
1 garlic clove, peeled and crushed
⅔ cup water
1 tablespoon light soy sauce
2 teaspoons lemon juice or vinegar
2 teaspoons sugar

60 g (2 oz) snow peas, topped and tailed (optional)
To garnish:
few fried onion rings
chopped coriander leaves*

METHOD: Put the bean curd in a bowl and mash to a smooth paste. Mince or finely chop the prawns, then add to the bean curd, together with the garlic (if using) the cornflour, egg and salt and pepper to taste. Mix well, then form into small balls, about the size of walnuts.

Heat the oil in a wok or deep frying pan to 180°C/350°F. Add the prawn balls and deep-fry until golden brown. Remove from the pan with a slotted spoon and drain on kitchen paper towels.

Meanwhile, make the sauce. Put the tomatoes, shallots, garlic and water in a pan. Bring to the boil, and boil for 5 minutes. Strain the mixture into a clean pan, then add the remaining sauce ingredients, with salt and pepper to taste. Return to the heat and simmer for 3 minutes.

Add the prawn balls to the sauce and simmer for about 1 minute until heated through, stirring gently. Garnish with dried onion rings and chopped coriander and serve immediately.
SERVES 4

KELIA AYAM
INDONESIAN CHICKEN CURRY

This dish can be cooked in advance and reheated just before serving.

8 brown shallots or 2 medium onions, peeled and sliced
2 garlic cloves, peeled and sliced
4 macadamias or kemiri*, chopped
2 tablespoons water
2½ cups thick santen* (coconut milk)
1 teaspoon grated fresh ginger*
1 teaspoon chilli powder
1 teaspoon ground turmeric
1 salam leaf*
salt
1 chicken, weighing 1.5 kg (3 lb), cut into serving pieces

METHOD: Place the shallots, garlic, macadamias and water in an electric blender and work until smooth. Transfer the liquid to a wok or deep frying pan and add the coconut milk, spices, salam leaf, salt and chicken.

Simmer the mixture for 1 to 1½ hours until the sauce is thick, then taste and add more salt if necessary. Serve hot.
SERVES 4

△ *Indonesian Chicken Curry (above); Fried Chicken Javanese-Style; Roast and Grilled Chicken with Soy Sauce*

AYAM GORENG JAWA
FRIED CHICKEN JAVANESE-STYLE
INDONESIA

Before frying chicken, the Javanese boil it in water or coconut milk with spices.

1 chicken, weighing 1.5 kg (3 lb), cut into serving pieces
1 onion, peeled and finely sliced
4 garlic cloves, peeled and finely sliced
2 teaspoons ground coriander
½ teaspoon ground cumin
pinch of ground sereh*

pinch of ground laos*
pinch of grated nutmeg
1 small cinnamon stick (optional)
1 bay leaf
1 teaspoon brown sugar (optional)
salt
4 cups water
vegetable oil for deep-frying

METHOD: Put all the ingredients except the oil in a heavy pan. Bring to the boil then lower the heat, cover and simmer for about 25 minutes until the chicken is almost tender; turn occasionally during cooking.

Remove the chicken from the pan and leave to cool. Heat the oil in a deep-fat fryer or wok to 180°C/350°F. Add the chicken and deep-fry for about 10 minutes until golden brown. Remove from the pan with a slotted spoon and drain on kitchen paper towels. Serve hot.

SERVES 4

AYAM PANGGANG KECAP
ROAST AND GRILLED CHICKEN WITH SOY SAUCE
MALAYSIA

1 chicken, weighing 1.5 kg (3 lb)
salt
2 tablespoons dark soy sauce
½ onion, peeled and finely sliced
2 garlic cloves, peeled and crushed
½ teaspoon chilli powder
juice of ½ lemon or lime
2 teaspoons sesame seed oil*
oil for basting (optional)

METHOD: Rub the chicken with salt, then roast in a preheated moderately hot oven (190°C/375°F) for 45 minutes or until golden brown. Leave to cool.

Cut the chicken into 4 pieces, then beat the flesh to loosen the fibres. Mix together the remaining ingredients, except the oil, and rub over the chicken. Cover and leave to marinate for 1 hour, turning the chicken pieces occasionally.

Just before serving, reheat the chicken under the grill, brushing it first with oil, if liked. Serve hot.

SERVES 4

▷ *Spiced Pork; Chicken with Shrimp Sauce*

AYAM PETIS
CHICKEN WITH SHRIMP SAUCE
INDONESIA

A spicy, rich chicken curry in a shrimp coconut sauce. Serve with rice and a few fresh sambals.

1.5 kg (3 lb) chicken joints (breasts, thighs)
1 onion, peeled and quartered
4 garlic cloves, peeled
2.5 cm (1 inch) piece of fresh ginger*, peeled and chopped
3 red chillis, seeded and quartered
1 tablespoon water
3 tablespoons vegetable oil
1 teaspoon ground turmeric
1 teaspoon freshly ground black pepper
½ teaspoon terasi* (dried shrimp paste)
½ teaspoon ground laos*
1 stalk lemon grass* or 2 strips lemon rind
2 teaspoons patis* or Chinese shrimp sauce
1½ teaspoons salt
1½ cups santen* (coconut milk)
1 tablespoon palm or raw sugar
2 tablespoons lime or lemon juice

METHOD: Cut chicken into pieces approximately 4 cm (1½ inches). In a *cobek* or blender put the onion, garlic, ginger and chillis with the water and work until well chopped, almost a paste.

Heat the oil in a large frying pan or wok and gently fry the onion mixture, stirring, for about 3 to 4 minutes. Add the turmeric, pepper, shrimp paste and laos and cook a minute longer. Add the lemon grass, patis, salt and chicken pieces and stir-fry over medium heat until chicken is well coated and starting to brown.

Add coconut milk and sugar and bring slowly to the simmer. Cover and cook over a gentle heat for about 30 minutes until chicken is tender and the gravy has thickened.

If gravy is not thick enough, remove chicken, keep warm and reduce gravy over a high heat, stirring constantly until reduced a little and thickened. Add lime juice and spoon over the chicken.
SERVES 4

RENDANG DAGING
BEEF IN COCONUT
MALAYSIA

A lovely thick spicy sauce coats the meat. It needs very little oil for frying the meat as the oil comes out of the coconut milk to help cook the meat and give the right sauce.

750 g (1½ lb) beef topside or chuck steak
1 onion, peeled and quartered
2.5 cm (1 inch) piece of fresh ginger*, peeled and sliced
6-8 dried red chillis
2 stalks lemon grass* or strip lemon peel
2 garlic cloves, peeled
1 tablespoon water
2 tablespoons vegetable oil
6 tablespoons freshly grated coconut or 4 tablespoons desiccated
2 cups santen* (coconut milk)
1 teaspoon salt
1 teaspoon sugar

METHOD: Trim the beef and cut into cubes. In a *cobek* or blender place the onion, sliced ginger, red chillis, lemon grass, garlic and water and grind to a smooth paste.

Heat the oil in a pan and gently fry the ground chilli mixture for 3 to 4 minutes. Add the coconut, cook for a minute or two, then put in the beef and stir-fry until it changes colour. Add the coconut milk, salt and sugar and bring to the boil. Reduce heat and simmer, uncovered, until meat is tender, about one hour. If the sauce threatens to dry out add a little hot water.
SERVES 4

cup water and the salt, cover and simmer gently until pork is just tender, about 30 minutes.

Add coconut milk and simmer uncovered for 10 to 15 minutes, stirring from time to time. Add sugar and lime juice.

SERVES 4-6

DENDENG PEDAS
FRIED STEAK WITH CHILLI
INDONESIA

In Indonesia, dendeng is thinly sliced meat which is coated in spices, then dried in the sun. The slices are coated with crushed red chillis, which make the meat pedas, or chilli-hot. Dendeng should be tender and brittle as a result of the exposure to many hours of hot sunshine. It is sold ready to cook in packets in Indonesian shops and markets, but outside Indonesia a good Dendeng Pedas can be made using this recipe.

600 g (1¼ lb) rump steak or beef topside
2 teaspoons ground coriander
2 tablespoons tamarind water*
1 teaspoon brown sugar
salt
freshly ground black pepper
8 red chillis, seeded and chopped
4 brown shallots or 1 onion, peeled and chopped
2 garlic cloves, peeled and chopped
6 tablespoons vegetable oil
1 teaspoon lemon juice

METHOD: Slice the meat thinly across the grain, then cut the slices into 5 cm (2 inch) squares. Arrange in a single layer on a plate and sprinkle with the coriander, tamarind water, sugar and salt and pepper to taste.

Press each piece with your hands so that the spices are thoroughly absorbed into the meat, then spread the slices out on the plate again. Leave to stand for 2 to 3 hours (in the sun if possible).

Put the chillis, shallots and garlic in a *cobek* or blender and work until broken, but not reduced to a paste.

Heat the oil in a heavy frying pan. Add the meat and fry until evenly browned and cooked through. Remove from the pan with a slotted spoon and keep hot.

Add the pounded mixture to the oil remaining in the pan and fry for 2 to 3 minutes, stirring constantly. Return the meat to the pan and stir to coat with the spice mixture. Add the lemon juice and salt to taste and stir well. Serve hot with rice and accompaniments such as Acar Kuning (see page 176), Serundeng and Krupuk (see page 163) and Sambals (see page 180).

SERVES 4

SAMBAL BABI
SPICED PORK

A dish developed by the Chinese from the Malay Straits, known as Nonyas.

500 g (1 lb) lean pork
6-8 brown shallots or 1 onion, peeled and chopped
6 dried red chillis, soaked, or 1½ tablespoons sambal ulek*
1 teaspoon terasi* (dried shrimp paste)
2 tablespoons vegetable oil
¼ cup tamarind water*
1 teaspoon sugar
½ teaspoon salt

METHOD: Cut meat into short finger-length strips. Put shallots, chillis, shrimp paste and 1 tablespoon water in a blender and grind to a paste.

Heat the oil in a deep frying pan or wok and gently fry the paste, stirring, for 3 to 4 minutes. Add the pork strips and stir-fry until they change colour. Add the remaining ingredients with 1 cup water. Simmer, uncovered, stirring frequently until the meat is tender and the sauce has reduced and thickened, about 45 minutes.

SERVES 4

BABI LEMAK
PORK IN COCONUT MILK
MALAYSIA

A Nonya dish, blending two cuisines – the Chinese love of pork and the Malaysian use of coconut milk.

750 g (1½ lb) lean pork
10 brown shallots or 2 onions, peeled and quartered
8 dried red chillis
6 macadamias or kemeri
½ teaspoon terasi* (dried shrimp paste)
2 tablespoons vegetable oil
1 teaspoon salt
1 cup thick santen* (coconut milk)
1 tablespoon sugar
2 tablespoons lime or lemon juice

METHOD: Trim pork and cut into 2.5 cm (1 inch) cubes. Put shallots, chillis, macadamias, shrimp paste and 1 tablespoon water in a *cobek* or blender and grind to a paste.

Heat the oil in a pan and gently fry the chilli paste, stirring, for 3 to 4 minutes. Add the pork and cook until it changes colour and is well coated with the paste. Add 1

SATE BABI
PORK SATE
SINGAPORE

There are endless sate* variations, using different meat and marinade combinations. Try to include a little fat with each piece of meat, or the sate will become dry when cooked. For optimum flavour, use a charcoal barbecue for cooking.

750 g (1½ lb) pork fillet or loin
2 tablespoons light soy sauce
2 garlic cloves, peeled and crushed
2 brown shallots or ½ onion, peeled and chopped
2 teaspoons five spice powder*
1 tablespoon clear honey
freshly ground black pepper

METHOD: Cut the pork into 2.5 cm (1 inch) cubes, then slice each cube in half so that the chunks of meat are quite thin. Put the pork in a bowl with the remaining ingredients and mix well. Marinate for 2 to 3 hours.

Divide the pork pieces equally between 8 kebab skewers, then place the skewers on a wire rack. Put the rack on a baking tray and roast in a preheated moderate oven (180°C/350°F) for 30 minutes. Transfer to a preheated hot grill and grill for 5 to 8 minutes, turning frequently. Serve hot.
SERVES 4

KAMBING KORMA
LAMB CURRY
MALAYSIA

4 brown shallots or 1 onion, peeled
3 garlic cloves, peeled
6 macadamias or kemeri*
2 cups thick santen* (coconut milk)
600 g (1¼ lb) boned leg of lamb, cut into small cubes
salt
3 tablespoons vegetable oil
1 small onion, peeled and finely sliced
1½ teaspoons ground coriander
½ teaspoon ground cumin
1 teaspoon grated fresh ginger*
pinch of ground laos*
4 whole cloves
2.5 cm (1 inch) piece of cinnamon stick
3 cardamom pods
1 salam leaf*
1 stalk sereh* (lemon grass), bruised, or ½ teaspoon ground sereh*
3 tablespoons tamarind water*
½ teaspoon freshly ground white pepper

METHOD: Chop the shallots, garlic and macadamias, then transfer to an electric blender, add 2 tablespoons coconut milk and work to a smooth paste.

Put the mixture in a bowl, add the lamb and a little salt and mix well. Leave to marinate for 30 minutes.

Heat the oil in a pan, add the onion and fry gently until soft. Add the spices, salam leaf and lemon grass. Stir-fry for a few seconds then add the meat and marinade and fry for 2 minutes. Add the tamarind water, salt and pepper. Cover and cook gently for 15 minutes, stirring every 5 minutes to prevent burning. Stir in the remaining coconut milk and simmer for 40 minutes or until the meat is tender and the sauce is quite thick.

Discard the salam leaf, lemon grass stalk if using, cloves, cinnamon stick and cardamoms. Serve hot.
SERVES 4

BABI KECAP
PORK IN SOY SAUCE
SINGAPORE

4 garlic cloves, peeled
2 tablespoons plain flour
1 tablespoon light soy sauce
750 g (1½ lb) pork fillet, cut into cubes
90 g (3 oz) Chinese dried mushrooms*, soaked in warm water for 30 minutes, or 125 g (4 oz) button mushrooms, sliced
7 tablespoons vegetable oil
1 teaspoon grated fresh ginger*
5 green shallots, thinly sliced
freshly ground black pepper
3 tablespoons dark soy sauce
1 teaspoon white vinegar
2 tablespoon rice wine* (optional)

METHOD: Crush 2 garlic cloves and mix with the flour and light soy sauce. Coat the pork with this mixture, then leave to stand for at least 30 minutes. Meanwhile, drain the Chinese mushrooms, if using, then discard the hard stalks and cut each mushroom cap into 4 pieces.

Heat the oil or fat in a wok or deep frying pan. Add half the meat and fry for 6 to 8 minutes until browned on all sides, turning frequently. Fry the remaining meat in the same way. Remove from the pan with a slotted spoon and drain.

Pour off all but 2 or 3 tablespoons oil from the pan, then add the mushrooms and fry for 3 minutes. Slice the remaining garlic and add to the pan with the ginger. Stir, then add the meat, green shallots, pepper, soy sauce and vinegar. Stir-fry for 2 minutes, then add the rice wine, if using. Serve hot, with accompaniments, such as Tumis Buncis (see page 177).
SERVES 4

BEBEK HIJAU
DUCK IN GREEN CHILLI SAUCE
INDONESIA

This dish improves if it is prepared 24 hours before required so the fat can be skimmed off. If a milder sauce is preferred, use green peppers instead of chillis.

10 green chillis, seeded and chopped
8 macadamias or kemiri*, chopped
3 tablespoons peanut oil
10 brown shallots or 2 onions, peeled and finely sliced
4 garlic cloves, peeled and finely sliced
2 teaspoons grated fresh ginger*
½ teaspoon ground turmeric
pinch of ground laos*
1 stalk sereh* (lemon grass) or ½ teaspoon ground sereh*
1 duck, weighing 1.75 kg (3½ lb), skinned and cut into 8 pieces
3 tablespoons tamarind water*
1 daun kunyit* (optional)
3 daun jeruk purut* (optional)
1 bay leaf
salt
freshly ground black pepper
1¼ cups water
2 tablespoons snipped chives

METHOD: Put the chillis and macadamias in a *cobek* or blender and work to a very smooth paste.

Heat the oil in a pan, add the shallots and garlic and fry gently until lightly browned. Add the chilli and macadamia paste, stir-fry for 1 minute, then stir in the spices and lemon grass. Add the remaining ingredients except the water and chives. Stir well, then cover and simmer gently for 45 minutes.

Remove the lid, increase the heat and boil for 10 minutes, stirring occasionally. Add the water and chives and cook for 15 minutes.

Discard the lemon grass, daun kunyit, daun jeruk purut and bay leaf. Correct the seasoning. Leave to cool, then chill in the refrigerator overnight.

Skim off the fat, reheat and serve hot with rice and accompaniments, such as Oseng-Oseng Wortel dan Bloemkool (see page 175).
SERVES 4

▷ *Duck in Green Chilli Sauce, served with Sauté of Carrots and Cauliflower (see page 175) and Boiled White Rice (see page 179); Pork in Soy Sauce, served with Spiced Green Beans (see page 177)*

RENDANG PADANG
A TRADITIONAL SUMATRAN BEEF DISH
INDONESIA

1.5 kg (3-3½ lb) chuck steak, cut into large chunks
7 cups thick santen* (coconut milk)
2 onions, peeled and sliced
4 garlic cloves, peeled and crushed
2 teaspoons grated fresh ginger*
4 teaspoons chilli powder or 2 tablespoons sambal ulek*
1 teaspoon laos powder*
1½ teaspoons ground turmeric
2 salam leaves*
1 daun kunyit* (optional)
salt

METHOD: Put all the ingredients in a wok or deep frying pan. Simmer, uncovered, for 1 to 1½ hours or until the sauce becomes very thick, stirring occasionally.

Taste and add more salt if necessary, then simmer for a further 1½ hours until the meat becomes dark brown and has absorbed almost all the liquid in the pan, stirring frequently.

Serve Rendang Padang hot or cold, with rice and accompaniments such as Urap (see page 177).

SERVES 8-10

▽ *Aromatic Lamb Stew, served with Cooked Salad with Coconut Dressing (see page 177) and Boiled White Rice (see page 179)*

SATE KAMBING
LAMB SATE

Make sure that some fat is included with the meat or the sate* will be dry. Use bamboo skewers if available.

As with all sates, a charcoal barbecue should ideally be used for cooking, but an ordinary gas or electric stove will give satisfactory results.

This recipe gives two sauces – either or both may be served with sate – in separate bowls so that guests can help themselves. Sate Kambing is particularly good served with Lontong (see page 178).

1 kg (2-2½ lb) boned leg or shoulder of lamb, cut into small cubes
Marinade:
2 tablespoons dark soy sauce
2 tablespoons tamarind water*
1 onion, peeled and finely sliced
3 garlic cloves, peeled and crushed
½ teaspoon chilli powder
1 teaspoon grated fresh ginger*
1 teaspoon ground coriander
1 teaspoon brown sugar
Peanut sauce:
5 tablespoons vegetable oil
½ cup whole shelled peanuts
3 brown shallots or 1 small onion, peeled and chopped
1 garlic clove, peeled and chopped
1 teaspoon terasi* (dried shrimp paste)
pinch of chilli powder
salt
1 tablespoon peanut oil
1¼ cups water
1 tablespoon tamarind water*
1 teaspoon brown sugar
Chilli sauce:
3 tablespoons dark soy sauce
½ onion, peeled and sliced
1 garlic clove, peeled and crushed
1 green chilli, finely chopped, or ½ teaspoon chilli powder
juice of ½ lemon
1 teaspoon olive oil (optional)
½ teaspoon brown sugar

METHOD: Put the lamb in a bowl with the marinade ingredients. Stir well, then leave to marinate for at least 2 hours, preferably overnight.

Divide the lamb cubes equally between 12 skewers. Grill for 5 to 8 minutes, turning frequently.

To make the peanut sauce, heat the vegetable oil in a small frying pan, add the peanuts and fry for about 5 minutes until just brown, shaking the pan constantly. Remove from the pan and leave to cool,

then work to a powder in a *cobek* or food processor.

Put the onion, garlic and shrimp paste in a *cobek* or food processor and work to a very smooth paste. Add the chilli powder and salt to taste and mix well.

Heat the peanut oil in a pan, add the spice paste and fry gently for a few seconds, stirring constantly. Add the water and bring to the boil, then add the ground peanuts, tamarind water and sugar. Stir, then taste and add more salt if necessary. Continue boiling until the sauce is thick, stirring constantly.

To make the chilli sauce, put all the ingredients in a bowl and mix well. Serve the sate hot with the sauces for dipping. (Illustrated on page 159.)
SERVES 6

OSENG-OSENG WORTEL DAN BLOEMKOOL
SAUTÉ OF CARROTS AND CAULIFLOWER
INDONESIA

6 carrots, peeled and sliced diagonally
185 g (6 oz) cauliflower florets
2 tablespoons vegetable oil or melted butter
1 garlic clove, peeled and crushed
1 teaspoon dried terasi* (dried shrimp paste) (optional)
4 green shallots, chopped into 1 cm (½ inch) lengths
1 tablespoon light soy sauce
pinch of chilli powder
pinch of ground ginger
salt

METHOD: Add the carrots and cauliflower to a pan of boiling water. Boil for 3 minutes, then drain.

Heat the oil or butter in a wok or deep frying pan. Add the garlic and shrimp paste and fry for a few seconds. Stir in the shallots and soy sauce, then add the carrots and cauliflower. Add the remaining ingredients and cook for 2 minutes, stirring constantly. Serve hot.
SERVES 4

GULE KAMBING
AROMATIC LAMB STEW
INDONESIA

This is a very liquid stew, which can be served as a spicy, meaty soup.

4 macadamias or kemiri*, chopped
1 small onion, peeled and chopped
3 garlic cloves, peeled and chopped
2 teaspoons ground coriander
1 teaspoon grated fresh ginger*
½ teaspoon ground turmeric
pinch of white pepper
pinch of cayenne pepper
pinch of chilli powder
pinch of ground laos*
2 tablespoons vegetable oil
1 kg (2-2¼ lb) boned leg or shoulder of lamb, cut into small cubes
1 teaspoon brown sugar
4 tablespoons tamarind water*
salt
1 stalk sereh* (lemon grass), bruised
1 small cinnamon stick
3 whole cloves
1 salam leaf*
2 cups water
2 cups thick santen* (coconut milk)

METHOD: Put the macadamias, onion and garlic in a *cobek* or blender and work to a very smooth paste. Add the spices and mix well.

Heat the oil in a pan, add the spice paste and fry for 1 minute, stirring constantly. Add the lamb and stir-fry for 1 to 2 minutes, then stir in the sugar, tamarind water and salt to taste. Cover and simmer for 4 minutes.

Add the remaining ingredients except the coconut milk. Cover and simmer for a further 20 minutes. Add the coconut milk and a little salt if necessary, then cover and simmer for 20 to 25 minutes, stirring occasionally. Discard the lemon grass, cinnamon, cloves and salam leaf. Pour into a warmed soup tureen. Serve hot, with rice and accompaniments, such as Urap (see page 177).
SERVES 6-8

SAYUR LEMAK
VEGETABLE STEW
MALAYSIA

| ½ small marrow, peeled |
| 2 medium potatoes, peeled and quartered |
| 3 brown shallots or 1 small onion, peeled and thinly sliced |
| 1 garlic clove, peeled and thinly sliced |
| 1 green chilli, seeded and thinly sliced |
| 6 tablespoons water |
| 1 teaspoon ground turmeric |
| 1 teaspoon ground ginger |
| 1 stalk sereh* (lemon grass) bruised |
| salt |
| 2 cups beef or chicken stock |
| 1½ cups coarsely shredded cabbage |
| ¼ cup thick santen* (coconut milk) |

METHOD: Cut the marrow into chunks about the same size as the potato quarters, discarding the seeds.

Put the shallots in a pan with the garlic, chilli, water, turmeric, ginger, lemon grass and a little salt. Bring to the boil and boil for 2 minutes, then add the potatoes and half the stock.

Cover and simmer for 4 minutes, then add the cabbage, marrow and remaining stock. Simmer for 6 minutes, then add the thick coconut milk and stir until dissolved. Taste and adjust the seasoning. Serve hot.
SERVES 4

ACAR KUNING
COOKED VEGETABLE SALAD

| 185 g (6 oz) green beans, topped and tailed |
| 3 medium carrots, peeled |
| 1 cucumber |
| 3 macadamias or kemiri*, chopped |
| 2 green shallots, chopped |
| 1 garlic clove, peeled and chopped |
| ½ teaspoon ground turmeric |
| ½ teaspoon ground ginger |
| pinch of chilli powder |
| 2 tablespoons vegetable oil |
| 10 small white onions, peeled |
| ¼ cup white vinegar |
| 1 cup water |
| 3 large cauliflower florets |
| 1 red chilli, cored, seeded and cut into strips |
| 2 teaspoons brown sugar |
| 1 teaspoon dry mustard |
| salt |

METHOD: Cut each bean into 3 or 4 pieces, then cut the carrots into pieces about the same size. Cut the cucumber in half lengthwise, scoop out the seeds and discard, then cut the flesh into pieces the same size as the carrots and beans.

Put the macadamias, shallots and garlic in a *cobek* or blender and work to a very smooth paste. Add the ground spices and stir thoroughly.

Heat the oil in a pan, add the spice paste and fry for 1 minute, stirring constantly. Add the onions, stir-fry for a few seconds, then add the vinegar and a little of the water. Cover and cook for 2 minutes, then stir in the carrots and beans. Cover and cook for 3 minutes, then add the cauliflower and chilli.

Add the remaining water, cover and cook for a further 6 minutes. Add the sugar, mustard and cucumber, stir, then cover and cook for 2 minutes. Remove the lid and cook for 2 to 3 minutes, stirring constantly. Taste and add salt if necessary. Serve hot or cold.
SERVES 4

◁ *Fried Steak with Chilli, served with Shrimp Crackers (see page 163), Roast Grated Coconut with Peanuts (see page 163), Relish (see page 180-1) and Cooked Vegetable Salad*

GADO-GADO
COOKED MIXED SALAD WITH PEANUT DRESSING

You will find Gado-Gado wherever you go in Malaysia, Singapore or Indonesia.

Sauce:
vegetable oil for deep-frying
½ cup whole shelled peanuts
1 teaspoons terasi* (dried shrimp paste)
½ onion, peeled and chopped
1 garlic clove, peeled and chopped (optional)
salt
½ teaspoon chilli powder or sambal ulek*
½ teaspoon brown sugar
1¾ cups water
2 tablespoons thick santen* (coconut milk) (optional)
1 tablespoon lemon juice
Salad:
1 cup shredded cabbage
2 medium carrots, peeled and sliced
2 small cauliflower florets
20-24 green beans, topped, tailed and sliced
2 cups bean sprouts
1 medium potato, peeled and sliced
¼ cucumber, sliced
To garnish:
1-2 hard-boiled eggs, sliced
Krupuk (see page 163) broken into pieces
few fried onion slices
1 lettuce

METHOD: To make the sauce, heat the oil in a wok or a deep frying pan and fry the peanuts for 5 to 6 minutes. Drain thoroughly on kitchen paper towels. Allow to cool, then work to a fine powder in an electric blender or with a pestle and mortar.

Put the shrimp paste, onion and garlic, if using, in a *cobek* or blender. Work to a very smooth paste, then add a little salt. Heat 1 tablespoon vegetable oil in a pan, add the paste and fry for 1 minute, stirring constantly. Add the chilli powder or sambal ulek, sugar and water, bring to the boil, then add the ground peanuts. Stir well, then simmer until thick, stirring occasionally. Add the coconut milk, if using, and stir until dissolved. Keep hot.

Cook the cabbage, carrots, cauliflower, beans, bean sprouts and potato separately in boiling water for 3 to 5 minutes; they should still be crisp. Drain thoroughly.

Arrange the vegetables on a large serving dish; place the cabbage on the dish first, then the carrots, cauliflower, beans and bean sprouts. Arrange the cucumber and potato slices around the edge, then garnish with the egg slices, krupuk and fried onion. Garnish the edge of the dish with lettuce leaves.

Stir the lemon juice into the sauce, then either pour over the vegetables or hand separately. Serve warm.
SERVES 6-8

URAP
COOKED SALAD WITH COCONUT DRESSING
INDONESIA

For this salad, you can vary the combination of vegetables as you wish. Do not overcook them or they will lose their crispness and flavour.

1 teaspoon terasi* (dried shrimp paste)
2 garlic cloves, peeled and chopped
1 green shallot, sliced
½ teaspoon chilli powder
1 teaspoon brown sugar
1 tablespoon tamarind water*
salt
125 g (4 oz) grated white coconut flesh
125 g (4 oz) cabbage, shredded
125 g (4 oz) green beans, topped and tailed
2 medium carrots, peeled and sliced
125 g (4 oz) bean sprouts
To garnish:
few watercress sprigs
few cucumber slices

METHOD: Spread shrimp paste on a small piece of foil and grill for 1 minute. Scrape off, put with garlic and shallot in a *cobek* or blender and work to a very smooth paste. Add the chilli powder, sugar, tamarind water and salt and mix well. Combine with the coconut.

Cook the cabbage, beans, carrots and bean sprouts separately in boiling water for 3 to 5 minutes; they should still be crisp. Drain thoroughly.

Just before serving toss the vegetables in the coconut mixture and pile the salad into a serving bowl. Garnish with a few sprigs of watercress and cucumber slices. Serve the salad warm.
SERVES 4

TUMIS BUNCIS
SPICED GREEN BEANS
INDONESIA

2 tablespoons vegetable oil
3 brown shallots or ½ onion, peeled and finely sliced
1 garlic clove, peeled and crushed (optional)
1 teaspoon ground ginger
pinch of chilli powder
pinch of grated nutmeg
500 g (1 lb) green beans, topped, tailed and halved
salt
freshly ground black pepper
6 tablespoons strong chicken stock, or 1 chicken stock cube dissolved in 6 tablespoons water

METHOD: Heat the oil in a pan, add the shallots and garlic, if using, and fry gently for 1 minute. Stir in the remaining ingredients, except the stock; cook for 2 minutes.

Stir in the stock, cover and simmer gently for 5 minutes. Remove the lid and cook for a further 2 to 3 minutes, stirring constantly. Correct the seasoning. Serve hot.
SERVES 4

LONTONG
COMPRESSED BOILED RICE
INDONESIA

Traditionally, people in Java eat lontong as part of their celebration of the Muslim New Year; but it is a popular way of cooking rice at any time all over Indonesia.

The grains of rice are compressed by prolonged boiling inside a casing or packet. In the tropics, this casing is usually a banana leaf; another variation, called ketupat, is made in a similar way in a casing woven from palm fronds.

This is a perfectly satisfactory method of preparing lontong, but remember that as lontongs are served cold the cooking needs to begin at least 8 hours before the meal is eaten.

2 cups short grain rice
3 cups water
banana leaf or aluminium foil
oil for greasing

METHOD: Place the rice and water in a heavy-based pan. Bring to the boil, stirring once or twice. Cover with a tight-fitting lid and cook over low heat for 35 minutes or until all the water has evaporated.

Meanwhile cut two pieces of banana leaf or aluminium foil to fit a small baking dish or cake tin about 25 × 35 cm (10 × 15 inches). Lightly oil the dish and banana leaves and line the bottom of the tin with one piece of leaf. As soon as the rice is cooked stir vigorously with a wooden spoon and turn into the lined tin, pressing rice firmly, and smooth top. Place the second piece of leaf on top and press firmly with your hand. Cover with a board or tin and place weights on top.

Leave at room temperature until firmly set. When ready to serve remove weights, board and banana leaf and cut with a wet knife into 5 cm (2 inch) squares.
SERVES 6

NASI LEMAK
WHITE RICE IN SANTEN

In Indonesia this kind of rice is called Nasi Uduk (see right) or Nasi Gurih.

1½ cups long grain rice
2½ cups thick santen* (coconut milk)
½ teaspoon salt

METHOD: Wash and cook the rice as for Nasi Putih (see right), boiling it with the santen and salt instead of the water; stir several times during boiling. When all the santen has been absorbed by the rice, continue cooking for 10 minutes as for Nasi Putih, either in a rice steamer or pan with a tight-fitting lid. Serve hot.
SERVES 4-6

NASI KUNING
SAVOURY YELLOW RICE

This is a brightly coloured dish which is often served at feasts and celebrations. It can be served simply as an alternative to Nasi Putih (see right), or garnished with the same ingredients as Nasi Goreng (see right).

1½ cups long grain rice
2 tablespoons vegetable oil or ghee*
1 teaspoon ground turmeric
2½ cups chicken stock
1 teaspoon coriander powder
½ teaspoon ground cumin
1 cinnamon stick
1 whole clove
1 salam leaf*

METHOD: Soak the rice in cold water for 1 hour, wash thoroughly under cold running water, then drain.

Heat the oil or ghee in a pan, add the rice and fry for 2 minutes. Stir in the turmeric and fry for 2 minutes, then add the remaining ingredients and boil until the rice has absorbed all the liquid. Continue cooking for 10 minutes as for Nasi Putih (see right), either in a rice steamer of a pan with a tight-fitting lid. Serve hot.
SERVES 4-6

NASI UDUK
RICE IN SPICED SANTEN
INDONESIA

This rich and spicy rice dish may be served with Ayam Goreng Jawa (see page 168) and sambals.

1½ cups long grain rice
2½ cups santen* (coconut milk)
1 teaspoon salt
1 onion, peeled and finely chopped
1 garlic clove, peeled and chopped
1 teaspoon ground turmeric
1 teaspoon ground cumin
2 teaspoons terasi* (dried shrimp paste)
1 teaspoon grated lemon rind

METHOD: Wash rice well under running water. Put all remaining ingredients in a saucepan and, stirring frequently, bring slowly to the boil. Add the rice and bring back to the boil, stirring once or twice. Cover, reduce heat to low, cover and steam for 20 minutes. Uncover, fork rice lightly, replace lid and steam for a further 5 minutes. Serve hot.
SERVES 4-6

▷ *Fried Rice; Compressed Boiled Rice*

NASI PUTIH
BOILED WHITE RICE

For cooking rice, choose a saucepan with a thick, heavy base. During the final stage of cooking a thin layer of rice may stick to the bottom of the pan, unless you use a non-stick saucepan or invest in a rice steamer.

A rice steamer is simply a pan with holes in it, which is placed inside a pan of boiling water. The rice is first boiled in an ordinary pan as described below, then transferred to the steamer when it has absorbed all the water. Leftover rice can be kept in a steamer for up to 24 hours after boiling, then reheated by gentle steaming.

1½ cups long grain rice
2½ cups water

METHOD: Wash the rice thoroughly under cold running water. Drain, then place in a pan with the water; do not add salt. Bring to the boil, stirring once or twice, then lower the heat and simmer, uncovered, until all the water has been absorbed into the rice. Stir once, then lower the heat and cover the pan with a tight-fitting lid – it should be as near airtight as possible. Cook very gently for 10 minutes. Serve hot.
SERVES 4-6

NASI GORENG
FRIED RICE

The ingredients in this basic recipe can be varied according to taste and availability. Fried rice may be served as an alternative to Nasi Putih (see left), or as a satisfying meal in itself – if suitably garnished. It is usually eaten with meat or fish and vegetables and is particularly popular served with baked or grilled fish, or any kind of sate*.

The chillis or chilli powder in this recipe give the rice a good red colour, but they do make it hot – substitute paprika if you prefer milder rice.

On a restaurant menu, Nasi Goreng Instimewa usually indicates that the rice is well garnished and topped with a fried egg.

1¼ cups long grain rice
2 cups water
2 tablespoons vegetable oil, ghee* or pork fat
4 brown shallots or 1 onion, peeled and thinly sliced
2 red chillis, seeded and thinly sliced, or 2 teaspoons sambal ulek* (optional)
60 g (2 oz) chopped pork, beef or bacon
1 tablespoon light soy sauce
1 teaspoon tomato sauce or tomato paste (optional)
salt
To garnish:
few fried onion slices
1 plain omelet, made with 1 egg, cut into strips
few coriander leaves* or parsley leaves
few cucumber slices

METHOD: At least 2 hours before the dish is required, wash the rice thoroughly, then cook in the water as for Nasi Putih (see left).

Heat the oil in a wok or deep frying pan, add the shallots and chillis, if using, and fry for 1 to 3 minutes. Add the meat or bacon and fry for 3 minutes, stirring constantly, then add the rice, soy sauce, tomato sauce or paste and sambal ulek, if using. Fry, stirring, for 5 to 8 minutes, then taste and add salt if necessary.

Transfer to a warmed serving dish and garnish with the onion, omelet, coriander or parsley and cucumber. Serve immediately.
SERVES 4

SAMBAL BAJAK
HOT RELISH
INDONESIA

This sambal will keep for a long time, and is one of the most popular of the hot relishes.

20 red chillis, seeded and chopped
10 brown shallots or 1 large onion, peeled and chopped
2 garlic cloves, peeled and chopped
5 macadamias or kemiri*, chopped
1 teaspoon terasi* (dried shrimp paste)
2 tablespoons vegetable oil
1 teaspoon grated fresh ginger*
1 teaspoon brown sugar
3 tablespoons tamarind water*
salt
⅔ cup thick santen* (coconut milk)

METHOD: Put the chillis, shallots, garlic, macadamias and dried shrimp paste in a *cobek* or blender and work to a very smooth paste.

Heat the oil in a pan, add the paste and fry for 2 minutes. Add the ginger, sugar, tamarind water and salt to taste, stir well, then add the coconut milk. Simmer for about 15 minutes until the sambal is thick and oily, stirring occasionally. Increase the heat and stir-fry for a further 2 to 3 minutes, then serve hot or cold.

SAMBAL TERASI OR BLACAN
HOT RELISH
INDONESIA/MALAYSIA

This sambal should be eaten on the day it is made.

6-8 green or red chillis
1 brown shallot, peeled and chopped
1 garlic clove, peeled and chopped
1 teaspoon terasi* (dried shrimp paste), grilled
½ teaspoon brown sugar
2 teaspoons lemon juice
salt

METHOD: Cook the chillis in boiling water for 6 to 8 minutes, then drain. Discard the seeds and chop the flesh, then pound in a *cobek* or blender with the shallot, garlic and dried shrimp paste. Add the sugar, lemon juice and salt to taste. Mix well. Serve cold.
SERVES 4-6

SAMBAL BRINJAL
EGGPLANT WITH CHILLI PRAWN
MALAYSIA

A delicious side dish, this enlivens plain rice. Watch out for the dried prawns, they taste stronger than they look!

4 long, thin eggplants
½ cup plus 3 tablespoons vegetable oil
4 tablespoons dried prawns, soaked
4-6 brown shallots or 1 small onion, peeled
3 garlic cloves, peeled
1 teaspoon chilli powder
1 tablespoon water
2 teaspoons vinegar
2 teaspoons sugar
¼ teaspoon salt

METHOD: Cut stems off eggplants. Cut in half lengthwise. Heat ½ cup oil in a large frying pan and fry the eggplants for a few minutes on either side until soft. Drain on kitchen paper towels and set aside.

Put the drained prawns, shallots, garlic, chilli powder and water in an electric blender and blend to a paste. Heat 3 tablespoons of oil and gently fry the paste, cooking for a few minutes. Add the vinegar, sugar and salt and cook a few minutes more. Spread a little of this mixture over each eggplant. Serve warm.
SERVES 4-6

▽ *Hot Relishes and Coconut Relish (centre)*

SAMBAL KELAPA
COCONUT RELISH

This sambal should be eaten on the day it is made.

1 teaspoon terasi* (dried shrimp paste) fried or grilled
2 garlic cloves, peeled and chopped
3-5 lombok rawit* (hot chillis), finely chopped
1 tablespoon gula jawa* (palm sugar)
1 tablespoon tamarind water*
7 tablespoons freshly grated coconut
salt

METHOD: Put the dried shrimp paste, garlic, chillis and palm sugar in a *cobek* or blender and work to a very smooth paste. Add the remaining ingredients, with salt to taste, and mix well. Serve cold.
SERVES 4-6

PISANG GORENG
FRIED BANANAS

Do not use over-ripe bananas for this dish.

¾ cup rice flour*
2 tablespoons melted butter
¾ cup thick santen* (coconut milk)
pinch of salt
4 medium bananas
3 tablespoons ghee*

METHOD: Put the flour, melted butter, coconut milk and salt in a bowl and stir well to make a smooth, liquid batter.
 Peel the bananas and cut each one in half lengthwise or slice into rounds. Roll the banana pieces in the batter until they are well coated. Heat the ghee in a large frying pan, add the banana pieces and fry until golden, turning frequently. Serve hot.
SERVES 4-6

LEPAT BUGIS
COCONUT CREAM CUPS
INDONESIA

In Malaysia and Indonesia, these cups are usually made from banana leaves. If fresh coconut is not available, desiccated coconut may be substituted.

2 cups rice flower*
1½ cups santen* (coconut milk)
pinch of salt
Filling:
½ cup brown sugar, finely packed
1 cup water
2 cups freshly grated white coconut flesh
1 tablespoon glutinous rice flour*
Coconut cream:
1 cup very thick santen* (coconut milk)
pinch of salt

METHOD: Put the rice flour in a pan, pour in the coconut milk and mix well. Add the salt and cook until the mixture begins to thicken, stirring occasionally. Cook for a further 5 minutes, stirring constantly, then remove from the heat.

To make the filling, put the sugar and water in a pan and heat gently until dissolved. Stir in the coconut, then simmer for a few minutes until it has absorbed all the water. Stir in the glutinous rice flour and cook for 2 minutes, stirring constantly.

To make the coconut cream, put the coconut milk and salt in a heavy pan and boil for 3 minutes, stirring constantly.

Spoon about 2 teaspoons of this cream into 8 ramekins or individual heatproof dishes. Pour 1 tablespoon of the rice flour mixture on top, then spoon over the filling. Divide the remaining rice flour mixture between the dishes, then top with the remaining coconut cream. Steam for 10 to 15 minutes, then serve hot or cold.
SERVES 4-8

RUJAK
SPICED FRUIT SALAD

Kedondong is a tropical fruit with firm, crisp flesh. If unobtainable, use crisp eating apples instead. Jeruk bali is a large citrus fruit with red flesh. It is only available in Asia; blood orange or grapefruit may be used as a substitute in Australia.

1 under-ripe mango
2 kedondong, or crisp eating apples
½ fresh pineapple
½ teaspoon salt
½ jeruk bali, or 1 orange or grapefruit
½ cucumber, peeled and sliced
Bumbu:
1 lombok rawit* (hot chilli), chopped, or pinch of chilli powder
1 teaspoon terasi* (dried shrimp paste), grilled
125 g (4 oz) gula jawa* (palm sugar)
pinch of salt
1 tablespoon tamarind water*

METHOD: Wash, peel and slice the mango, kedondong or apples and pineapple, then place in a bowl. Add just enough water to cover and stir in the salt. Peel the jeruk bali or other fruit, and divide into segments.

To make the bumbu, put the chilli, dried shrimp paste and palm sugar into a *cobek* or blender and work until smooth. Add the salt and tamarind water and stir well.

Drain the fruit and arrange in a serving bowl with the jeruk bali, or other fruit, and cucumber. Pour the bumbu over the fruit and fold gently to mix.
SERVES 4-6

KUE DADAR
COCONUT PANCAKES
SINGAPORE

185 g (6 oz) gula jawa* (palm sugar)
5 cups water
4 cups freshly grated white coconut flesh
pinch of ground cinnamon
pinch of grated nutmeg
pinch of salt
2 teaspoons lemon juice
Pancakes:
1 cup plain flour
pinch of salt
1 egg, beaten
1¼ cups milk
lard for greasing

METHOD: To make the filling, put the palm sugar and water in a pan and heat gently until the sugar has dissolved. Add the remaining ingredients, except the lemon juice, and mix well. Simmer gently for a few minutes until the coconut has absorbed all the water, yet is still moist.

To make the pancakes, sift the flour and a pinch of salt into a bowl. Add the egg, then gradually beat in the milk to make a smooth batter.

Grease an 18 cm (7 inch) frying pan and place over moderate heat. Pour in just enough batter to cover the base thinly, tilting the pan slightly to spread it. Cook for 1 minute, then turn the pancake and cook the other side. Repeat with the remaining batter, to make 8 pancakes.

Add the lemon juice to the filling and divide equally between the pancakes. Roll up and serve warm or cold.
SERVES 4-8

AGAR-AGAR DENGAN
SEAWEED PUDDING

5 tablespoons (7 g/¼ oz) agar-agar* flakes
5 cups water
⅓ cup caster sugar
Serikaya:
3 small eggs
60 g (2 oz) gula jawa* (palm sugar)
salt
2½ cups thick santen* (coconut milk)

METHOD: Soak the agar-agar in just enough cold water to cover for at least 2 hours, preferably overnight.

Drain the agar-agar, then put in a large pan with the water. Add the sugar and simmer for a few minutes until the agar-agar and sugar have dissolved, stirring occasionally. Strain through a fine nylon sieve or muslin then pour into a 5 cup mould. Leave to cool, then store in the refrigerator until required.

To make the serikaya, put the eggs and gula jawa in a bowl over a pan of hot water and whisk until thick and fluffy. Add the salt and coconut milk and whisk thoroughly. Pour into a heatproof bowl. Place in a steamer or large pan, containing 2.5 cm (1 inch) boiling water, and steam for 10 to 15 minutes until thick.

Turn the agar-agar out onto a serving plate. Serve accompanied by the hot or cold serikaya.
SERVES 8-10

▷ *Coconut Pancakes; Spiced Fruit Salad*

GLOSSARY

Aburage (JAPAN) Fried soy bean cake. It is prepared in thin sheets and is sold frozen – unlike the Chinese type (dow foo pok) which comes in cubes.

Agar-Agar (BURMA/CHINA/JAPAN/MALAYSIA) Known as *kanten* in Japan. A kind of seaweed available in long white strands or powdered form. Use in very small quantities, as a little will quickly set a large volume of liquid. It has almost no taste or colour. Powdered gelatine may be substituted, allowing 4 tablespoons gelatine to 25 g/1 oz agar-agar. Available from Oriental stores and some health food shops.

Akamiso (JAPAN) Soy bean paste, reddish brown in colour.

Ata (INDIA) A type of wholemeal flour used in the preparation of Indian unleavened breads. Sometimes sold in Australia as *chappati* flour. Available from Indian stores.

Azuki (JAPAN) Red beans. Sweetened azuki beans are available in cans.

Bagoong (PHILIPPINES), see Fish paste.

Balachan (MALAYSIA), see Terasi.

Bamboo shoot, dried (VIETNAM) Not a substitute for fresh or canned bamboo shoots. Dried bamboo shoots have their own special flavour and texture. Soak in hot water for at least 2 hours before using.

Bamboo shoots, canned (CHINA/INDONESIA/JAPAN/MALAYSIA) Known as such in China, *takenah* in Japan, *rebong* in Malaysia, and *rebung* in Indonesia. The tender shoots which appear at the base of bamboo are gathered at the end of the rainy season, parboiled and canned. After opening, store in a jar of water in the refrigerator changing the water daily. They will keep for about 10 days. For preference use the small winter shoots.

Bean curd (CHINA/INDONESIA/KOREA/MALAYSIA) Known as *tofu* in Japan, *tahu* or *taukwa* in Indonesia/Malaysia. Made of puréed and pressed soya beans, its texture is like soft cheese. Sold in 10 cm (4 inch) × 7.5 cm (3 inch) and 2.5 cm (1 inch) thick cakes, or cut into cubes, in tubs or packets, weighing about 300 g (11 oz). It will keep fresh for several days if stored in water in the refrigerator. Dried bean curd skin is also available, in packets of sheets or sticks: soak overnight in cold water or in warm water for 1 hour before using. Available from Oriental stores and some health food shops. *Tofu* is also available in instant powdered form, easy to prepare.

Beans, salted (INDONESIA/MALAYSIA/THAILAND) Known as *tao chiew* in Thailand, *tauco* in Indonesia/Malaysia. Black soya beans which have been steamed, spiced and preserved in salt. Sold in cans and packets. Should be transferred to an airtight jar and stored in the refrigerator; will then keep for up to 1 year.

Bean Sauce (CHINA) Also known as yellow bean sauce and brown or black bean sauce. Crushed yellow soya beans, mixed to a paste with flour, vinegar, spices and salt. Sold in jars and cans. Once opened, store the sauce in covered container in refrigerator. If it seems to dry out, add a little oil to top.

Bean threads (CHINA/JAPAN/KOREA/THAILAND/VIETNAM), see Mung bean threads.

Belimbing wuluh (MALAYSIA) A sour kind of fresh fruit. Common in South-East Asia, but unobtainable in Australia. Lemon, lime or rhubarb may be used as a substitute.

Beni-shoga (JAPAN) Red salt-preserved ginger.

Besan (INDIA) A very fine flour made from ground chick peas. It must be sieved before using as it tends to become lumpy on standing.

Blacan (MALAYSIA), see Terasi.

Boo (BURMA/KOREA) A long white radish resembling a parsnip in appearance. It has a mild flavour and English radishes should not be used as a substitute. Available in high-class greengrocers or in areas where there are Chinese, Japanese and Korean shops. If unobtainable, use tender white turnips as a substitute.

Buah keras (MALAYSIA), see Kemiri.

Bumbu (MALAYSIA) A general term for any mixture of ingredients that gives a strong flavour to a dish. It can refer to the dry ingredients, or to the sauces that are made from them.

Bün tâu (VIETNAM), see Mung bean threads.

Cabé rawit (MALAYSIA) Small, very hot chillis – red, green or sometimes white in colour.

Candlenut (MALAYSIA), see Kemiri.

Cellophane noodles (CHINA/JAPAN/KOREA/THAILAND/VIETNAM), see Mung bean threads.

Chilli sauce There are two main chilli sauces used in Oriental cooking. Chinese chilli sauce is made from chillis, salt and vinegar; this has a hot flavour. The Malaysian, Singaporean or Sri Lankan chilli sauce is a mixture of hot, sweet and salty flavours and generous quantities of garlic and ginger are added. It is cooked with vinegar. Both types of sauce are readily available.

Chinese parsley, see Coriander.

Cilantro, see Coriander.

Citronella, see Lemon grass.

Cloud ear (CHINA), see Wood ear.

Coconut milk (INDIA/MALAYSIA/THAILAND/VIETNAM) Known as *narial ka doodth* in India, *santen* in Indonesia and Malaysia. Best made from fresh coconuts: grate the flesh of 1 coconut into a bowl, pour on 2½ cups boiling water, then leave to stand for about 30 minutes. Squeeze the flesh, then strain before using. This quantity will make a thick coconut milk, add more or less water as required. Desiccated (shredded) coconut can be used instead of fresh coconut: use 4 cups to 2½ cups of boiling water. Use freshly made coconut milk within 24 hours. Canned coconut milk is also available.

Coconut sugar (THAILAND) Also known as palm sugar. Brown sugar may be substituted.

Coriander (ALL COUNTRIES) Also known as *pak chee* (THAILAND), *dhania* (INDIA), *ngô* (VIETNAM), Chinese parsley and cilantro. Widely used in South-East Asian cooking in the form of leaves, roots, stems, seeds and powder. In Vietnam, Laos and Kampuchea, only the fresh leaves and stems are used and are indispensable to these cuisines. The fresh leaves are usually chopped, the roots are washed and dried, then grated. The roots will keep in an airtight jar and the leaves in a jar with 1 cm (½ inch) of water in the refrigerator. Can easily be grown outdoors in summer. Parsley is often substituted for fresh coriander although it does not impart the same flavour. Available at many greengrocers and Oriental and Continental stores.

Creamed coconut (BURMA/MALAYSIA/THAILAND) Sold in packets, tubs, slabs and cakes. More concentrated than coconut milk. Cut up roughly before using, then heat gently with water added until melted, stirring frequently. Use as coconut milk.

Culantro (VIETNAM) Also known as *ngô tay*, a member of the coriander family. Each stem has 1 elongated leaf which grows in a dark green cluster.

Daikon (JAPAN) A long white radish. Sometimes referred to as the 'workhorse' of the Japanese diet, it is a basic vegetable in Japanese cooking. Use both raw and cooked.

Dal (INDIA) The general name given to a variety of pulses grown in the Indian sub-continent. Along with rice, these pulses form the staple diet of millions of peasants. There are several varieties – *moong, urhad, chenna,* and, the dal which most people in the West are familiar with, the lentil. They are all interchangeable, and the cooking method is the same for each.

Daun jeruk purut (MALAYSIA) The leaf of a fruit similar to a lime.

Daun kunyit (MALAYSIA) Turmeric leaf.

Dhania (INDIA), see Coriander.

Dow foo pok (CHINA) Chinese-style fried bean curd sold in Oriental stores.

Dried mushrooms (CHINA/JAPAN/KOREA/THAILAND/VIETNAM), see Mushrooms, dried.

Ebi (MALAYSIA) Tiny uncooked dried shrimps.

Fish paste (KAMPUCHEA/PHILIPPINES)
Known as *bagoong* in the Philippines. It is a paste made from fermented fish or shrimps and salt. Used in small quantities as a relish. Kampuchean fish paste is made from whole preserved anchovies which are strained when required. Available from Oriental stores in two varieties, thick and thin.

Fish sauce (KAMPUCHEA/LAOS/ PHILIPPINES/THAILAND/VIETNAM)
Known as *patis* in the Philippines, *nam pla* in Thailand, *nuoc cham* or *nuoc mam* in Kampuchea, Laos and Vietnam. As important to these schools of cooking as salt is in the West. Prepared from fresh anchovies and salt which are layered in wooden barrels and left to ferment. The liquid that is drained off initially is light and clear and considered to be the best quality; the two subsequent extractions are darker and of a poorer quality. Available from Oriental stores.

Five spice powder (CHINA/MALAYSIA) A reddish-brown aromatic powder, made from a combination of ground spices – anise, fennel, cloves, cinnamon and szechuan pepper. These spices are also sold as 'five spices', ready-mixed but whole. Will keep indefinitely in an airtight container.

Fried bean curd, see Aburage and Dow foo pok.

Galingale (MALAYSIA/THAILAND/ VIETNAM) Known as *laos* in Malaysia, *kha* in Thailand. It is the root of a plant resembling ginger, creamy white in colour, with a delicate flavour. Used fresh, but only dried galingale is available in Australia. Soak in hot water for 1 hour before using in cooking, then remove before serving. Galingale (*laos*) powder is also available.

Garbanzo beans (PHILIPPINES) Chick peas.

Ghee (INDIA) Clarified butter. To make pure ghee: heat 1.5 kg (3 lb) unsalted butter over low heat in a heavy pan. Skim off any impurities, then maintain the heat at just below simmering point for 1 hour. Strain through several layers of cheesecloth, then store in a cool place. It will keep for several months. Many Indian cooks use a ghee substitute derived from vegetable oil. Ghee can be bought in packets and cans from most supermarkets. Vegetable oil may be used as a substitute.

Ginger (ALL COUNTRIES) Fresh ginger, sometimes referred to as 'green ginger'. Peel before using, then slice, crush or chop finely. To keep fresh, peel, then wash and place in a jar, cover with pale dry sherry, seal and store in the refrigerator. Ground ginger is not an acceptable substitute, but dried root ginger may be used, in which case the quantity should be decreased as it is sharper in taste.

Glutinous rice (JAPAN/KAMPUCHEA/ LAOS/MALAYSIA/THAILAND/VIETNAM)
Known as *mochigome* in Japan. Also sometimes referred to as 'sticky rice', because it becomes very sticky when cooked. Used in stuffings, cakes and puddings. In Laos it is used in place of long grain rice and served with all meals.

Glutinous rice flour (JAPAN/KAMPUCHEA/ LAOS/MALAYSIA/THAILAND/VIETNAM)
Known as *mochiko* in Japan. Made from ground glutinous rice. There is no substitute. Obtainable from Chinese supermarkets.

Gobo (JAPAN) Edible burdock roots.

Goma (JAPAN), see Sesame seeds.

Goma abura (JAPAN), see Sesame seed oil.

Goma jio (JAPAN) Salted sesame seeds. Dry fry 1 tablespoon black sesame seeds in a hot frying pan until they 'jump', shaking the pan constantly. Transfer to a bowl, then sprinkle with 2 teaspoons salt.

Gula jawa (MALAYSIA) Also known as *gula malaka*. Brown palm sugar, sold in thin blocks. Brown sugar may be used as a substitute.

Gyoza skins (JAPAN) Round in shape. *Wun tun* (wonton) skins may be used as a substitute.

Hakusai (JAPAN), see Napa.

Harusame (JAPAN) Soya bean noodles. Can be used instead of mung bean threads if these are unobtainable.

Hijiki (JAPAN) Brown algae seaweed.

Hoi sin (hosin) sauce (CHINA) Also known as Chinese barbecue sauce. Made from soya beans, flour, sugar, spices and red food colouring. Available in jars or cans from Chinese supermarkets. It will keep for several months in the refrigerator.

Horapa (THAILAND) A member of the *ocimum* family, like sweet basil. Use fresh rather than dried. Sweet basil may be used as a substitute.

Hundred year eggs Duck eggs which are coated with a mixture of clay, ashes and salt, then buried for 100 days. This preserves them. When shelled they are firm and jellied and usually served dipped in soy sauce and finely grated ginger.

Jelly mushrooms (THAILAND), see Wood ear.

Kamaboko (JAPAN) Japanese fish cake.

Kanten (JAPAN), see Agar-Agar.

Kapi (THAILAND), see Terasi.

Kasu (JAPAN) Rice wine lees. Sold in Asian stores.

Katsuobushi (JAPAN) Dried bonito fish. Used in making Dashi (basic stock).

Kecap (INDONESIA/MALAYSIA) Soy sauce. It is darker and sweeter than Chinese dark soy sauce and quite different from Chinese light soy sauce, which is very salty, also known as *ketjap*.

Kemiri (MALAYSIA) Also known as *buah keras* and candlenuts. Used in many South-East Asian dishes. Pale yellow nuts, roughly the same size as chestnuts. They are usually shelled before being exported and the kernels break into fragments. If '2 kemiri' are specified in a recipe, this means the equivalent of 2 whole nuts.

Kentjur (Kachai) (THAILAND) Thick root of a tropical Asian plant of the ginger family. Sold dried, sliced or chopped, in jars, by importers of Indonesian speciality foods or some Oriental food stores.

Kha (THAILAND), see Galingale.

Kochujang (KOREA) Hot bean mash paprika paste. Nearest equivalent is mashed onions and chilli powder fried in oil. Available in cans from Oriental stores.

Kombu (JAPAN) Tangle or kelp seaweed. Used in making Dashi (basic stock).

Konnyaku (JAPAN) Tuber root cake.

Laksa (MALAYSIA), see Rice vermicelli.

Laos (MALAYSIA), see Galingale.

Lemon grass (BURMA/MALAYSIA/ THAILAND/VIETNAM) Known as *serai* or *sereh* in Malaysia, *takrai* in Thailand. Also known as *citronella*. Fresh lemon grass is available from Oriental food stores. The lower third of the stalk, the bulb-like portion, is the part to use when a recipe specifies 'chopped or sliced lemon grass'. Alternatively the whole stalk may be bruised and added during cooking, but then it should be removed before serving. Dried lemon grass is a good substitute; soak in hot water for about 2 hours before using, then remove from the dish before serving. (1 tablespoon dried lemon grass is roughly equivalent to 1 stalk fresh.) Powdered lemon grass is also available, or substitute 2 strips of lemon peel.

Lentil flour (BURMA) Made from ground or pounded lentils. Can be made at home using an electric blender or pestle and mortar.

Lily buds (CHINA) Kown as yellow flower or golden needles in China. A dried bud, golden-yellow in colour and crunchy in texture. Soak in water before using. It keeps indefinitely.

Lime leaves (THAILAND/VIETNAM) Fresh lime leaves are preferred. Dried lime leaves are available from Oriental stores.

Lombok (MALAYSIA) Chilli. *Lombok merah* are red, *lombok hijau* are green, *lombok rawit* are hottest and are available in dried form in Australia.

Makrut (THAILAND) An ugly-looking citrus fruit with very strongly flavoured peel and leaves. The peel is ground with other ingredients in curry pastes and the leaves are used in soup. Lemon leaves can be used as a substitute.

Matcha (JAPAN) Powdered green tea used for the traditional Japanese tea ceremony. This tea is made from the most tender tea leaves of the first spring picking, and is processed by a very expensive, tedious method.

Mint (THAILAND), see Saranae.

Mirin (JAPAN) Sweetened *sake* (rice wine) used in cooking and for seasoning. If unavailable, substitute dry sherry and sugar in the proportion of 3 tablespoons (¼ cup) sherry to 1 tablespoon sugar.

Miso (JAPAN), see Soy bean paste.

Miti (PHILIPPINES) Wide egg noodles. Fresh egg noodles can be used as a substitute.

Mochigome (JAPAN), see Glutinous rice.

Mochiko (JAPAN), see Glutinous rice flour.

Monosodium glutamate (CHINA/JAPAN/KOREA/THAILAND) Known as *oji-no-moto* in Japan and Korea, *veh t'sin* in China. A chemical compound sometimes known as 'taste essence'. It is used to bring out the natural flavours of food, and is entirely optional in all recipes where it is specified. It is widely used in restaurants, but should be used sparingly at home: ¼-½ teaspoon is ample in any recipe. Obtainable from most Oriental stores.

Mung beans (KOREA/VIETNAM) Dried mung beans are very small and green in colour. Dried split peas may be used as a substitute, although mung beans are usually available at good health food shops. When their green husks have been removed, dried mung beans are yellow in colour.

Mung bean threads (CHINA/JAPAN/KOREA/THAILAND/VIETNAM) Known as *saifun* in Japan, *wun sen* in Thailand, *bún tàu* in Vietnam. Also known as Chinese bean threads or cellophane noodles. They are very fine dried noodles made from mung bean flour. Sold in packets. Soak in water for about 10 minutes before using.

Mushrooms, dried (CHINA/JAPAN/KOREA/THAILAND/VIETNAM) Known as dried *shiitake* in Japan. Chinese and Japanese dried mushrooms (*lentinus edodes*) are sold in plastic bags in Oriental stores. They are very fragrant, and will keep almost indefinitely in an airtight jar. They have an entirely different flavour from their fresh counterparts. Soak in warm water for 30 minutes before using. Ordinary mushrooms do not make a good substitute.

Mushrooms, dried jelly (THAILAND), see Wood ear.

Nam pla (THAILAND), see Fish sauce.

Napa (JAPAN) This is *hakusai* or Chinese cabbage, sometimes referred to as celery cabbage. Not to be confused with Chinese leaves. Napa has very delicate leaves and is used both raw and cooked. Chinese leaves can be used as a substitute.

Ngapi (BURMA), see Terasi.

Ngô (VIETNAM), see Coriander.

Ngô tay (VIETNAM), see Culantro.

Nori (JAPAN) Dried seaweed. Often toasted, then shredded and used as a garnish.

Nuoc cham/Nuoc mam (KAMPUCHEA/LAOS/VIETNAM), see Fish sauce.

Oyster sauce (CHINA) A thickish brown sauce with a rich flavour. Made from oysters and soy sauce. It keeps indefinitely in the refrigerator.

Pak chee (THAILAND), see Coriander.

Paku (MALAYSIA) Also known as *pakis*. Young edible fern shoots, called 'fiddlehead ferns' in North America. Young curly kale may be used as a substitute.

Panko (JAPAN) Coarse breadcrumbs.

Patis (PHILIPPINES), see Fish sauce.

Prawns, dried (THAILAND) Sold in packets in Chinese supermarkets. Best kind are bright pink in colour because they are the freshest. Rinse before use to remove dirt and excess salt.

Radish, white Chinese (BURMA/KOREA), see Boo.

Rice flour (BURMA/INDIA/MALAYSIA) Made from ground rice. Can be made at home using an electric blender, coffee mill or pestle and mortar.

Rice papers, dried (VIETNAM) Known as *banh trang*. A thin, brittle, disc-like pancake. Used in many ways, to make spring rolls and as a wrapper for a variety of foods. Must be moistened with water or egg to make them flexible before using. Mostly imported from Thailand. If unavailable, use Chinese spring roll wrappers.

Rice powder (MALAYSIA) Known as *tepung beras*. Extremely fine powdered rice. When specified in a recipe it must be assumed that rice flour may not be used.

Rice vermicelli (MALAYSIA/THAILAND/VIETNAM) Known as *laksa* in Malaysia, or rice sticks. These are noodles made from rice flour which come in various sizes. In soups, the very thin string-like variety called *bun*, are used. The different sizes can be interchanged in recipes if it is difficult to obtain the exact type specified.

Rice wine (CHINA/JAPAN/KOREA/MALAYSIA) The two most popular wines in China are the white and yellow wines made from rice. The ordinary yellow rice wine called *shaosing* is used for cooking.

Rijsttafel (MALAYSIA) Rice table. The name given by the Dutch to a variety of Indonesian dishes that are all served together.

Saifun (JAPAN), see Mung bean threads.

Sake (JAPAN/KOREA) Rice wine. Dry sherry makes an excellent substitute. Sold in Oriental stores.

Salam (MALAYSIA) The leaves of this plant are used extensively in Malaysian cooking. Bay leaves can be used as a substitute.

Salt fish, dried (BURMA) Sword fish is the commonest fish used. Rinse well to remove excess salt before using. Available at Oriental stores.

Salted duck eggs (VIETNAM), see Hundred year eggs.

Sambal ulek (INDONESIA) Used as an accompaniment and in cooking. Made by crushing red chillis with a little salt: remove the seeds from the chillis, chop finely, then crush with salt, using a pestle and mortar. Three chillis will make about 1 tablespoon *sambal ulek*. Also available ready-prepared in small jars from Oriental stores and some delicatessens.

Sansho (JAPAN) *Zanthoxylum pieratum*. Fresh leaves of this bush are used for fragrance and garnish. Powdered sansho, a fragrant pepper, is also available.

Santen (MALAYSIA), see Coconut milk.

Saranae (THAILAND) Mint. Always use spearmint (*mentha spicata*) in preference to other types of mint for Thai recipes.

Saté (MALAYSIA) Also known as *satay*. A general name for any kind of meat, poultry, or fish that is grilled on a skewer.

Serai/Sereh (MALAYSIA), see Lemon grass.

Sesame seed oil (CHINA/INDIA/JAPAN/KOREA/THAILAND/VIETNAM) Known as *goma abura* in Japan. A strongly flavoured seasoning oil made from roasted sesame seeds. Used for its fragrance and the flavour it imparts to other foods. Sold in bottles. Keeps indefinitely.

Sesame seeds (BURMA/JAPAN/KOREA/VIETNAM) Known as *goma* in Japan. There are 2 types – white (*kurogoma*) and black (*shirogoma*). Can be used raw or toasted. To toast sesame seeds, dry fry in a hot frying pan until they 'jump', shaking the pan constantly.

Shichimi (JAPAN) A mixture of 7 spices, ground to a spicy hot powder. Not to be confused with five spice powder. Used on noodles and other cooked dishes.

Shiitake, dried (JAPAN), see Mushrooms, dried.

Shiitake, fresh (JAPAN) Japanese mushrooms, which have an entirely different, more delicate flavour than their dried counterparts. Vitamin-packed and exalted 'the elixir of life' in many countries. Ordinary mushrooms do not make a good substitute.

Shirataki (JAPAN) Yam noodles. Sold in cans. Mung bean threads may be substituted.

Shiromiso (JAPAN) White soy bean paste.

Shoyu (JAPAN) Light soy sauce prepared from fermented cooked soya beans, wheat, malt and salt. Do not substitute Chinese or other soy sauces, their flavour is completely different and will spoil the dish.

Shrimp-flavoured soy sauce (BURMA) Also known as fish sauce. It gives a fishy taste to dishes. Ordinary soy sauce can be used as a substitute. Available from Chinese stores.

Shrimp paste (BURMA) Made from salted dried shrimps. Greyish pink in colour. Anchovies mixed with a little vinegar may be used as a substitute, but this is not very satisfactory. Available in jars from Chinese stores.

Shrimps, dried (BURMA) Available whole, pounded or powdered, from Oriental stores.

Silver leaf (INDIA), see Varak.
Somen (JAPAN) Very thin thread-like wheat vermicelli.
Soy bean paste (CHINA/JAPAN/KOREA) Known as *miso* in Japan. A basic seasoning made from cooked soya beans, malt and salt. Sold in plastic packs and jars at Oriental stores and some health food shops.
Split pea flour (BURMA) Made from ground or pounded split peas. Can be made at home using an electric blender or pestle and mortar.
Su (JAPAN) Rice vinegar, distilled from white rice. It has a very sweet aromatic quality and is much milder than cider vinegar. If unobtainable, substitute distilled white vinegar and mix with water. Seasoned rice vinegars, with sugar and monosodium glutamate added, are also available.
Szechuan preserved vegetable (CHINA) A vegetable pickled in salt and chilli, which is therefore very hot and salty to the taste. Sold in cans, it should be transferred to an airtight jar once opened, then it will keep for several months in the refrigerator.

Tahu/Taukwa (INDONESIA/MALAYSIA), see Bean curd.
Takrai (THAILAND), see Lemon grass.
Tamarind (BURMA/INDIA/MALAYSIA/THAILAN/VIETNAM) Also known as *asam* or *assem*. An acid-flavoured fruit resembling a bean pod. Sold as dried tamarind pulp in blocks, it is dark brown in colour. The dried tamarind pulp must be made into tamarind water before using: Soak about 30 g (1 oz) tamarind pulp in 1¼ cups water for 5-10 minutes, then squeeze, strain and use the water. The longer the tamarind is left to soak, the stronger the flavour. The amount of tamarind pulp and water can be adjusted according to the thickness required; the thicker the water, the more sour it tastes. Lime, lemon or mango juice or vinegar may be used as substitutes but the flavour of the finished dish will not be the same. Tamarind paste is also available, packaged in plastic bags. It should be refrigerated once opened, in which case it will keep indefinitely. Both tamarind pulp and tamarind paste are available at Oriental stores.
Tao chiew (THAILAND), see Beans, salted.
Tauco (INDONESIA/MALAYSIA), see Beans, salted.
Tepung Beras (MALAYSIA), see Rice powder.
Terasi (MALAYSIA) Also known as *balachan/blacan* (Malaysia), *kapi* (Thailand) and *ngapi* (Burma). A kind of pungent shrimp paste, used in very small quantities. Depending on the recipe in which it is used, it can be crushed with spices to make a paste which is then sautéed in oil. Alternatively, it may be grilled or fried first, then added to other ingredients.

Tofu (JAPAN) Soy bean cake.
Tonkatsu sauce (JAPAN) A commercially prepared sauce, it is thick-brown and made from fruit and vegetables combined with spices and seasonings. Soy sauce or ketchup may be used as substitutes.
Transparent noodles (CHINA/JAPAN/KOREA/THAILAND/VIETNAM), see Mung bean threads.
Tree ear (CHINA/THAILAND/VIETNAM), see Wood ear.
Tung chai (THAILAND) Tiensin preserved vegetables. Obtainable from Chinese supermarkets.

Udon (JAPAN) A thick, broad noodle made from flour and water (without eggs).

Varak (INDIA) Known as silver leaf in the West. Used solely for decorative purposes, although it is said to aid digestion. Available from some Oriental shops.

Wakame (JAPAN) Lobe leaf seaweed. Traditionally, the heavy vein is removed. The vein can be eaten, but it is rather chewy.
Wasabi (JAPAN) A green horseradish grated from the root of the Eutrema Wasabi. Use green horseradish powder, which is very pungent and hot, for convenience, as fresh wasabi is both difficult to obtain and very expensive. Dry mustard mixed to a paste with a little water may be used as a substitute.
Water chestnut (CHINA/JAPAN) A walnut-sized bulb with brown skin; the inside flesh is white and crisp. Canned water chestnuts are ready-peeled and will keep for about 2 weeks in the refrigerator, changing water frequently.
Wood ear (CHINA/THAILAND/VIETNAM) Known as tree ear in North America, cloud ear in China, jelly mushrooms in Thailand. A dried fern fungus. Use only in small quantities. Soak in warm water for about 20 minutes before using, until they become glutinous and crinkly. The dried fungi will keep indefinitely. Available at Chinese supermarkets.
Wun sen (THAILAND), see Mung bean threads.
Wun tun skins (KOREA/MALAYSIA) Also known as wonton skins. Paper-thin squares or circles of dough. Can be made at home, or bought ready-rolled and trimmed at Chinese supermarkets. Store in the refrigerator or freezer.

INDEX

ACKNOWLEDGMENTS

Special Photography: Robert Golden 12-21, 24-31, 34-37, 40-45, 50-51, 54-61, 64-67, 70-71, 74-79, 86-88, 92-101, 104-112, 120-121, 124-125, 133-147, 152-153, 163-169, 173-177; Ian O'Leary 14, 22-23, 32-33, 38-39, 52-53, 62-63, 68-69, 72-73, 81, 90-91, 102-103, 114-115, 122-123, 127, 130-131, 150-151, 154-157; Clive Streeter endpapers, 1-5, 9, 10, 47, 49, 83-85, 117-119, 129, 149, 159-160, 170-171, 178-183.

Food prepared by Caroline Ellwood, Susumo Okado, Jackie Burrow and Maureen Pogson.

Photographic stylists: Antonia Gaunt and Sue Brown.

The Publishers would also like to thank the following for loan of accessories:
Ajimura Japanese Restaurant, 27 Endell St WC2; Collet's Chinese Gallery & Bookshop, 40 Great Russell St WC1; Craftsmen Potters Association, William Blake House, Marshall St W1; David Mellor, 26 James St WC2; Frida 111 Long Acre WC2; Ikeda Japanese Restaurant, 30 Brook St W1; Mitsukiku, 15 Old Brompton Road SW7; Neal Street East, 5 Neal St WC2; New Neal Street Shop, 23 Neal St WC2; Nice Irma's Floating Carpet, 46 Goodge St W1; Paul Wu Ltd, 64 Long Acre WC2.